Christoph A. Stumpf

The Grotian Theology of International Law

W
DE
G

Religion and Society

Edited by
Gustavo Benavides and Kocku von Stuckrad

Volume 44

Walter de Gruyter · Berlin · New York

Christoph A. Stumpf

The Grotian Theology of International Law

Hugo Grotius and the Moral Foundations of International Relations

Walter de Gruyter · Berlin · New York

♾ Printed on acid-free paper which falls within
the guidelines of the ANSI to ensure permanence and durability.

ISBN-13: 978-3-11-019120-2
ISBN-10: 3-11-019120-2

ISSN 1437-5370

Library of Congress Cataloging-in-Publication Data

A CIP catalogue record for this book is available from the Library of Congress.

Bibliographic information published by the Deutsche Nationalbibliothek

The Deutsche Nationalbibliothek lists this publication in the Deutsche Nationalbibliografie; detailed bibliographic data are available in the Internet at http://dnb.d-nb.de.

Printed in Germany
Cover design: Christopher Schneider, Berlin

Acknowledgments

In writing this book I have received enourmous support from many sides, for which I am greatly indebted: In particular, I am grateful for the help, support, and patience of The Revd. Oliver O'Donovan, Regius Professor of Moral and Pastoral Theology and Canon of Christ Church, who has encouraged and accompanied my work on Grotius. Gratitude is also due to Professor David Fergusson of the School of Dinivity of the University of Edinburgh, as well as to Dr Andrew Hurrell, Department of Politics and International Relations of the University of Oxford, and furthermore to Dr Karma Nabulsi, Nuffield College, each of whom has contributed to my work with extremely helpful advice and counsel. Furthermore, I am thankful to my college, Christ Church, for providing me with an inspiring environment.

My work has received generous material support from the Fritz-Thyssen-Stiftung, through a scholarship; from the Becket Institute at St. Hugh's College, which appointed me as a Junior Scholar; from the Faculty of Theology; and from my family – I feel very much obliged to all of them.

I am grateful to the editors of *Religion and Society*, Professors Gustavo Benavides and Kocku von Stuckrad, for offering me to publish the book in this distinguished series. Furthermore, I am indebted to Dr Thomas Thornton who gave invaluable technical help, as well as to Dr Claus-Jürgen Thornton and Dr Albrecht Döhnert of Walter de Gruyter who have patiently assisted in the publication of this book.

I also would like to thank my friends in and beyond Oxford, who encouraged me in my work and who made my time in Oxford truly enjoyable. To name some means to do injustice to others, but still a few need to be mentioned especially: Kathryn Bevis; my sister-in-law, Dr Zoë Laidlaw; and my brother, Dr Michael Stumpf; all of whom have helped to shepherd me through the subtleties of the English language.

Finally, I am grateful for being blessed with the greatest family one could hope to have, not only when writing books. Hence, I would like to thank my sister, Alexandra Schörghuber, not only for generous support and extensive hospitality, but also for being the sister that she is, and my brother, Michael, who is certainly the best natural scientist one could wish for a brother, but also a great brother as such. Most of all, I would like to express my sincere gratitude to my parents, Dr Annedore Stumpf and Dekan Hans Rudolf Stumpf, for their unwavering support and never-failing love, which made this work possible. This book is dedicated to them.

Lübeck-Travemünde, Trinity 2006 — Christoph A. Stumpf

Table of Contents

Introduction

There are two characteristic features of modern public international law which are the cause for numerous problems in international practice: First, as a general rule modern public international law acknowledges as legal subjects only states to which rights and obligations pertain.[1] Individual human beings are only accorded a limited legal status under public international law, which is mainly derived from their respective relation to the state of which they are citizens. They are not in the position to assert any rights against states, which makes it hard to accommodate a satisfactory concept of international human rights. At the same time individuals are not held to be personally responsible for any contraventions against international legal standards: breaches of international law remain a matter directly between states, whereas there is as yet no general possibility of addressing the personal responsibility of private individuals. This concentration of modern public international law on states as exclusive legal subjects faces mounting criticism, for this concept fails to answer numerous problems in international relations today, such as human rights issues or matters of international criminal law.[2]

A second feature of public international law, which is both a blessing and a curse for the modern international society of nations, is the strict reliance on consensus as the exclusive source of international law. This is most obvious for international treaties which require the consent of the parties to become binding.[3] The same is true for international customary law, which has to be supported by the *opinio iuris* of the parties concerned in order to be acknowledged as part of public international law.[4] Finally, general legal

---

1 Cf. J. Kokott, "Naturrecht und Positivismus im Völkerrecht – sind wir auf dem Wege zu einer Weltverfassung?", in: C. J. Meier-Schatz (ed.), *Recht und Internationalisierung*, pp. 3 et seq.; M. Nettesheim, "Das kommunitäre Volkerrecht", *Juristenzeitung*, 57 (2002), pp. 569 et seq.; K. Hailbronner, "Der Staat und der Einzelne als Völkerrechtssubjekte", in W. Graf Vitzthum (ed.), *Völkerrecht*, pp. 161 et seq.; 171 et seq.

2 Cf. E. Klein, *Menschenrechte: Stille Revolution des Völkerrechts und Auswirkungen auf die innerstaatliche Rechtsanwendung*; H. Mosler, "Die Erweiterung des Kreises der Völkerrechtssubjekte", *Zeitschrift für ausländisches Recht und Völkerrecht*, 22 (1962), pp. 1 et seq., 30 et seq.; cf. J. Kokott, "Naturrecht und Positivismus im Völkerrecht", pp. 18–19.

3 K. Zemanek, "Das Völkervertragsrecht", in H. Neuhold, W. Hummer, C. Schreuer (eds.), *Österreichisches Handbuch des Völkerrechts*, pp. 55 et seq.

4 K. Wolfke, *Custom in Present International Law*, pp. 23 et seq.; B. Simma, "Das Völkergewohnheitsrecht", in H. Neuhold, W. Hummer, C. Schreuer (eds.), *Österreichisches Handbuch des Völkerrechts*, pp. 43 et seq.

principles as the third core element of public international law also have to be accepted by the legal subjects of public international law; otherwise, they cannot be deemed legally binding.[5] While consensus as the ultimate basis for public international law is, of course, advantageous for its universal acceptance, it also makes the principles of public international law the least common denominator of the international society.[6]

Both of the aforementioned features are relatively new to international law: they both are a consequence of the secularisation within the European legal tradition in the course of the 17th century, and of the emergence of the concept of a territorial state in Europe. Previously there prevailed, at least in the European history of Christian legal thought, an understanding of law as a metaphysical system, which was supplemented by a Christological concept of legislation. This concept included rights and obligations in the strict sense as well as certain moral standards pertaining to the inward dispositions of the respective moral agent. The identification of law with metaphysics corresponded to the focus of this Christian tradition of international law on the personal responsibility of the individual as moral agent. Hence, any individual was taken to be obligated personally by the respective moral obligations according to his respective status as ruler or subject.[7]

The traditional Christian concept of international law entails various parallels to similar religious systems of international law. The most prominent example for such systems, which is still also one of the most relevant factors for the modern society of nations, is the Islamic law of nations, which in its classic shape is termed *siyar*.[8] The Islamic law of nations relies on a set of divine laws which God revealed to mankind[9] through his prophet. Here we have no international law, but divine law. The respective rights and obligations under this divine law pertain to the individual faithful Muslim, whereas at least in its classic shape the Islamic law of nations did not account for states as legal entities.

---

5 M Rotter, "Die allgemeinen Rechtsgrundsätze", in H. Neuhold, W. Hummer, C. Schreuer (eds.), *Österreichisches Handbuch des Völkerrechts*, pp. 883 et seq.; M. M. Whiteman, "Jus Cogens in International Law", *Georgia Journal of International and Comparative Law*, 7 (1977), pp. 609 et seq.

6 On the moral inadequacies of the traditional understanding of international relations see A. Hurrell, "Order and Justice in International Relations: What is at Stake?", in R. Foot, J. Gaddis, A. Hurrell (eds.), *Order and Justice in International Relations*, pp. 31 et seq.

7 H. G. Walther, *Imperiales Königtum, Konziliarismus und Volkssouveränität: Studien zu den Grenzen des mittelalterlichen Souveränitätsgedankens*, pp. 10 et seq.

8 Khadduri, *The Islamic Law of Nations*, pp. 5 et seq.

9 The use of the term "mankind" instead of the more fashionable "humankind" or "humanity" throughout this thesis is a mere linguistic choice that by no means implies the exclusion of women. Similarly, the use of "he" and "his" instead of "he or she" and "her or his" serves the sole purpose of preserving readability.

Meanwhile, the contemporary debate on public international law also reveals an inclination to develop its principles further so as to overcome the problems of its moral relativity and its blindness to individuals.[10] One of the most interesting of the recent proposals brought forward by liberal authors is the "Law of Peoples" as described by John Rawls.[11] Rawls endeavours to pierce the veil of statehood by transferring the idea of a social contract from the domestic to the international level: through an international discourse amongst the "well-ordered" societies – that is to say, whose political structures provide a "decent consultation hierarchy" – the common good is to be found for the international society, and consequently given a legal shape. While the details need not interest us in this context, it should be noted that the modern idea of a public international law in the sense of a law as agreed between states is only one potential answer to the question of how to organise the international relations for all of mankind.

As it is, international relations – the interaction between states and peoples on an international level and its legal framework – are in the modern secular approach taken by most of the so-called "Western" scholars regarded as a domain of the legal and the political sciences. The interest of "Western" lawyers and of "Western" political scientists lies with certain political and legal principles which govern international relations. These lawyers and political scientists conventionally restrict their attention to the question of which rules are acknowledged in international affairs, and which consequences will effectively result from non-compliance with such rules. In the secular environment of the "Western" tradition, legal and political scholars rather concentrate on external acts than on the agents' internal sentiments or thoughts. The personal motivation of the agents in international relations and their perception of the moral quality of international rules, which determine their conduct as internal factors, remain unfocused. Though it is certainly acknowledged in the "secularised" legal and political sciences that religious beliefs shape the moral values of the individual agents, matters related to philosophical, moral, or metaphysical aspects are ignored. Yet, remarkably enough, such metaphysical or theological aspects of international relations are only rarely addressed even by modern theological scholars. There are, of course, issues of international relations which are discussed in the contemporary theological debate, such as, for example, human rights, the use of force between states, humanitarian crises, or economic justice. Nonetheless, the question what the legal framework of the international society of states might look like from a Christian perspective and how the

---

10 See for example F. Tesón, *A Philosophy of International Law*. Buchanan, Allen. *Justice, Legitimacy, and Self-Determination: Moral Foundations of International Law*.

11 J. Rawls, *The Law of Peoples*; on Rawls' concept of international relations see F. Tesón, "The Rawlsian Theory of International Law", pp. 79-99.

Church as political community can contribute to the identification of an international moral order receives only very limited attention by the theologians of our time.[12] The reluctance of many modern theologians to attend to the fundamental question of the international legal order contrasts significantly to that of preceding generations, in particular to the church fathers, from Isidor of Seville, to Augustine, to Thomas Aquinas, to such canon lawyers as Gratian or Hostiensis, and in particular to the Spanish moral theologians of the School of Salamanca.

In this respect a most conspicuous position is held by the Dutch theologian and lawyer Hugo Grotius. As a polymath Grotius took an interest in a wide range of subjects, reaching from theology and law, to classical literature and philology, through to historiography and ethnological studies. Contemporary jurists still praise Grotius as the father of modern public international law; numerous modern theologians continue to appreciate Grotius' contributions to the fields of exegesis and of early ecclesiastical history. However, the combination of jurisprudence on the one hand and moral theology and philosophy on the other in Grotius' work rarely attracted any keen interest by legal or theological scholars, even though Grotius regarded any human jurisprudence which did not account for the respective framework of Divine Right as crippled and mutilated.[13]

Succeeding generations of jurists and theologians appear to have agreed implicitly to share Grotius and his works in roughly equal pieces. International jurists, in particular many of his Dutch followers, concentrated on those parts of Grotius' system in which they could find support for their own ideas. Hence Grotius could be celebrated as inventor of the freedom of the high seas, as human rights advocate, as innovator in the fields of international criminal justice, or as eminent legal historian on the theory of just war. Many theologians have relished seeing Grotius as one of the entrepreneurs of historical critical exegesis, who combined a vast knowledge of oriental history with immense philological skill. The bridges Grotius himself built between the fields of law and theology had, however, rarely tempted disciples of either discipline to cross the lines: Grotius' analysis of moral theological aspects of the just war doctrine thus maintained as much a

---

12 Nonetheless, the perception of the Church as *Politeia* next to other political communities already reaches back to the anonymous apologetic Epistle to Diognetus around A.D. 130, cf. O. M. T. O'Donovan, J. Lockwood O'Donovan, *From Irenaeus to Grotius: A Sourcebook in Christian Political Thought*, pp. 12 et. seq.; on this tradition as venturing point for a communitarian understanding of the Church see D. Fergusson, *Community, Liberalism and Christian Ethics*, pp. 18 et seq.; see also E. Herms, "Lage und Perspektive der Kirchen im Zusammenhang der europäischen Einigung am Ende des 20. Jahrhunderts: Eine evangelische Selbsteinschätzung", in C. A. Stumpf, H. Zaborowski (eds.), *Church as Politeia: The Political Self-Understanding of Christianity*, pp. 285 et seq.

13 Cf. D. M. Sprackling, "Divine and Human Law in Hugo Grotius", p. 81.

life in the shadows of scholarly light as his considerations on penal justice in the context of his theory of divine atonement. Grotius' interpreters frequently explained the respective cross-references from legal arguments to theological precedents and vice versa as illustrations of his ambition to impress his readers with his humanist literacy, or as attempts to clothe his legal or philosophical arguments in theological garments, so as to make them acceptable for a pious audience. However, a prevailing view on Grotius' theory of international relations amongst contemporary jurists and political scientists is that he tried to create an international legal order, relying on a minimalist legal ethics which was designed in a way to be amenable to a wide range of ethnical and ethical backgrounds.[14]

It is to be doubted whether such an interpretation of Grotius' theory of international relations can do justice to a jurist with such an immense theological interest. The interpretation of Grotius as an ethical minimalist contrasts strongly to Grotius' own dogmatic position in the theological controversies in the Netherlands between the Remonstrants and the Counter-Remonstrants. Moreover, it probably belies human nature to conceive of a scholar who is fully devoted to proposing a return to the fundamental dogmatics of the church fathers in elaborated theological treatises on one day, just to free himself of any such theological preconditioning in order to display himself as the avant-garde of a secular jurisprudence the next day.

Meanwhile, there have been some attempts to reconcile the theology and the law in the historical interpretation of Grotius' works on international relations. For example, the excellent evaluation of Grotius' theory of just war by Peter Haggenmacher illustrates the Grotius' indebtedness to the theological traditions of the late Scholastics as well as the Reformation[15]; a recent research project undertaken by Onuma Yasuaki highlighted the links of Grotius to the political theology of the Salamancan school.[16] In addition to the aforementioned historical evaluations of Grotius' theory, there are also more conceptual interpretations of Grotius, which illustrate the interweaving of theological and legal concepts in his works, for example the work of Karma Nabulsi on the traditions of war, which present the Grotian just war theory as *via media* between the martial and the republican traditions of war respectively[17], as well as the history of the right of war and peace by Richard Tuck[18] and by Edward Keene[19], both of which endeavour to identify Grotius'

---

14 See, for example, R. Tuck, *Natural Rights Theories: Their Origins and Development*, pp. 58 et seq.; id., *Philosophy and Government*, p. 185. On the 'orthodox' perception of Grotius see E. Keene, *Beyond the Anarchical Society. Grotius, Colonialism and Order in World Politics*, pp. 12 et seq.

15 P. Haggenmacher, *Grotius et la doctrine de la guerre juste*.

16 Y. Onuma (ed.), *A Normative Approach to War*.

17 K. Nabulsi, *Traditions of War*.

18 R. Tuck, *The Rights of War and Peace*.

theory of international law as one of the keystones within a greater mosaic of respective concepts in the history of international legal thought.

One particularly noteworthy conceptual interpretation of Grotius to be noted in this respect is that offered by the political theorist Martin Wight, who has described Grotius' concept in a rather brief sketch as a "dual" or "concentric" system of international relations[20]: The first, inner circle of nations in Grotius' system followed the idea of a society of Christian nations, the *respublica Christiana,* which corresponds to the political society described by medieval canon law. The second, wider, circle of nations then follows the concept of a universal human fellowship, stressing the membership in the human race regardless of the religious conviction of the individual as cause for the acknowledgement of rules of the law of nations. This idea had been put forward primarily by such Spanish moral theologians as Vitoria and Suarez. Consequently, the outer circle encompasses both Christian and non-Christian nations; it conceives of a worldwide family of nations, bound together simply by the bond of human fellowship. According to Wight, Grotius combines both ideas and perceives a distinction between international relations amongst Christian nations on the one hand and non-Christian nations on the other. Yet Wight obviously believes that Grotius' distinction drew a geographical borderline between the Christian group of nations that was bound by the law of Christ, and other states.

These rather sketchy observations by Martin Wight will provide the venturing point from which we will embark to revisit Grotius' theory of international relations as a theology of international law and its framework of Divine Right (*Ius*), which indeed disregards geographical borderlines.

As a first step we shall investigate Grotius' concept of Natural Right (*Ius naturale*) as Right of creation. We shall analyse the origin of Natural Right and its main principles of justice and Natural Religion, and their respective consequences for the international intercourse between states. For Grotius, Natural Right is the right of creation, valid for mankind in its entirety, and thus is applicable to anyone regardless of the individual's religious affiliation.

The analysis of Grotius' position on Arbitrary Divine Right (*Ius voluntarium divinum*) as Right of revelation will be the second step. Here we shall look at the sources and functions of Arbitrary Divine Right. Furthermore, we shall focus on the content of the Law of the Gospel as most central code of Arbitrary Divine Right. The Law of the Gospel provides a specific legal standard peculiar to Christians, to Christian rulers as well as to Christian subjects.

---

19 E. Keene, *Beyond the Anarchical Society. Grotius, Colonialism and Order in World Politics.*

20 M. Wight, *Systems of States*, pp. 125–128.

The third step will be the examination of Human Right (*Ius humanum*) and human rule as presented by Grotius. For this we shall explore Grotius' position with respect to the origin and structure of established political rule. Moreover, we will inquire into the role which Grotius accords to the state in relation to religious affairs. For Grotius, the state is a purely human institution. However, God approves of the human establishment of the state, which is why its political organisation is accommodated in the wider context of divine justice.

As a fourth step we shall ask what relevance proprietary rights have for Grotius. Here we shall examine the consequences of Grotius' theory of proprietary rights for the establishment of territorial authority. Proprietary rights are for Grotius also a purely human institution. Nonetheless, they are legitimate in the post-lapsarian state of the world, but at the same time they are limited by the overarching framework of Divine Right.

Finally, we shall turn to the procedural aspects of Grotius' theology of international law by delving into his outlook on war. In particular, we shall deal with Grotius' just war, the legitimacy of war, its functions in international relations, and his attempts to provide for moderation of war-faring practice. For Grotius, peace provides the normal state, whereas war is only a remedy to restore the rule of justice. As such the Right of War as well as the Right in War are altogether embedded in the fundaments of Divine Right.

The examination will primarily rely on Grotius' treatises on the law of nations. Pertinent works of Grotius on the law of nations are *De Iure Praedae Commentarius*, written in 1603, and *De Iure Belli ac Pacis*, the first edition of which had appeared in 1625. While in *De Iure Praedae Commentarius* Grotius aims to justify the use of violence by the Dutch East Indian Company against the Portuguese and Spanish fleet in the East Indies, which was criticised by the company's pacifist shareholders, the treatise *De Iure Belli ac Pacis* was mainly motivated by Grotius' wish to undertake a comprehensive general survey of the law of war, including the principles of the law of nations. The picture of Grotius' legal theory that may be drawn from the aforementioned treatises on public international law will be supplemented by references to Grotius' work on the jurisprudence of Holland, *Inleiding tot de Hollandsche Rechtsgeleertheyd*, written during his imprisonment in Loevestein in 1620 in the wake of the confessional controversies in the Netherlands.

However, no examination of Grotius' legal theory will be able to do completely without reference to his works specifically devoted to theological matters. For our purposes his works on the relationship between state and Church, namely *De Ordinum Hollandiae ac Westfrisiae Pietas Vindicata* and *De Imperio Summarum Potestatum circa Sacra*, will be of particular importance. *De Ordinum Hollandiae ac Westfrisiae Pietas Vindicata* is a rather polemic refutation of the attacks of Sibrand Lubbert on the states of Holland, completed and published in 1614. Here Grotius is not so much concerned with theological questions or theoretical issues as such. Rather he endeavours to show that the state of Holland had the competence to decide upon theological disputes legitimately. Interesting in this context is Grotius' comparison between the views of the Dutch Counter-Remonstrants and the English Puritans.[21] The second important work by Grotius on the matter in question is *De Imperio Summarum Potestatum circa sacra*. It was also written mainly in 1614, but was revised until 1617 and published only posthumously in 1647.[22] In this treatise Grotius elaborates on the relationship between Church and state, and the role and the powers of civil magistrates in spiritual matters in a more sophisticated and irenic fashion.[23]

Of central interest for Grotius' theological approach to the theory of justice is his elaboration in *Defensio Fidei Catholicae de Satisfactione Christi*[24], dating from 1617. Furthermore, we shall take account of the exposition of Grotius' views on Natural Religion in comparison to Christianity in *Meletius sive de Iis Quae inter Christianos Conveniunt Epistola*[25], written in 1611, and his apologetically orientated *De Veritate Religionis Christinianae*[26] compiled in 1627.

Hence the general object of this examination will be the demonstration that the system of international law as perceived by Grotius indeed presents

---

21 Cf. H. Grotius, *De Ordinum Pietas*, 112b et seq. Grotius noted that Sibrandus and his friends were keen on avoiding to be identified with the Puritans as they hoped to attract support from King James I of England, who was known to be fervent opponent of Puritanism. Nevertheless, in Grotius' opinion the Puritans of England, "hominibus ... duricervicibus", were similar to the Counter-Remonstrants with respect to three distinct characteristics: they did not acknowledge the head of the state as simultaneously the head of the external Church; they did not approve of the respective government of the Church; and they did not rely on ancient sources but solely on recent authors.

22 Cf. on the genesis of *De Imperio Summarum Potestatum circa Sacra* H.-J. van Dam, "De Imperio Summarum Potestatum circa Sacra", in H. Nellen, E. Rabbie, *Hugo Grotius, theologian: Essays in Honour of G. H. M. Posthumus Meyjes*, pp. 19 et seq.; A. Caspani, "Il De Imperio summarum potestatum circa sacra di Grozio", *Revista di Filosofia Neo-scolatica*, 79 (1987), pp. 218–249, pp. 382–419.

23 A description of how Grotius endeavoured to return to a milder and more peaceful tone in *De Imperio*, in contrast to the more aggressive style exposed in *De Ordinum Pietas*, can be found in H.-J. van Dam, "De Imperio Summarum Potestatum circa Sacra", in H. Nellen, E. Rabbie, *Hugo Grotius, theologian*, pp. 34 et seq.

24 Cf. E. Rabbie, "Some Remarks Concerning the Textual History of Hugo Grotius' De Satisfactione", *Grotiana*, 7 (1986), pp. 99–120.

25 Cf. Posthumus Meyjes and H. M. Guillaume, "Hugo de Groot's 'Meletius' (1611), His Earliest Theological Work, Rediscovered", *Lias*, 11 (1984), pp. 147–150.

26 Cf. F.-J. Niemann, "Die erste ökumenische Fundamentaltheologie", *Catholica*, 37 (1983), pp. 203–215.

a theology of international law. We will concentrate on three different aspects in particular:

Firstly, Grotius did not establish his theory of international law in an intellectual vacuum. His concept of international law is indeed firmly rooted in a longstanding tradition of Christian legal thought, which in Grotius' works shines through in a typical humanist fashion. The indebtedness of Grotius' legal theory to the Christian traditions will be illustrated by reference to various examples of medieval Christian theology as well as of the canon law tradition.

Secondly, even though Grotius' theory of international law is profoundly Christian in nature and in tradition, it is at the same time compatible with modern liberal concepts of international law. Indeed, Grotius' international legal ethics might well serve as a theological supplement to a more contemporary legal system in a modern society of nations. To this effect Grotius' theology of international law will be compared to the modern liberal concept of the Law of Peoples by John Rawls, in particular in one regard: the modern positivist legal system relies on a negative definition of freedom – hence freedom is essentially what is not prohibited by law. We are free to act irrationally, to behave unreasonably, to display bad manners, as long as we do not cross the borderline of established legal regulations, e.g. by breaching our obligations vis-à-vis others or the state. However, Grotius' idea of freedom is a positive one: we have to accept the moral responsibility entailed in freedom, and hence in deciding upon how to act we have to take into consideration not only legal prohibitions or commandments, but also the consequences of our actions for others and for our relationship with God.

Thirdly, while being profoundly Christian in content and at the same time distinctly modern in shape, Grotius' theology may also provide bridges to other religious concepts of international relations, such as that in classic Islamic jurisprudence. Indeed, the aforementioned distinction between an inner circle of Christian nations and a wider circle of nations connected through the universal fellowship of human beings might serve as a Christian answer to the Islamic idea of a realm of Islam (*dār al-Islām*) – a realm that comprises all faithful Muslims and adheres to the fullness of God's law on the one hand, and a realm of war (*dār al-Harb*) on the other which contains everyone else and in which a more general equity may be expected.

In this sense Grotius' theory of international law is then truly a Christian theology of international law, and as such it may provide assistance in overcoming the aforementioned problems of contemporary public international law and even help to build bridges to other religious cultures of international law.

Chapter 1

Natural Right

I. Introduction

All of the more important theories of international law have a global approach in that they provide a set of rules which are universally applicable, regardless of the individual circumstances of the legal subjects and objects concerned. Regulations of international law naturally have to be acceptable to a wide range of legal cultures shaped by diverse traditions, social structures, and values. Yet, at the same time nearly all major theories of international relations conceive of a separation of states into at least two groups, one of which provides the model for member states (or more traditionally: member peoples) of the international community, and thus may be used as a standard for determining "proper" international conduct; for easy reference we may call these "decent states". The other states (or peoples) do not adhere to the same standards, and thus are conceived of as objects of international law – or, rather, as proof that certain standards of international law need to be defined so that the well-being of the international community of states (or of peoples) can be ensured. Such states (or peoples), which we may refer to as a "non-decent realm" (not necessarily, but possibly "indecent" or "outcast" realm), are as necessary for any theories of international law as murderers, thieves, and swindlers are requisite for establishing any criminal law. The distinction between a decent realm and a non-decent realm is not an end in itself: theories of international law, just as any other legal theories, reflect a certain concept of right and wrong of those developing these theories. Truth entails the possibility of untruth, potentially correct conduct in the international arena entails potentially incorrect conduct, and a commandment entails the potential of disobedience. Any theory of international law thus has to take account of potential breaches of its legal principles.

Such a distinction between a decent political realm in international relations and a "non-decent", if not "indecent", one is surely present in the Christian legal tradition. Regardless of the different veins pursued by Christian authors who have dealt with international law intensively, an underlying feature of all of the more important works on international relations in the history of Christian political thought since the Constantinian period is the emphasis on Christian nations, peoples, or states as distinguished body politick (or bodies politick), which are distinguished from non-Christian, infidel, or pagan nations, peoples, or states. In one way or the other this tradition is apparent in the writings of Augustine, who distinguishes between the divine city and the earthly city[1]; in the canon lawyers, especially of the thirteenth century, with their views on wars against Muslim rulers[2]; in the late Scholastics with their interest in warfare against unbelievers in territories overseas[3]; and in Humanist writers such as Erasmus, with his strict opposition against wars amongst Christian princes and mild favouring of wars against non-Christians.[4] If one applies the distinction between a decent realm and a non-decent realm, the former category consists of the Christian states, peoples, and nations, while the latter category is identical with the non-Christian realm.

A similar distinction is notoriously to be found in the Islamic concept of international law, which presupposes a distinction between the realm of Islam (*dār al-Islām*), which includes all areas which are already under Islamic domination, and the realm of war (*dār al-Harb*), where Islam is not yet dominating.[5] There is a necessary antagonism between the former and the latter. Leaving aside all different streams of this tradition and its diverse shapes in the history of Islamic legal thought, this distinction is a traditional feature forging the Islamic law of nations, from Shaybani[6] to modern Islamic scholars of public international law.[7] The decent realm may be identified with the realm of Islam, whereas the realm of war presents the non-decent realm.

Yet, not only the religious traditions of a law of nations with their inherent strong emphasis on a specific moral truth presuppose such distinctions between a decent and a non-decent realm in the international arena: modern liberal concepts of international law rely on similar distinctions as well. While a liberal legal concept naturally can do without defining a religious truth, it nevertheless presupposes a truth of its own:

---

1 Cf. A. Augustinus, *De civitate Dei*, XI on the respective origins of the divine city and the earthly city.

2 Cf. J. A. Brundage, *Medieval Canon Law*, pp. 162 et seq.; C. A. Stumpf, "Völkerrecht unter Kreuz und Halbmond: Muhammad al-Shaybani und Hugo Grotius als Exponenten religiöser Völkerrechtstradition", *Archiv des Völkerrechts*, 41 (2003/1), pp. 93 et seq.

3 Cf. R. Tuck, *The Rights of War and Peace*, pp. 65 et seq.

4 Cf. J. Lockwood O'Donovan, "The Christian Pedagogy and Ethics of Erasmus: A Poesis for the Present?", in C. A. Stumpf, H. Zaborowski (eds.), *Church as Politeia: The Political Self-Understanding of Christianity*, pp. 103, 112 et seq.

5 Cf. Stumpf, "Völkerrecht unter Kreuz und Halbmond", pp. 93 et seq.

6 Cf. Khadduri, *The Islamic Law of Nations*, pp. 38 et seq.

7 Cf. M. Rohe, "Rechtliche Perspektiven eines deutschen und europäischen Islam", *Rabels Zeitschrift für ausländisches Privatrecht*, 64 (2000/2), pp. 258, 267 et seq.

liberal theories of law naturally are not so much interested in the material truth of a certain content of law, but they nevertheless require a more institutionally orientated legal concept, meaning, for instance, that such modern liberal theories regard certain information and consultation procedures as necessary for the legitimacy of any legal order[8]: they are more concerned with justice in procedure than in material justice. Consequently, John Rawls, one of the most important liberal theorists of modern international law, is distinguishes between liberal peoples and non-liberal peoples: liberal peoples, according to Rawls, consist of citizens that are united by common sympathies and by a common moral nature. They have a reasonably just constitutional democratic government that serves their fundamental interests.[9] Non-liberal peoples, on the other hand, lack one or several of these features. The concept of international relations presented by Rawls is developed from the standpoint of the liberal peoples. Consequently, Rawls takes an interest in how liberal peoples can come to terms with other peoples in a peaceful international society, and in how liberal peoples are to relate to peoples that are not organised in a liberal way.

One of the typical problems with such distinctions between a decent realm and a non-decent one is the scope of the respective definitions of such states: the establishment of rule will have to take into account the exceptions it entails – e.g. it will be difficult to establish a rule of monogamy in a society overwhelmingly forged by polygamic relationships. Or, to use a rather profane example, a vegan concept of international law very likely will meet an overwhelming majority of carnivorous transgressors of its principles. Fundamentalist veganism as basis of a theory of international law will very likely be bound to fail in its extreme demands. To reach his ultimate end at least somewhere half-way, a considerate representative of international veganism will therefore ask how an acceptable common denominator can be found with other positions that do not endorse his own strict views. Pushing this example further, one may expect that some other intermediary dietary concept will be used to enhance the acceptance of a specific international standard.

This is exactly what has happened in the existing traditions of international law as well, though the solutions offered by and within these traditions are manifold: in the Christian tradition, for example, certain authors have taken the opinion that even without fully accepting the Christian faith, unbelievers may be accorded the status of legal subjects in international law.[10] The acknowledgement of a rightful dominion of pagan

---

8 Cf. W. Graf Vitzthum, "Begriff, Geschichte und Quellen des Völkerrechts", in W. Graf Vitzthum, *Völkerrecht*, pp. 9 et seq.

9 J. Rawls, *The Law of Peoples*, pp. 23 et seq.

10 Cf. F. H. Russell, *The Just War in the Middle Ages*, pp. 294, 255 et seq.

rulers by the late Scholastics of the School of Salamanca is but one example for such an extension of legal principles beyond the traditional borderlines of the Christian faith.[11] In relation to the Christian tradition of international law it has to be remembered that early Christianity developed in a pagan environment without gaining political importance from the start. Given that the early Christians lived in a paganly dominated legal environment may have contributed considerably to the acceptance of the legitimacy of certain non-Christian legal structures.[12]

The situation for the Islamic law of nations was different from that of the respective Christian traditions. Nearly from the start it had a strong political dimension which had become manifest in the political rule exercised by Mohammed as chief Islamic prophet and his successors, in particular by the Caliphs. Very early on, Moslems encountered followers of different creeds inside and outside of the boundaries of the realm of Islam. This explains why the Islamic law of nations had already acknowledged at a rather early stage the access of unbelievers to Islamic justice inside the realm of Islam. In relation to the realm of war, the early Islamic lawyers expected to find only a rather vague kind of natural equity; only later did Islamic jurisprudence gradually begin to acknowledge treaty relations with non-Islamic rulers.[13] The Islamic law of nations finally developed this into the concept of a realm of agreement (*dār al-Sulh* or *dār al-Ahd*)[14]: the realm of agreement is not yet considered part of Islam, but at the same time does not meet the same fundamental hostility with which the realm of war is viewed.

A similar "intermediary" approach can be found in the modern liberal theory of international law. Again we may take a look at the respective concept of Rawls, who – while still taking the liberally organised people as ideal – seeks to find a common legal standard in a contractually organised society of peoples with "decent peoples". While decent peoples in the sense applied by Rawls do not meet the specific standards required from liberal peoples, they have nevertheless a "decent" consultation hierarchy or are otherwise "worthy of membership in a Society of Peoples" because their organisational structure is compatible with the underlying concept of justice as fairness to be applied as fundamental principle of the Society of Peoples.[15]

This short overview might suffice to illustrate the necessity for any sound theory of international law to identify certain fundamental principles which may adequately serve as common denominator for nations in their

---

11 Cf. E. Reibstein, *Johannes Althusius als Fortsetzer der Schule von Salamanca*, pp. 20 et seq.

12 Cf. Stumpf, "Völkerrecht unter Kreuz und Halbmond".

13 Ibid., pp 88 et seq.

14 S. Ramadan, *Das Islamische Recht*, pp. 168 et seq.; D. Macdonald, A. Abel, "dār al-Sulh", in *Encyclopedia of Islam* II, pp. 131 et seq.

15 J. Rawls, *The Law of Peoples*, p. 63.

international intercourse. Given the need for a global scope in its application to a variety of legal cultures, these fundamental principles will typically not represent the full truth as viewed by the author of such a theory, though they certainly may not be contrary to this truth either.

In Grotius' theology of international law, the function of fundamental principles of International Right (*Ius*) is performed by Natural Right (*Ius naturale*): Natural Right in Grotius' theology serves as the legal fundament of all international relations, whether amongst Christian nations or non-Christian nations. In the following we shall firstly view Grotius' legal taxonomy in general, before we turn to Natural Right as a distinct legal category which Grotius employs to identify a specific legal standard for Christian and non-Christian states alike. In particular, we shall examine how Grotius used the Christian tradition of justice in general and of International Right in particular to shape a common denominator for a global morality of international relations. Furthermore, we will endeavour to find out how the distinctly theological concept of international relations presented by Grotius could find acceptance by the modern "Western" system of puclic international law. At the same time we shall check the compatibility of the Grotian concept with other religious theories of the Right of Nations, namely the Islamic law of nations.

We shall see that Natural Right as a distinct category of Divine Right presents the overarching category in Grotius' theology of International Right: the principles of Natural Right have their source in the rationality of God's creation; consequently, matters of divine truth, which had only been revealed subsequently to creation, remain outside its scope. Thus Natural Right for Grotius does not represent the full divine truth, though it certainly is fully compatible with the divine will in its entirety.

The system of Right and of Natural Right developed by Grotius has sometimes been labelled "minimalist", meaning that it presents a kind of lowest common denominator for a universal culture of Right.[16] However, despite Grotius' concessions in the presentation of a divine truth in creation without the additions entailed by the divine revelation in the Holy Scripture, the Grotian concept of Natural Right provides a relatively high moral standard: Grotius presents an elaborate and comprehensive doctrine of justice, and he explicitly relies on the concept of a universally binding Natural Religion. Despite the importance which Grotius accords to consensus of the legal subjects in identifying principles of Natural Right on the epistemological level, which might indeed ultimately result in a somewhat minimalist code of principles, his greater emphasis is on the reason inherent in God's creation on the ontological level: this is certainly far from any moral

16 Cf. R. Tuck, *Philosophy and Government*, p. 185 et seq.; id. *Natural Rights Theories: Their Origins and Development*, pp. 58 et seq.

minimalism whatsoever. Grotius views a legal pattern by which human beings are connected to each other. This legal web penetrating mankind includes certain distinct principles of justice with God as legislator. Thus it seems appropriate to view Grotius as heir of a distinct Christian tradition of legal and political thinking, of which in particular Dante Alighieri may be seen as important representative[17]: like Dante in his *Monarchia*, so Grotius argues for an all-encompassing order as guarantee for the peaceful striving of human beings on earth. As regards the mode of practical implementation, Grotius, like Dante, accords great importance to the human intellect as a means to recognise the legal order provided already in creation. The main difference between Grotius and Dante is rooted in the scope of the legal order and the location of a supreme power within this legal order as envisioned by them respectively: Dante identifies the universal order with the Roman Empire: in Dante's opinion, the Romans had acquired universal rule by natural right, in particular by the natural virtue of the Romans, as well as by divine right, in particular by the divine designation of the Romans as universal rulers.[18] It is here that Grotius parts with Dante: as we shall see in this and in subsequent chapters in more detail, Grotius manages to create the idea of a universally applicable legal system without any particular institutionalised ruler other than God as legislator. It is probably this rulerless concept, besides other factors, which helped this part of Grotius' system to survive the further development of sovereign states which rendered any concept of an institutionalised rule without any actual manifestation.

Before embarking on an examination of Grotius' legal theory, a remark regarding the adaptation of Grotius' Latin vocabulary into English legal language seems in place: It is quite impossible to translate the Latin term *Ius* adequately into a truly corresponding English term which at the same time entails the abstract meaning of *Ius* as something including, but going beyond, *Lex* – law – and at the same time semantically conveys the inner connection between *Ius* and *iustitia* – justice or righteousness. The solution pursued here is to translate *Ius* with the capitalised English word "Right" or, when Grotius uses the plural, as "Rights", wherever he uses the word *Ius* in the sense of a law derived from the principle of justice. The lowercase term "right" will be used as the translation of a specific right of someone or to something; consequently, the English term "law" will only be used for the translation of *lex* as a code of particular legal rules.[19] This method of translation is sup-

17 Cf. Dante Alighieri, *De Monarchia*, I. iii., v. et seq.

18 Cf. ibid., II.ii. et seq.

19 It should be noted that the problem of translating *lex*, *ius* and *iustitia* is peculiar to the English language. Dutch, Grotius' mother tongue, provides a distinction, similar to the Latin terminology, between *wet*, *recht* and *gerechtigheid*, as does French, the language conventionally used by Grotius for conversation, as it offers the terms *loi*, *droit*, and *justice*.

ported by Grotius' own manuscript of *De Iure Belli ac Pacis*: Grotius himself writes the term *Ius* standardly with an initial capital, thus indicating an abstract noun, whereas he never uses the plural form *iura* except in literal quotations or when its meaning corresponds to the term "laws".

II. The Definition of Right

Traditionally the definitions of Right used by late Scholastic authors primarily followed Aristotle's distinction between justice in a general sense, comprising virtue in all its aspects, and in the particular sense of a partial virtue, relating to his concepts of commutative justice and distributive justice.[20] Thus, primarily two senses of Right were employed: Right in general and Right in the strict, particular sense. To these two meanings of Right, a third was added as a consequence of Jean Buridan's objections to the Thomist understanding of *Ius* in the sense of *iustitia*. Buridan had asserted that the term *Ius* had derived from the verb *iubere*, to command, and thus Right could also simply mean a law.[21] This implies a set of Right which derives its force not directly from an inherent principle of justice, but rather from the authority of the legislator. Yet, this still does not mean that Right in the meaning of "law" draws merely on a positive commandment: commandments by God as the source of morality certainly are perfectly compliant with a broader divine morality.

Compared to the ontological approach of medieval Christian jurisprudence, the modern Western liberal tradition of the Right of Nations primarily focuses on the epistemological level of the term "law". All three sources of international law acknowledged by Article 36 of the Statute of the International Court of Justice – treaty law, customary law, and general legal principles – refer in some way or other to an acceptance of any rule by the legal subjects concerned.[22] This is most obvious for treaty law: provisions of international agreements receive their legal force exclusively from their acceptance by the parties concerned. The same is true, however, for the two other sources: customary law draws for its validity on an underlying *opinio iuris* of the subjects of international law, and thus again requires its general acceptance in order to assume its legal force. *Prima facie*, general legal principles imply an objective obligatory force regardless of any subjective acceptance. Yet, no general legal principle will be able to demand observance as long as it is not accepted at least in a general way by the greater part of the

---

20 Cf. E. Reibstein, *Johannes Althusius als Fortsetzer der Schule von Salamanca*, pp. 17 et seq.; cf. J. Brundage, *Medieval Canon Law*, pp. 173 et seq.

21 Cf. J. Buridan, *In metaphysicam Aristotelis questiones*, 12.4.

22 Cf. W. Graf Vitzthum, "Begriff, Geschichte und Quellen des Völkerrechts", pp. 62 et seq.

subjects of international law. While thus the acceptance of a rule as obligatory under international law is decisive for attaining its legal force, the ontology of international law entailing the question of whether or not such a rule is "right" has only secondary importance. Surely, the question of whether a legal subject will accept a certain rule depends very much on whether this rule is deemed appropriate, whether it is accepted as "just", adequate, or equitable. However, such considerations on the moral value of a rule of international law merely concern the subjective motivation of legal subjects participating in legal discourse, whereas they cannot assume immediate relevance for the legal quality of any rule.[23] Thus, modern international law primarily relies on legal positivism as prerequisite for the efficacy of international regulations, whereas metaphysical reflections on the ontology of Right are beyond the interest of the relevant legal practice.[24]

In his definitions of "Right", Grotius is still indebted to medieval Christian jurisprudence, but he also prepares the way for a modern concept of international law: Grotius is essentially concerned with the substance of Right, with its link to justice, and to metaphysics, whereas epistemological matters, such as the recognition of any rule as International Right, are outside the scope of his attention in this respect. Grotius thus stands in the Aristotelian legal tradition of the late Scholastics, though, as we shall see, he certainly moves beyond them.

Within Grotius' works, the first chapter of *De Iure Belli ac Pacis* presents the most developed exposition of, and at the same time the most original elaboration upon, a definition of Right which is to be found in Grotius' works.[25] Grotius offers three different definitions of Right, which find their root in the traditional Aristotelian account of legal taxonomy, but go far beyond that.

While in his other expositions of the legal terminology, in particular in *De Indis* and *The Jurisprudence of Holland*, Grotius had more or less followed traditional definitions, a shift of emphasis can be recognized in *De Iure Belli ac*

---

23 Cf. J. Kokott, "Naturrecht und Positivismus im Völkerrecht – sind wir auf dem Wege zu einer Weltverfassung?", in C. J. Meier-Schatz, R. J. Schweizer (eds.), *Recht und Internationalisierung*, pp. 3 et seq.

24 Cf. H. Neuhold and C. Schrummer, "Westliches Völkerrecht: Geschichte, Methoden, Positionen", in H. P. Neuhold, W. Hummer, C. Schrummer (eds.), *Österreichisches Handbuch des Völkerrechts*, pp. 19 et seq.; W. Graf Vitzthum, "Begriff, Geschichte und Quellen des Völkerrechts", pp. 80 et seq.

25 In Grotius' other main work on International Right, *De Iure Praedae*, II.i., he is more concerned with the meaning of Right than with the definition of the term. However, in this work Grotius offers a philological explanation of the term *Ius*, which he believes to have been derived from *Jove* as the Stoics had already suggested; this is repeated in IBP, "Prolegomena" 12. Cf. for this in greater detail, O. M. T. O'Donovan, "The Justice of Assignment and Subjective Rights in Grotius", in: O. M. T. O'Donovan, J. Lockwood O'Donovan (eds.), *Bonds of Imperfection: Christian Politics, Past and Present*, pp. 167 et seq.

Pacis: The first sense of Right is presented here by Grotius as the original sense, from which the two other meanings of the word follow. Consequently, Grotius parts with the traditional distinction between a general and a particular sense of Right: the distinction is now one between an objective sense of Right and a subjective sense, with the traditional distinction between a general and a particular sense of Right being relocated to the distinction between two types of subjective Right.

1. Right is Nothing but what is Just

The first definition of Right offered by Grotius is a doubly negative one: *Ius hic nihil aliud quam quod iustum est significat*[26] – Right is nothing but what is just, and just is what is not unjust. Right is therefore to be determined negatively from what is not injustice. In this context injustice is described as what contradicts the nature of a society of those who use reason. Thus Grotius sees a connection between the negation of sociality in sin and the establishment of Right, in which he follows a Scholastic tradition.

Two aspects of this definition are remarkable: Firstly, the establishment of a relationship between Right and justice or, to be more precise, between Right and the absence of injustice. Hence Right, according to this definition, is not an abstract concept of universal rules that require obedience even if there is no one to obey. Indeed, the term "Right" is tied to and depends on the existence of human beings.

Secondly, this definition of Right excludes from its scope those virtues which do not involve any relation to justice as such, even though the practice of such virtues might be praiseworthy. There is then in this respect a notion of a paralegal morality implied by such virtues, though – as we shall see in due course when discussing Grotius' views on attributive justice – these virtues may indeed be included in a wider sense of justice. Yet, Grotius, in offering a first definition of Right alongside the Aristotelian general sense of justice, is at the same time restricting its scope to justice in a rather strict sense by excluding the virtues converging on the common good, which Aristotle had included in his understanding of general justice. In so doing, Grotius has reshaped the Scholastic understanding of the general sense of Right in a way that has become more compatible with the modern understanding of Right as law in a justiciable sense. Thus, duties which spring from virtues other than justice in the strict sense find no place in this first definition of Right. While this definition of Right still has a strong link to morality, it nevertheless is more compatible with the modern concept of international law than with much of the respective Christian tradition.

26 Cf. IBP, I.I.iii.1.

2. Right as Moral Quality

Grotius' second definition of Right is closely related to and developed from the first definition: *Quo sensu ius est Qualitas moralis personae competens ad aliquid iuste habendum vel agendum.*[27] Right is a moral quality attached to a person, by virtue of which quality this person is entitled to have or do something justly. Hence, while the first definition of Right referred to justice as a moral quality in the sense of the moral value of a certain state of affairs, this second definition of Right focuses on the admissibility of human beings having or doing something under the principles of justice. While the first definition described Right in an objective dimension, the second definition now turns to the subjective sense of Right.

Grotius here introduces two types of moral qualities which can be distinguished from each other by their respective degrees of perfection and thus in their respective subjective quality. A perfect moral quality is an ability or faculty (*facultas*). Here Grotius uses the Gersonian term for Right in a strict subjective, proprietorial sense. A less perfect moral quality is a fitness (*aptitudo*). These terms correspond in metaphysics to the terms reality (*actus*) and possibility (*potentia*).[28]

For example, a property right typically presents a faculty which grants a multitude of potential legal options: the owner can, for example, relinquish his ownership, he can destroy the object to which the property right relates, he can transfer the property right to the object to someone else, and so forth.

Grotius' introduction of fitness as legal category may be explained by the example of the appointment of candidates to a certain office: if someone is legally trained, he is fit to become a judge, or he may appear as legal practitioner before a court of law. This distinguishes the candidate from other candidates who lack the same fitness. However, the actual appointment of a certain candidate to a particular office does not correspond to a respective claim of the candidate for appointment. Instead this decision rests with others, e.g. with those who have a faculty to appoint suitable candidates to an office.

2.1. Faculty as Subjective Right in a Strict Sense

Grotius identifies faculty with what is called "one's own" (*sui*) by lawyers: something that belongs to someone. Faculty therefore presents a right in a genuine and strict sense, which may consist of various kinds of powers –

27 Cf. ibid., I.I.iv.

28 Cf. ibid., I.I.iv.

potestas[29]: First, a faculty can be the power over oneself, which is to be identified with liberty. Second, it can be the power over other human beings, like the power of the father over his children or the power of the master over his servants. Third, it can be the power over things, full as well as limited power. Fourth, it can be the claim of the creditor against the debtor in the sense of an entitlement to do or to have something.

There are two different aspects of a faculty: a faculty exists as a common faculty in coordinative relationships, as well as an eminent faculty in subordinate relationships.[30] Faculties in the latter sense are stronger than faculties in the former sense, for these present rights entailing claims of the community against individual parts and their goods. Thus, just as anyone is more obliged to the state than to one's creditor, a king has for the sake of the common good a more eminent power over things than an owner has over his own property.[31] We shall return to this issue in greater detail when we arrive at Grotius' treatment of rule and property. For the moment it should suffice to illustrate the eminent power by taking two examples from Grotius' further elaboration of the Right of peace and war: Though we have the entitlement to defend ourselves against an act of injustice committed against us, this right is monopolised after the establishment of human rule in the institution of the government.[32] Moreover, while we may acquire individual proprietary rights, in certain cases the ancient communal proprietary right may prevail.[33]

2.2. Fitness as Suitability

Grotius states that fitness is what Aristotle had named dignity (αξιαν)[34] and what Michael of Ephesus had called equitable.[35] The interpretation by Michael of Ephesus might be helpful to grasp Grotius' understanding of fitness. What Michael of Ephesus calls "equitable" does not, strictly speaking, pertain to dignity itself, but to its identification in practice: distributing according to the dignity of the recipients is equitable. Compared to faculty, fitness entails a minor degree of perfection in the sense that it does not in

29 Cf. ibid., I.I.v.

30 Cf. ibid., I.I.vi.

31 K. Nabulsi, *Traditions of War*, concludes from this passage that Grotius here defines liberty as subsidiary right to sovereign authority; cf. ibid., p. 151. However, Grotius is here not concerned with a definition of liberty or sovereignty; he merely comments on hierarchical structures of power.

32 Cf. IBP, I.IV.ii. et seq.

33 Cf. ibid., II.II.xviii.

34 Cf. Aristoteles, V.6.

35 Cf. IBP, I.I.vii.36 Cf. ibid., I.I.ix.1.

itself imply a full entitlement to do or have something, but only a suitability of being allowed to do something or to receive something. It merely signifies the suitability of someone or something for a certain purpose; it does not constitute rights in a strict sense.

Fitness means aptness to be something, to do something, or to have something, without actually putting the fit person into a position to enforce this. Compared to the rather "active" legal position contained in the faculty, the fitness is a comparatively "passive" legal position. This can be illustrated by the granting of relief from debts and the forgiving of wrongdoings: a debtor who has paid his debts to the creditor in so doing receives a faculty against the creditor no longer to be held liable for the cleared debt. An offender may obtain the fitness to be discharged from his guilt and spared from punishment if he displays repentance, thus giving satisfaction.

This becomes relevant, in particular, for Grotius' position in relation to the atonement of the sins of mankind in the death of Christ, which – as we shall see in due course – is also important for Grotius' general conception of justice. The attack of Faustus Socinus in *De Iesu Christo Servatore* against the Catholic doctrine of vicarious satisfaction, as expounded by Anselm of Canterbury and upheld by the Calvinists, mainly addressed the conventional thesis that God received a satisfaction for the sins of mankind by Christ's death. According to Socinus, God merely forgives sins just as creditors relieve debtors of their debt. Grotius, however, holds that punishment is not a personal right, but an actualisation of justice: thus satisfaction has to be granted through punishment. Yet it is not for the offender to enforce his fitness for mercy. Forgiveness cannot be concluded solely from the fitness of the offender for such mercy, though repentance as satisfaction is certainly necessary for the exercise of mercy.

2.3. Right and Justice

As Grotius distinguishes between faculty and fitness as aspects of Right, he likewise makes a distinction between expletive justice (*iustitia Expletrix*) and attributive justice (*iustitia Attributrix*). Faculty pertains to expletive justice, while fitness is an aspect of attributive justice. We shall return to these two types of justice linked to faculty and fitness respectively and to their roots in the Aristotelian distinction between commutative justice and distributive justice when we discuss Grotius' views on Natural Right in greater detail. For the moment it suffices to summarise the differences between expletive justice and attributive justice by their respective grade of obligatory nature: expletive justice describes what human beings are obliged to do, while attributive justice explains what human beings will do, provided that they let their judgement be guided by equity.

3. Right as Law

In the third definition of Right Grotius equates Right with law (*lex*). Grotius points out that he applies a wide sense of law for the purpose of this definition. Thus, law is here to be understood as a rule of moral actions which obliges to do what is right. Grotius points out that any regulation of law must have an obligatory nature. Mere counsels and other prescriptions are therefore not part of Right in the sense of law.[36] Rules of moral actions oblige to do what is right, not only what is lawful or in compliance with a certain law. Right is not restricted to the mere notion of justice, but also extends to areas of other virtues. This definition of Right as law obviously hints at the aspects of attributive justice and expletive justice, to which we will return later. The definition of Right as law thus exceeds the concept proposed by Jean Buridan, which was merely based on an understanding of law as commandments regardless of their moral value. Likewise, this sense of Right as law applied by Grotius goes beyond the modern positivism of the "Western" liberal idea of international law, which merely focuses on a rightful promulgation of laws according to an appropriate consultation procedure while refraining from asking for the substantive moral value of the contents of laws.[37] For example, Rawls' concept of justice as fairness ultimately is a concept of justice in procedure: Rawls believes that the common good can be identified through an appropriate discourse within society. If the discourse is performed properly, then the outcome will be just. Grotius, on the other hand, is not really concerned about whether any special procedure is followed: Right is derived from the relevant rules of morality and thus is just; it is comparatively irrelevant how such rules are identified.

The obligation to do what is right, which is at the core of Grotius' third definition, deserves some further attention. An obligation is either a commandment to do something or to leave something undone. From a modern legal perspective, we might find this restricted definition wanting: neither permissions, which grant the freedom to do something legally, nor rights to claim to do something, or to have someone else do something, appear to be contained herein. However, according to Grotius, permission is not a legal position in his concept, as it is not in the strict sense effected by an act of law; rather it is the absence of a legal rule to prohibit a certain conduct.[38] An example for Grotius' understanding of Right in the sense of law as commandment can be taken from the Right of the seas. Grotius takes the use of the high seas for navigation to be permitted to everyone, because

---

36 Cf. IBP, I.I.ix.1.

37 Cf. as an example the concept of J. Rawls, *The Law of Peoples*, pp. 61 et seq.; see also Rawls' more general concept in *A Theory of Justice*, pp. 73 et seq.

38 Cf. IBP, I.I.ix.1.

everyone is obligated not to impede the use of the high seas by others.[39] The notion of subjective rights in the sense of an entitlement to claim something is indeed absent from this definition: though Grotius takes account of subjective rights in the sense of certain claims of human beings against other human beings, these are mostly rights granted by human laws. Grotius' third definition of Right works without any recourse to subjective rights or claims: if someone has damaged someone else, he is under an obligation to pay compensation, for which purpose it is irrelevant whether or not there is a corresponding claim of the person damaged. Notwithstanding this, the obligee will not be under the obligation if the obligor has discharged him of this obligation. The same concept becomes relevant for the competence for exacting punishment. According to Grotius, no one has a subjective right to exact punishment. Thus he denies the possibility of a mere waiver of punishment. The state is entrusted with the task of punishing; however, this does not mean that a subjective right to punish in the strict meaning of the word has been conferred to the state. By being entrusted with the task of punishing wrongdoings, the judge appointed by the state is obliged to exercise punishment as far as punishment is due. Correspondingly, the offender is obligated to accept punishment.

In expounding his theory of Rights, Grotius mainly applies the third definition of Right as a law obligating to do what is right. Grotius includes in the term of "Right" as "law" principles which are beyond the traditional legal taxonomy as employed by the classical Roman lawyers and medieval Canonists: in traditional Roman and canon law, the term "law" could only mean rights and obligations in a very strict sense; some lawyers had even excluded equity from the scope of the term "law".[40] This is the case, for example, with Giovanni de Andreae, according to whom perfect justice could not be attained; Right was therefore as close as one could get to perfection, but inevitably had to fall short of the ideal. Equity consequently was mitigation, designed to soften harsh effects of a strict application of the law. One notable exception in this respect was Hostiensis, who undertook to present a rather more differentiated picture of the various forms of law, including the natural law of reason, beyond of what his contemporaries acknowledged as elements of law in the strict sense.[41]

Grotius therefore follows the medieval theological tradition against the corresponding canon law tradition, in that he effectively includes metaphysics in the term "law". His inclusion of attributive justice in justice allows

39 Cf. ibid., II.II.iii., or even more famously, *De Iure Praedae*, XII – "Mare Liberum".

40 Cf. G. d'Andreae, *Commentarius: Liber Extra*, 45.5; cf. J. Brundage, *Medieval Canon Law*, pp. 156 et seq.; R. Weigand, *Die Naturrechtslehre der Legisten und Dekretisten von Irnerius bis Accursius und von Gratian bis Johannes Teutonicus*, pp. 24 et seq.

41 Hostiensis, *Summa super titulos decretalium, Liber Extra*, 23.5.

Grotius to explain how virtues beyond justice in the proper sense may supplement law. Thus Grotius also moves beyond the aforementioned understanding of "Right" in the sense of law as commandment proposed by Jean Buridan: Right thus has by definition a moral import; it is not merely an abstract formulation of commandments and prohibitions, but is always inherently linked to morality.

4. Conclusion

Summing up the definitions of Right Grotius offers in *De Iure Belli ac Pacis*, we can see that for Grotius Right derives from justice in a wider moral sense as opposed to a narrower legal one. Comparing these definitions with the modern understanding of law as rules establishing enforceable obligations, one is bound to realise two remarkable differences in relation to the Grotian concept:

4.1. Right as Obligatory Rules on an Objective Level

First, Grotius' definitions of Right include obligatory rules on an objective level only. The notion of an establishment of claims of legal subjects appears to be absent from these definitions, even though Grotius certainly allows for the creation of subjective claims under Human Right, and even though he acknowledges a subjective dimension of Right in his second definition of the term. The Grotian terminology restrains itself to objectivity with respect to the definition of Right. It covers commandments as well as prohibitions, but it always does so by obligating someone to act in a certain way. Hence, there are not necessarily any subjective claims that correspond to these obligations entailed by the aforementioned definitions. For example, human beings are under an obligation not to harm others, but there is not necessarily any corresponding subjective claim of human beings not to be harmed. In Grotius' terminology Right exists as an obligatory rule whether or not there are claims by which obligations could be enforced individually.[42] Whewell's translation of *De Iure Belli ac Pacis* thus misses Grotius' distinction between

42 This problem seems to be neglected by R. Tuck, *Natural Rights Theories: Their Origins and Development*, pp. 58 et seq., in his interpretation of the term *dominium*, which is used by Grotius in the context of his discussion on private property in *De Iure Praedae*, p. 18; Tuck does not provide substantial evidence for his assumption that *dominium* was not only the objective power of an individual to do something, but was also accompanied by an individual right; cf. D. M. Sprackling, "Divine and Human Law in Hugo Grotius", pp. 146–159; we shall return to this misinterpretation below.

the objective and general law on the one hand and the subjective and individual right, as it frequently renders *Ius* as "right" or "rights".[43]

This is not to say that Grotius' concept of Right lacks any individual or subjective component altogether. From his second definition of Right it is clear that Grotius is aware of individual powers that are established and regulated by Right and enable human beings to do something legally; he exemplifies this by referring to the debt of the debtor that corresponds to the claim of the creditor. Human Right may, of course, contain provisions for claims of someone to something or against someone else, such as the *vindicatio rei* as the right of the owner of an object against the possessor for return of this object. However, such claims can also be accommodated in the above-mentioned definition by taking them as obligations to perform certain acts, which corresponds to the determination of these obligations by a sole act of will by the counterpart. The *vindicatio rei* then is an obligation of the possessor of an object to return that object to the owner, if the owner so requests. In any case, Grotius' definitions of Right do not take any specific interest in the position of the counterparts of the addressees of legal obligations. Claims that correspond to obligations are not integrative parts of his definitions of Right.

While Grotius certainly has a concept of subjective rights, as becomes clear from his second definition of Right, he nevertheless emphasises the objective aspects of Right. From this it seems that Grotius is somewhat distancing himself from earlier ideas which endorsed subjective legal constructions, for which the fabric of subjective rights and entitlements under canon law, glued together by the principle of *epikeia*, brought forward by Jean Gerson is probably one of the most prominent examples.[44]

Given this emphasis on the objective obligation as core element of his understanding of Right, it seems inappropriate to label Grotius as "modern human rights entrepreneur", as frequently done by modern authors of international law.[45] Grotius proposes not a system of human rights, but of human obligations. For example, he certainly postulates that no one may kill

---

43 See, for example, the rather misleading translation in W. Whewell, *Grotius on the Right of War and Peace*, I.I.i, ii.

44 Cf. J. Gerson, *Tractatus de ecclesiastica potestate & origine iuris ac legume*, 1, 8, 13; G. H. M. Posthumus Meyjes, *Jean Gerson: Zijn Kerkpolitiek en ecclesiologie*, pp. 206 et seq.; R. Weigand, *Die Naturrechtslehre der Legisten und Dekretisten von Irnerius bis Accursius und von Gratian bis Johannes Teutonicus*, pp. 26 et seq., 339 et seq.; Gerson probably derived the concept of epikeia from William Ockham, cf. *Dialogus inter militem et clericum* I, VI c. 100.

45 Cf. R. J. Vincent, "Human Right and Interventions", in: H. Bull, B. Kingsbury, A. Roberts (eds.), *Hugo Grotius and International Relations*, pp. 241 et seq., who claims that Grotius was a propagator of human rights in his second definition of Right, though the author complains about Grotius denying rights of resistance to put respective human rights of individuals into effect; a more moderate interpretation can be found in H. Suganami, *International Equality*, in: H. Bull, B. Kingsbury, A. Roberts (eds.), *Hugo Grotius and International Relations*, pp. 239 et. seq.

a human being without sufficient justification. However, the reason for this is that everyone is obligated not to kill someone illegitimately, not because any human being has a right not to be killed. Consequently, Grotius holds it to be perilous for a Christian to inflict punishment, in particular capital punishment, for his own benefit or for the commonwealth[46]; obviously, Grotius does not claim any human right of the convict not to be executed. One could argue that by such a system of human obligations one could also overcome the concept of so-called inalienable human rights: if there are fundamental obligations of any human being in relation to any other human being, then it will no longer be necessary to ask whether or not certain fundamental rights may be waived by their holder.[47] Compared with the concept of inalienable human rights, the Grotian concept of obligations to heed the position of other human beings appears more stringent.

4.2. Irrelevance of Enforceability of Right

This leads to a second feature, which presents a major difference between Grotius' definitions and modern concepts: in modern doctrines of public international law a rule will only be acknowledged as a rule of law if it can be enforced[48]. This distinguishes legal regulations from rules of morality.[49] Grotius, however, clearly takes the position that a rule of Right is not deprived of its legal quality if its breach will not or cannot be punished.[50] While any violation of a Right normally deserves to be punished, there are cases where punishment must not or need not be inflicted. This enables Grotius to deal not only with legal commandments and prohibitions, but also

---

46 Cf. IBP, II.XX.xiv.

47 As an example for the discussion on inalienable rights one might look at the question on whether lie-detectors may be used as evidence in criminal proceedings; cf. Günter Dürig, "Artikel 1: Menschenwürde", Art. 1, No. 23.

48 Cf. John Austin and Robert Campbell. *Lectures on Jurisprudence, or the Philosophy of Positive Law*, vol. I, p. 182; also on this issue Zemanek, "The Legal Foundation of the International System", *Recueil des Cours de l'Académie de droit international*, 266 (1997/IV), pp. 9, 37 et seq; A. Hurrell, "Order and Justice in International Relations: What is at Stake?", in R. Foot, J. Gaddis, A. Hurrell (eds.), *Order and Justice in International Relations*, pp. 31 et seq.

49 As example for the modern concept of public international law cf. Hanspeter Neuhold, Walter. Hummer and Christoph Schreuer, "Grundlagen und Rahmenbedingungen des heutigen Völkerrechts", in H. Neuhold, W. Hummer, C. Schrummer (eds.), *Österreichisches Handbuch des Völkerrechts*, pp. 2 et seq.

50 This may have been overlooked by Hersch Lauterpacht, "The Grotian Tradition in International Law", *British Yearbook of International Law*, 23 (1946), pp. 7, 9, who arrived at the opposite conclusion.

with licences which dispense from the strict compliance with a rule of Right. As we shall see later, Grotius believes that many rules of the Human Right in War only present exemptions by way of licences from the overarching legal categories of Natural Right and Arbitrary Divine Right. Hence he can criticise the ongoing practice in war amongst his contemporaries, without depriving the contemporary practice of war of legal efficacy. Grotius thus places himself in a Christian tradition of moral standards in international relations, while at the same time taking account of contemporary practice in warfare. At the same time Grotius' practical realism helped the modern perception of international law to hold his concept of international relations compatible with the practical needs of an international society in an increasingly sophisticated world. This enabled modern lawyers to return to the Grotian legal concepts when, for example, endeavouring to enhance international co-operation against war criminals.[51] We shall return to this in due course.

III. The Concept of Natural Right

Having examined Grotius' definitions of Right we shall now take a closer look at the different categories of Right which govern international relations within the Grotian concept. We will have to undertake a survey of these categories, and shall critically review their respective function, scope, and principal elements. We will start this task by turning to Natural Right.

The intellectual context within which Grotius worked on his theory of Natural Right was largely dominated by two main traditions of thought on Natural Right, each of which took particular interest in the use of force. One tradition we may briefly characterise as Natural Right in favour of the fittest: it implies that if nature favours anyone with more strength than someone else, then it is legitimate for the stronger to subject the weaker; as representatives of this line of thinking one might take Cicero and those of his followers, up to Machiavelli and Clausewitz, who followed a concept of *raison d'etat* in the sense that matters of utility could legitimise the use of force.[52] The second tradition, which was followed mainly by Christian

51 Cf. M. Schröder, *Verantwortlichkeit, Völkerstrafrecht, Streitbeilegung und Sanktionen*, in W. Graf Vitzthum, *Völkerrecht*, pp. 565 et seq.

52 Cf. C. v. Clausewitz, *Vom Kriege*, I.I.2: "… *Der Krieg ist also ein Akt der Gewalt, um den Gegner zur Erfüllung unseres Willens zu zwingen.* Die Gewalt rüstet sich mit den Erfindungen der Künste und Wissenschaften aus, um der Gewalt zu begegnen. Unmerkliche, kaum nennenswerte Beschränkungen, die sie sich selbst setzt unter dem Namen völkerrechtlicher Sitte, begleiten sie, ohne ihre Kraft wesentlich zu schwächen. Gewalt, d.h. die physische Gewalt (denn eine moralische gibt es außer dem Begriffe des Staates und Gesetzes nicht), ist also *das Mittel,* dem Feinde unseren Willen

authors of the canon law tradition, intended to restrict the use of force to clear breaches of universally applicable standards.[53] These applicable standards were closely tied to a specific moral concept relying on a strong notion of divine will.

Classic Islamic jurisprudence followed a quite similar approach: the divine will as revealed through the Prophet is the central source of Right.[54] Revelation is of primary importance for the identification of God's justice, whereas reason beyond revelation is mainly used as a legal method for the application of revealed legal rules to new facts.[55] For example, reason may help to draw analogies between questions which have been answered by the Prophet with pertinent revealed rules and such questions which arose subsequently. Yet, the mainstream jurisprudence in Islam was quite hesitant to accept reason as a legal source distinct from revelation, even though some Islamic legal scholars in the Shi'i tradition had held that unbelievers ignorant of the divine revelation could be bound by a law of natural reason.[56]

The modern theories of international law after World War II are in substance more similar to the second tradition of thought, without however being able or willing to take a "too restrictive" religious approach that would necessarily limit their acceptance in a multi-religious world. The basic problem for any modern theory of international law lies in the need to reconcile universally applicable moral standards with a diversity of legal cultures throughout the world. A theory with high moral standards risks only to achieve very limited acceptance; a theory which is widely accepted will risk having only a very low moral standard. As has already been pointed out above, modern liberal jurisprudence tends to pay more attention to institutions and procedures than to the substantive quality of Right: the performance of the right procedure and the involvement of the right institutions in the process of legislating thus indicates that a rule generated through this process is right in itself – for John Rawls justice is fairness, which means that everyone may contribute to the discourse through which the common good is identified.[57]

---

aufzudringen, *der Zweck*. Um diesen Zweck sicher zu erreichen, müssen wir den Feind wehrlos machen, und dies ist dem Begriff nach das eigentliche Ziel der kriegerischen Handlung. Es vertritt den Zweck und verdrängt ihn gewissermaßen als etwas nicht zum Kriege selbst Gehöriges."

53 Cf. F. H. Russell, *The Just War in the Middle Ages*, pp. 55 et seq.

54 B. Krawietz, *Hierarchie der Rechtsquellen im tradierten sunnitischen Islam*, pp. 88 et seq.

55 Cf. ibid., pp. 18 et seq., 21, 59 et seq.

56 Cf. Khadduri, *The Islamic Conception of Justice*, pp. 40 et seq., in particular on the Mu'tazila, who valued reason as a higher source of justice than revelation.

57 Cf. J. Rawls, *A Theory of Justice*, pp. 47, et seq., pp. 65 et seq.; *The Law of Peoples*, pp. 66 et seq.

Grotius here pursues a *via media* in between the afore-mentioned traditions: he presents Natural Right as Divine Right which is accessible to reason. He defines Natural Right as a Right that is dictated by right reason, which indicates whether a certain action is in itself morally shameful or morally necessary, and therefore commanded or prohibited by God as author of nature.[58] *Prima facie* this definition of Natural Right is predominantly related to the third definition of Right.[59] Natural Right is obviously concerned with moral rules regarding human acts and their moral quality. According to Natural Right, acts are indicated (or, alternatively, counter-indicated) in themselves, and are therefore regarded as necessarily commanded (or forbidden) by God. The notion of a commandment or a prohibition "in itself" is what distinguishes Natural Right from any form of voluntary Right, whether divine or human, in which prohibitions or commandments are not entailed by the nature of the action itself, but positively ordered by God or by man.[60]

Yet, Grotius also borrows from the first definition of Right: he claims that some parts of Natural Right are not rules of morality that command or prohibit actions, but are rather the absence of rules. Natural Right does therefore not only command or prohibit actions, but also allows actions by its mere silence; this silence can be taken as permissiveness conveyed to man through conscience.[61] On the other hand, the term "Natural Right" cannot be applied to behaviour, which is more appropriate and better than its opposite, but not commanded as obligatory.[62]

In relation to the Grotian concept of Natural Right we shall first examine the function of God as its legislator in creation, before we analyse the relationship between Natural Right and nature, the methodology to be employed in identifying rules of Natural Right, and the basic material principles of Natural Right in justice and Natural Religion. Finally we shall ask in how far Grotius takes account of subjective natural rights, and to which extent he believes principles of Natural Right to be enforceable.

1. God as Author of Nature

In its modern use the term Natural Right indicates that there is a set of legal rules which are valid regardless of history, regardless of their acceptance by

58 Cf. IBP, I.I.x.1.

59 P. Haggenmacher, *Grotius et la doctrine de la guerre juste*, pp. 523 et seq., nevertheless claims that Grotius in this context mostly uses the first definition.

60 Cf. IBP, I.I.x.2.

61 Cf. IBP, I.I.x.3.

62 Cf. IBP, I.I.x.3.

human beings, and ultimately also regardless of the existence of a divine legislator: indeed, various interpreters of Grotius have labelled him a "seculariser" of Natural Right, and thus modern secular natural law theorists frequently adopt Grotius as one of their earliest ancestors.[63] This interpretation of Grotius is conventionally sought to be corroborated by the famous remark in the Prolegomena of *De Iure Belli ac Pacis* according to which certain principles of natural justice would be valid even if God did not exist or if God did not attend to the world. We will return to this remark and its meaning later.

However, Grotius firmly stands in the older Christian tradition of Natural Right: while there had been a broad variety of different Natural Right theories in the history of Christian legal thought, all theorists agreed that God was ultimately the legislator of Natural Right. There had certainly been disagreement about the content of Natural Right amongst Christian authors, but there was unanimous consensus on the quality of Natural Right as expression of divine will.[64] This is also true for other religious concepts of Right, such as those brought forward by Islamic jurisprudence: the various Islamic schools differed on the relationship between reason and revelation, but there was ultimately agreement on any legal principle having to be in compliance with the divine will.[65]

Grotius thus adheres to the older Christian tradition in contending that Natural Right is enacted by God as author of nature. This implies that just as God created nature, he also created a respective legal order, the order of Natural Right. Natural Right is on the one hand determined by nature and dominating nature on the other. Thus in creation God acts as a legislator. Consequently, Natural Right is Right entailed by divine creation. According to Ernst Reibstein it was probably Suarez who, *inter alia* by claiming God's authorship of nature, had influenced Grotius through his treatise *De legibus et legislatore Deo*, written in 1619, and thus effected the careful "re-theologisation" of the profane natural rights theories, which ensured that this doctrine then became acceptable to the Protestant orthodoxy.[66] However, Reibstein probably gives too much credit to the originality of Suarez: it should be noted in this respect that Grotius had already claimed in *De Iure*

63 Cf. W. Graf Vitzthum, "Begriff, Geschichte und Quellen des Völkerrechts", p. 56.

64 Cf. Rufinus, *Summa Decretorum*, I. D. 1; see also F. H. Russell, *The Just War in the Middle Ages*, pp. 56 et seq.; E. Reibstein, *Johannes Althusius als Fortsetzer der Schule von Salamanca*, pp. 17 et seq.

65 Cf. C. A. Stumpf, "Die Freiheit des Religionswechsels als Herausforderung für das religiöse Recht des Islam und des Christentums", *Zeitschrift für evangelisches Kirchenrecht*, 48 (2003/2), pp. 129–148.

66 E. Reibstein, *Johannes Althusius als Fortsetzer der Schule von Salamanca*, pp. 57 et seq.; H. F. Köck, *Der Beitrag der Schule von Salamanca zur Entwicklung der Lehre von den Grundrechten*, p. 23.

Praedae Commentarius, written shortly after 1603, that the will of God is not only revealed supernaturally, but above all in the very design of the creator, and that it is from this source that the law of nature is derived.[67] Grotius himself analyses the activity of God as legislator in creation in *Meletius*, which had been written in 1611. Though this idea may not be original in itself, it certainly was not taken from *De legibus et legislatore Deo*, but in *De Iure Praedae Commentarius* was taken from Justinian's *Institutes*, and in *Meletius* was developed rather independently.[68] The same distinction between creation and legislation by God is already present in Melanchthon's *Loci Communes*.[69] It is in substance an element of the natural law tradition of the Middle Ages, which had been inherited by the Western Church, and thus Suarez cannot be credited as originator of this view.

Grotius does not venture to analyse the activity of God as legislator in *De Iure Belli ac Pacis* in detail; here he concentrates on the task of dealing with the Right of War and Peace, and not so much on arguing theologically about the nature of God and his legislative activities. Thus it will be helpful to turn to Grotius' theological works for a moment in order to gain a broader view on how Grotius perceives the function of God as legislator. It is in *Meletius*, a fairly early theological treatise focusing on the basic laws of Christian faith and doctrine, where Grotius also touches on the issue of God as lawgiver. Though Richard Tuck argues that in *Meletius* Grotius was taking a minimalist approach to Natural Religion by arguing in favour of certain religious principles that could be acceptable to any kind of society, whether Christian or not[70], this interpretation is not supported by the text itself: in fact, in *Meletius* 5 Grotius states that it was Patriarch Meletius' intention to identify what was regarded best in any philosophical school or among popular institutions and to prove that this was shared by all Christians.[71] Accordingly Grotius points out that there are important differences between Christians on the one side, and Jews as well as Turks on the other. In *Meletius* Grotius is eager to establish an ecumenical point of view with respect to the basic principles of what Christians are and what they are not required to believe. The litmus-test for him is the question whether a principle of faith can be approached by reason.

In order to find out more about Grotius' views on God's role as legislator with respect to Natural Right, we first need to ask if and to what extent this role is different from that of God as legislator in Arbitrary Divine Right.

---

67 H. Grotius, *De Iure Praedae*, II.i.

68 *Corpus Iuris Civilis, Iustiniani Institutiones*, I.II.ii.

69 P. Melanchthon, *Loci Communes*, VII.

70 R. Tuck, *Philosophy and Government*, p. 185.

71 Cf. H. Grotius, *Meletius* 2 and 5; cf. D. M. Sprackling, "Divine and Human Law in Hugo Grotius", pp. 48–51.

Consequently, we shall have to examine Grotius' perception of Natural Religion, and ask what it has in common with Christianity and how it differs from it. In *Meletius*, Grotius starts his exposition with the question of what Christianity has in common with other faiths[72], in fact, with all religions, including the false ones as well as those that are true but less perfect than Christianity, namely what he calls the primary Natural Religion and Judaism.[73] Of particular interest for our examination of Natural Right are Grotius' observations on Natural Religion, which he regards as the religious basis already contained in creation and providing the primary source for any religion, including but not limited to Christianity. According to Grotius, Natural Religion presupposes that there is one God and that God is ready to reward those that wish to please him. This means that God sanctions the compliance of human acts with his laws – which is true for acts by Christians and non-Christians alike. Though we have seen that earthly sanctions are no prerequisite in Grotius' definitions of Right, the assumption that God himself ultimately rewards compliance and punishes non-compliance with his laws is used by Grotius in order to illustrate God's attention to his creation.

The assumption that God rewards those that wish to please him implies that God has intelligence and takes an interest in his creation.[74] Grotius believes that God's intelligence is proved by his superiority to his creation, as the maker is generally superior to what he makes. Thereby Grotius refutes the Stoics, who had claimed that God himself was subordinate to fate. Moreover, Grotius disagrees with those who believe that God can be described in formulas – he holds that these people profess God in words, but deny him in fact. Again: Grotius believes these arguments to hold for both Christians and non-Christians.

God attends to his creation, including all things celestial and earthly or human, in an effortless way.[75] Hence Grotius refutes the Epicureans, who held that it was an effort to apply intelligence and free will. As God, according to Grotius, is omnipotent, he can rule effortlessly. Rule requires effort only if the ruler is somewhat incompetent. Yet, God is omnipotent and thus faces no difficulties in ruling the universe. The admirable order of the

72 Cf. H. Grotius, *Meletius* 6. Though the word *multis* in 6 is of rather ambivalent meaning and could refer to people or faiths, we may conclude from the context that Grotius actually meant faiths; Christianity was not just another people; yet D. M. Sprackling, "Divine and Human Law in Hugo Grotius", p. 51, seems to be doubtful about the exact meaning.

73 Grotius summarises the contents of the first chapter in *Meletius* 12: "Haec illa sunt principia quae comunia habet christiana religio et cum falsis omnibus, et cum veris quidem, sed minus oerfectis, qualis est primum naturalis religio, inde mosaica."

74 Cf. ibid., 7.

75 Cf. ibid., 8.

universe shows that God is founder as well as ruler – again it may be added that for Grotius this is manifest to Christians and non-Christians alike.

In order to establish a reason for rewards we must, according to Grotius, presume that man is a rational being possessing free will – once again, this holds true for Christians and non-Christians alike. If man had no free will, it would be pointless to incite him to good behaviour through reward, as it would not be for him to decide whether or not to behave in a morally acceptable fashion. Grotius sees this presumption justified by experience, and therefore rejects the Stoic doctrine of fate.[76] If everything that happens in the future were dependent upon necessary causes, man would have received his free will in vain. To suppose that God has furnished man with free will in vain is to accuse God of incompetence.

From this Grotius concludes that we have to acknowledge God as legislator. God has free will and so has man. But God is superior, man inferior. Consequently, the superior influences the inferior, for the superior is destined to act, the inferior to be acted upon. Therefore God acts upon man in exercising his free choice. This acting by the superior toward the inferior is law or authority.[77] Grotius sees the most striking evidence for this thesis in the existence of conscience in human beings. Consequently, Grotius believes that human conscience is aware of the divine legislation, which for Grotius is again a valid supposition for both Christians and non-Christians.

From here Grotius moves on to a discussion of reward: someone who keeps and obeys the law shall be rewarded, and someone who violates it shall be punished[78] – which is once more true for Christians and non-Christians. God, Grotius assumes, is just and acts justly. Every legislator expects his laws to be obeyed, and does what can be done in order to enforce them. Yet nothing is more effective as an incentive to obedience than a reward. God is competent to reward, whereas human legislators are not, at least not always.

Grotius sees the principles that have been outlined here as common principles of all religions, the false religions as well as the true one. These principles are common property both of Christianity and of the primary Natural Religion. Grotius praises religion – religion in a general sense, not merely Christianity – for being able to prompt man to act honestly and correctly, whereas human laws cannot achieve this quite as effectively, since human thoughts and deeds evade them. Amending the poetic quotation "It is profitable that there be gods, let us therefore assume that they exist", Grotius states: "It is profitable that there be religion, therefore religion exists; God as

76 Cf. ibid., 9.
77 Cf. ibid., 10.
78 Cf. ibid., 11.

wise ruler did not fail to institute those things like religion, which were of greatest use for human beings".[79]

A crucial point for Grotius is the question of whether Christianity can be reconciled with right reason. The method Grotius applies here is, first, the search for religious principles that can be discerned by reason alone. Such principles constitute Natural Religion. Grotius then, secondly, checks the validity of specific Christian principles by their compatibility with logic. This leads Grotius to the question from where these specific Christian principles were derived. The answer can be found in his treatment of the Holy Scripture in *Meletius*[80]: Christian principles have been revealed by Christ as recorded in the Gospel.[81] Therefore it was the revelation by Christ in the Gospel that made Christianity more perfect than Natural Religion: revelation added to creation; the divine will added to nature. While Natural Right finds its principles in nature and in natural reason, Christianity has additionally been favoured by the revelation in Christ. The difference between Natural Religion and Christianity therefore lies not so much in quality of truth, but in quantity of truth: Christianity combines principles that are already entailed by creation with principles that are revealed in the Gospel. Both are accessible by reason; though some of the principles revealed in Christ could not have been found by reasoning alone, all of these principles are certainly consistent with reason. The image of God as a superior being with intelligence, free will, and an interest in his creation is an underlying feature of both Natural Right and Arbitrary Divine Right. For Grotius it is not necessary to be a Christian in order to believe in the principles of creation, for they are already substantial elements of the primary Natural Religion. Christianity then differs from Natural Religion only in what has been added through the revelation by Christ.

We can now return to *De Iure Belli ac Pacis* using the insights about the function of God as legislator gained from *Meletius*. We have already seen that God acted as legislator when he created the world. Rules of Natural Right are defined by creation itself; the imposing of rules of Natural Right cannot be separated from nature's coming into existence in creation. This leads to the question of whether God can amend Natural Right, or alter it in any way. The assumption that God has free will might lead to the conclusion that God can indeed alter Natural Right. Grotius, however, claims that Natural Right is immutable. Though the power of God is immense, Grotius states that there are nevertheless certain areas to which it does not extend. Grotius is aware of the danger of contradicting himself, yet he argues that this question is rather a matter of words than a problem of substance. For Grotius the point is that

79 Cf. ibid., 12.
80 Cf. ibid., 51–57.
81 Cf. ibid., 51.

God cannot contradict himself: not even God can effect two to be four; likewise God cannot turn something which is bad due to its intrinsic nature into something which is not bad.[82] Grotius therefore remains coherent in defending the free will and the omnipotence of God, while nevertheless denying God's capacity to alter Natural Right.

In describing God's function as legislator Grotius thus takes a specific Christian point of view in relation to Natural Right in viewing God as legislator. But the Islamic concepts of Right certainly also accept the legislating function of God, given the strong notion of a divine law inherent in Islamic legal theory.[83] However, Islamic legal theory focuses on the divine legislation through revelation, whereas creation is only of relatively minor importance in this regard. Consequently, the use of reason and the accessibility of divine commandments by rational reasoning are not as important for Islamic jurisprudence as it is for Grotius.

While Grotius places himself in a particular Christian tradition of thought about Natural Right, this is not to say that his approach is wholly incompatible with modern theories of Natural Right: modern theories of international law are generally willing to accept a diversity of religious convictions amongst the members of the society; they seek to enable a peaceful living together of individuals with different religious views; they neither contend nor refute any religious positions.[84] Thus, while none of the so-called liberal theories would endorse a legislative activity by God, it seems that they still could very well accept the individual's view of God as legislator. Grotius' concept is thus compatible with modern liberal positions; however, Grotius differs from modern concepts of Natural Right as in his concept God as legislator also shapes the content of Natural Right through creation, while modern liberal jurisprudence contents itself with the justice of certain procedures and institutions for the identification of Right, regardless of the moral value of the respective rules.

2. The Relationship between Natural Right and Nature

If God is the author of nature through creation, and thus acts as legislator of Natural Right as the legal order of creation, we are bound to ask how Natural Right and nature relate to each other. As already mentioned, there was a strong tradition in the history of legal thought according to which nature itself favours some by furnishing them with more strength than others, and

82 Cf. IBP, I.I.x.5.

83 Cf. B. Krawietz, *Hierarchie der Rechtsquellen im tradierten sunnitischen Islam*, pp. et seq.

84 Cf. W. Graf Vitzthum, "Begriff, Geschichte und Quellen des Völkerrechts", pp. 35 et seq.; see also R. Song, *Christianity and Liberal Society*, pp. 213 et seq.

thus nature legitimises the subjection of the weak by the strong. For Grotius, however, this is a rather abhorrent vision: consequently, he distinguishes raw nature from the nature of rational human beings, as do most of the religious concepts of Natural Right in Christian and Islamic jurisprudence.[85]

Grotius deals with nature in paragraphs 5 and 6 of the Prolegomena of *De Iure Belli ac Pacis*. He then goes on to derive principles of Natural Right from the sociable and rational nature of human beings: nature provides the origin for the Right of Nature; Natural Right is a legal order of human nature. Though nature includes animals and human beings alike, only the latter are superior beings by virtue of their potential for rational reasoning. Thus only human beings are able to acknowledge a legal order. In consequence Grotius rejects the distinction in Roman legal literature between Natural Right in a narrower sense, which human beings share with animals, and the Right of Nations as Right peculiar to human beings.[86] Moreover, in Grotius' opinion the Right of Nations is not a Divine Right, but a positive human one.

We can see the difference between nature and Natural Right in Grotius more clearly when we examine Grotius' observations on self-defence.[87] Starting point for his treatment is Cicero's statement that there is on the one hand a primary nature, which includes natural impulses, and that on the other hand there are subsequent rational principles which are designed to direct and limit natural impulses. One of these natural impulses is the desire to preserve oneself in one's natural state and to repulse anything that could cause harm. Grotius here presents a historic development of nature, in particular of human nature, referring to the relevant impulses sometimes just as *Natura*, at other times as *prima Natura*, but then also as *appetites*.[88] Natural impulses have to be brought into compliance with rationality. It is this compliance between rational principles and impulses that constitutes morality. Though natural impulses in general lead to morality, morality has to be dearer to human beings than natural impulses.[89] From this Grotius concludes that any examination of the Right of Nature (*Ius naturae*) has first to ask what is in compliance with natural impulses. Yet, in a second step, one has to check whether there is something more precious than these natural impulses that one has to strive for absolutely. If this is the case, this indicates a rule of Natural Right in the sense of a legal order of morality.

Morality can, according to Grotius, be absolutely precise. In this case, any deviation is immoral. On the other hand, morality can also allow for a latitude of alternatives; compliance with one alternative may then be

85 Cf. Stumpf, "Völkerrecht unter Kreuz und Halbmond", pp. 91 et seq.
86 Cf. IBP, I.I.xi.
87 Cf. ibid., I.II.
88 Cf. ibid., I.II.i.1.
89 Cf. ibid., I.II.i.2.

praiseworthy, but not absolutely necessary; we still are allowed not to act, or to act otherwise. Grotius illustrates this difference by using the image of colour: while in the former case, the difference between what is allowed and what is prohibited by nature is as sharp as between black and white, in the latter case there are a variety of shades of grey in between. Divine and human laws are mostly concerned with the latter case. As far was we consult the Right of Nature, we have to ask whether something can be done without injustice; injustice is what is contrary to the rational nature and contrary to society.[90]

Grotius examines, for example, whether war is contrary to nature, to natural impulses, or to natural appetites.[91] He comes to the conclusion that it is not, and that nature is in favour of war in any respect, for the ultimate end of war is the preservation of life and the defence or the acquisition of goods that are necessary for it. However, whether Natural Right is contrary to war, is another question, as both, right reason and the nature of society, are more eminent authorities than raw primary nature.[92] Nature is in favour of war under any circumstance, while Natural Right reflects the rationality of human beings and may therefore prohibit certain wars that are unjust even if they are "natural". Thus nature provides only the circumstances within which Natural Right can develop. Nature itself is not organised by rationality, yet it presents an arena in which human rationality can act, and provides the means by which rationality can govern the society of human beings. Now if Natural Right is to be distinguished from raw nature, the question arises of how we can recognise rules of Natural Right.

3. Recognition of Rules of Natural Right

Modern theories of international law offer various methods for the identification of specific legal principles. Most common to nearly all theories of international law is the acceptance of certain rules by the members of the international community.[93] Modern liberal jurisprudence consequently puts more emphasis on the process and institutions of identifying such rules than on their actual content. As Alasdair MacIntyre puts it: "The lawyers, not the philosophers, are the clergy of liberalism".[94]

---

90 Cf. ibid., I.II.i.3.

91 Cf. ibid., I.II.i.4.

92 Cf. ibid., I.II.i.5.

93 Cf. M. Rotter, "Die allgemeinen Rechtsgrundsätze", in H. Neuhold, W. Hummer, C. Schrummer (eds.), *Österreichisches Handbuch des Völkerrechts*, pp. 88 et seq.; W. Graf Vitzthum, "Begriff, Geschichte und Quellen des Völkerrechts", pp. 76 et seq.

94 Cf. A. MacIntyre, *Whose Justice? Which Rationality*, p. 344.

It is rather obvious that Grotius could hardly be satisfied with the mere acceptance of rules through the relevant legal subjects as primary method for the recognition of rules of Natural Right. Like most representatives of legal theory in Christianity Grotius is concerned with an ontological approach to rules which are universally applicable, and this approach also shapes his epistemological interest in International Right. We have seen that for Grotius Natural Right provides an objective order for international relations. To put it simply: rules of Natural Right are, in principle, valid regardless of their acceptance by legal subjects. Obviously, the recognition of legal rules by legal subjects and the acceptance of obligations by the respective obligors can, for Grotius, only indicate their existence as such. The epistemological approach for Grotius follows the ontological approach: if Natural Right follows the rational nature of the society of human beings, its rules will be accessible to reason.

Grotius presents two different methods that can be used in order to discern Natural Right. One method is direct and deductive, the other is indirect and empirical. The first method to discern Natural Right is the demonstration that something is necessarily in compliance with the rational and social nature of human beings. This constitutes an intellectual endeavour; we have to substantiate the imperatives of the rational and social nature of man, and if we do this correctly we will be able to deduce abstract principles that either command or prohibit certain ways of behaviour.[95] One might doubt the feasibility of this rather subtle and sophisticated method; whether results obtained by this method really can be verified through indisputable proof seems questionable. Yet, Grotius is optimistic about this: he is convinced that the principles of Natural Right are apparent and evident, provided that we pay attention to them, that we are furnished with healthy senses, and that we are sufficiently intelligent for this exercise.[96] Nevertheless, Grotius admits that such rational reasoning is difficult and consequently errors can be made in applying it.

The second method to discern principles of Natural Right suggested by Grotius is to compare the customs of nations, or at least of "civilised" nations, with each other. Where something is agreed upon by all nations to be Natural Right, there is, according to Grotius, a high probability that it actually does constitute Natural Right. A common effect presupposes a common cause; Grotius sees this common cause in common sense.[97] He praises the importance of the writings of philosophers, historians, poets, and rhetoricians for his project to present a compendium of the Right of War and Peace, as they often have stated the same on certain issues throughout all

95 Cf. IBP, I.I.xii.1.
96 Cf. ibid., "Prolegomena".
97 Cf. ibid., I.I.xii.1.

times and at all places. They have therefore provided evidence for the existence of certain rules.[98] Where similar statements have been made as a consequence of the nature of the subject, these statements suggest a rule of Natural Right. Grotius uses history and judgements for the same purpose, as these can provide evidence for principles of Right and illustrate such principles.[99]

Grotius calls this second method a more popular one than the first method: it is easier to make a survey and establish the customs of nations than to search for norms by rational reasoning. Yet it is less secure: it is possible, and Grotius himself eventually provides examples for it in the further course of *De Iure Belli ac Pacis*, that all nations, even the most civilised, err on a particular subject or do not comply with the rational and social nature of human beings. This becomes apparent particularly in the third book of *De Iure Belli ac Pacis*, in which Grotius deals with the Right in War. He criticises the Right of Nations that is practised amongst many nations from the point of view of Natural Right, which in his opinion is too often ignored. In substance this second method has a parallel in modern public international law, which also relies on the opinions of the most excellent legal scholars and on the customs of civilised nations as a secondary source of International Right.[100] However, while the empirical method of identifying rules may be regarded as the most appropriate in a system of Right which mainly relies on the acceptance of its rules by the legal subjects, it nevertheless is less apt for a system that traces the obligatory nature of its regulations to their respective roots in human rationality entailed by divine creation.

In *De Iure Belli ac Pacis* Grotius primarily uses the first method, and establishes rules of Natural Right by logical reasoning. He then re-examines these rules using historical examples or quotations by theologians, lawyers, philosophers, historians, poets, or rhetoricians, which are either cited as evidence if they support his opinion, or are criticised and dismissed as erring if they deviate. Grotius' examination of the legitimacy of war may be one of the best examples for a consequent application of both methods.[101]

Grotius' opinion on the recognition of Natural Right enables us to see that the rules of Natural Right are not only binding, but are also accessible to everyone. Therefore mankind is bound to observe them. In particular, acknowledging Christianity as true religion is no prerequisite for the obligation of all human beings to adhere to Natural Right. As rules of

98 Cf. ibid., "Prolegomena" 40.

99 Cf. ibid., "Prolegomena" 46.

100 Cf. W. Graf Vitzthum, "Begriff, Geschichte und Quellen des Völkerrechts", pp. 79 et seq.

101 Cf. IBP, I.II.

Natural Right can be discerned by the mere use of the human senses, no one can be excused for ignoring these rules. Natural Right does not contain any doctrines which would require faith rather than reason for their recognition. Rules of Natural Right are intelligible without any external assistance, e.g. by the Holy Ghost. They oblige man regardless of his position, whether he is ruler or subject. Therefore Natural Right, according to Grotius, constitutes a system of international relations which is universally applicable, comprising nations irrespective of their religious creeds. The discernment of the rules of Natural Right and their application to specific issues does not even require any particular degree of cultural development. Though Grotius does not spell this out expressly, any human being in any part of the world is able to use his reason. Natural Right obligates Christian European citizens as much as savages or infidels in any other part of the world. However, it should be noted that for Grotius reason is not simply a means to identify single items of knowledge that are all discernible to the same degree. Instead it is a progressive epistemology which governs the use of reason, starting with items that are clear and obvious, but finally leading into mystery. This already becomes apparent from Grotius' comments on the methods to identify rules of Natural Right. The mere use of rational reason may be difficult, and thus there may remain doubts whether a rule belongs to Natural Right. The method of identifying rules of Natural Right through their recognition by all or many nations faces the problem that tradition may be obscured or corrupted. Thus Grotius differs from modern jurisprudence in that he treats the recognition of legal principles as an intellectual exercise of using reason and of assessing tradition, whereas modern jurisprudence is more or less content with the observance of certain procedures through competent institutions for the identification of legal principles.

4. The Principles of Natural Right

Modern theories of international law regard certain rules as *ius cogens*[102]: hence these rules have the quality of a "modern" Natural Right, which is universally applicable and immutable.[103] In practice this becomes relevant for human rights, which are frequently viewed by "Western" liberal theories as substance of a universal system of international relations. Thus, modern concepts of a humanitarian intervention often rely on Natural Right doctrines as justification for the use of force in cases where human rights are sub-

102 Cf. K. Zemanek, "Das Völkervertragsrecht", in H. Neuhold, W. Hummer, C. Schrummer (eds.), *Österreichisches Handbuch des Völkerrechts*, pp. 77 et seq.; W. Graf Vitzthum, "Begriff, Geschichte und Quellen des Völkerrechts", pp. 28 et seq.

103 Cf. J. Kokott, "Naturrecht und Positivismus im Völkerrecht", pp. 3 et seq.

stantially violated.[104] Another important example for such traces of a Natural Right doctrine in modern international law is the incrimination of war criminals. Before the modern international conventions on crimes in war were adopted, courts in Western liberal countries, as well as the tribunals of Nuremberg and Tokyo after the Second World War, tried to establish principles of a penal law for war crimes from concepts of Natural Right. Traditionally, war crimes had not been covered by the earlier codifications of penal law; therefore the traditional liberal principle of *nulla poena sine lege* meant a major obstacle to the prosecution of incidents which were generally viewed as war crimes or as crimes against humanity.[105]

In this respect, various scholars have acclaimed Grotius for making Natural Right a moderating or a progressive force – others have accused of him of "using" Natural Right as a conservative element.[106] Both criticisms miss the point: Grotius certainly pursues certain aims in describing his system of Right as put forth in *De Iure Belli ac Pacis*. It is obvious that he endeavoured to moderate the rather harsh modes of warfare which had been in practice at his time. Perhaps the compilation of *De Iure Belli ac Pacis* may also have been driven by Grotius' personal vanity to set himself a memorial in the science of International Right. However, any interpretation of Grotius that acclaims – or defames, as the case may be – him for what has been made out of his work centuries later, will be bound to misjudge Grotius' approach in any case.[107] If any such adjectives as "progressive" or "restorative" are used in relation to Grotius' theory of Right, Grotius' perception of Natural Right may be viewed as restorative, because he uses this theory as a standard for criticising a corrupt practice, whereas in his system of Right the Law of the Gospel plays a progressive part in enhancing political morals.

In *De Iure Belli ac Pacis*, Grotius develops his views on Natural Right by making a comparison between human beings and animals, and in opposition to an anti-Stoic poetic statement by Horace according to which not even nature itself can distinguish what is just from what is inequitable[108]: man, according to Grotius, is not only an animate being, but an exceptional being

104 Cf. K. Hailbronner, "Der Staat und der Einzelne als Völkerrechtssubjekte", in W. Graf Vitzthum (ed.), *Völkerrecht*, pp. 230 et seq.

105 Cf. Green, "International Crimes and the Legal Process", *ICLQ*, 29 (1980), pp. 567 et seq.; M. Schröder (ed.), "Verantwortlichkeit, Völkerstrafrecht, Streitbeilegung und Sanktionen", in W. Graf Vitzthum, *Völkerrecht*, pp. 564 et seq.

106 On the discussion see H. Lauterpacht, "The Grotian Tradition in International Law", pp. 7 et seq.; P. Remec, *The Position of the Individual in International Law According to Grotius and Vattel*, pp. 63 et seq.; K. Nabulsi, *Traditions of War*, p. 145.

107 Hence, one may doubt whether Grotius deserves any honour or blame for what is called the "Grotian tradition"; cf. however H. Lauterpacht, "The Grotian Tradition in International Law", pp. 7 et seq.

108 Horace, *Satires* 1.3.

that is more distinguished from any other sort of creature than these are different from each other. The most important example of this is a distinct social and communal appetite (*appetitus societatis*) of human beings which leads to the establishment of an organised, tranquil, and intellectually determined form of society.[109] Therefore it is inappropriate merely to see individual utility as sole impulse for living beings. Though many animals appear to restrain themselves out of care for their fellow creatures, and exhibit characteristics like mercy, only human beings have the ability to gather in a society, and they do so because they are driven by an impulse for community. Human beings alone possess the necessary means of communication through language. They alone can organise themselves along certain precepts of behaviour. Only human beings can understand such precepts and act in accordance with them.[110] Society is therefore not just any kind of community, but a human community based on certain rules of behaviour, in which human beings comply with nature and in particular foster the natural desire for peace and order.

Before we move on to view the principles of Natural Right in more detail, a few words on Grotius' regulative methodology will be in place: For Grotius, Natural Right comprises commandments and prohibitions dictated by right reason. Natural Right either commands acts or prohibits acts; such commandments are given explicitly. However, Natural Right does not explicitly permit any acts. Instead the permissibility of acts is inferred from the mere silence of Natural Right on any particular matter. Hence, it is not only explicit commandments that constitute the body of Natural Right, but also their corresponding silence; here Grotius applies his first definition of Right as what is not unjust, by designating the absence of positive principles as Right in a "reductive" sense.[111] Thus, the inferences from the general principles are also encompassed by Natural Right and are accorded similar quality.[112]

Human care for society, which results from human rationality, is for Grotius the source of Right properly so called. Here Grotius uses his second definition of Right, according to which Right is a moral quality to have or to do something justly. In Prolegomena 8 to 11 Grotius names three particular areas of Natural Right, two of which are related to justice: expletive justice (*iustitia Expletrix*) and attributive justice (*iustitia Attributrix*); the third area is refers to faith in God, or more generally, to Natural Religion.

109 Cf. IBP, "Prolegomena" 6.
110 Cf. ibid., "Prolegomena" 7.
111 Cf. ibid., I.I.x.3.
112 Cf. P. Remec, *The Position of the Individual in International Law According to Grotius and Vattel*, pp. 63 et seq.

4.1. Expletive Justice

For Grotius expletive "justice is justice properly so called". In parallel to the faculty as perfect moral quality, he describes expletive justice as "justice in a genuine and strict sense".[113]

The first interesting aspect of Grotius' concept of expletive justice is its root in Aristotle's concept of justice as commutative justice – συναλλακτικη. However, Grotius finds the Aristotelian idea of commutative justice wanting. While expletive justice for Grotius surely includes a commutative dimension, as the term συναλλακτιχη already indicates, expletive justice is not restricted to this. Grotius therefore prefers the term επανορθωτικην as "restoring justice", which had been used by Aristotle on other occasions, as it could better describe the actual content of expletive justice. This is because expletive justice comprises more than merely an exchange of things or rights.

Expletive justice is a principle of restoring what is due another party, regardless of whether such restoration is accompanied by the consent of the parties involved. It is the force which is designed to implement the legal order of the natural society of rational human beings. However, expletive justice presupposes legal positions that already exist, and which are to be implemented or rectified if they are in disorder. This can be illustrated by an example from the contemporary law of the seas: expletive justice requires that a state renders a foreign vessel unjustly seized on the high seas to its flag state. Expletive justice is not concerned with the question of how ships are attributed legally to a flag state: it already presupposes that such legal positions exist under a different set of Right. Expletive justice then comes into play if such legal positions are violated: it orders the rectification of the legal position and provides a remedy.

For Grotius, rules of Natural Right are universally applicable. They do not depend upon divine revelation, or upon a consensus between the individuals concerned, for being obligatory to every human being. Taking up a medieval Scholastic tradition, Grotius states that expletive justice would govern Right properly so called even if God did not exist. This validity of expletive justice regardless of the existence of God should not be overstated, as had been done frequently by interpreters of Grotius throughout the ages: for Grotius it simply means that expletive justice requires no specific religious allegiance, but has to be observed by all and any human beings across the world, regardless of their cultural background, their economic situation, or their personal taste.

Grotius presents the following five rules as basic content of expletive justice as Right properly so called[114]: to abstain from the property of others; to

113 Cf. IBP, I.I.viii.1.

114 Cf. ibid., "Prolegomena" 8.

reimburse for taking the property of others; to adhere to one's promises; to compensate damages; and to take revenge through punishment. These principles are results of the human care for society and therefore also basic principles of Natural Right. They constitute rules of behaviour which are crucial for a society to function. However, in substance the examples Grotius gives in this context are more or less all built on the Roman understanding of civil law.[115] Grotius thus transfers these basic principles from the realm of private law to the sphere of international relations in abstracting them as general legal principles.

According to Grotius, any human being has to abstain from the property of others. At first glance this appears to constitute a status of property on the level of Natural Right. However, this would be a wrong conclusion: Grotius holds that proprietary rights have been introduced by man and are thus neither part of creation nor part of the rational nature of man. Yet, after proprietary rights have been introduced, observation of such rights is entailed by Natural Right in a reductive sense.[116] Therefore theft or any other infringements of human proprietary rights contravene the rational nature of human beings.

The reimbursement for taking or possessing the property of others as second principle of expletive justice is a consequence of the commandment to abstain from the property of others. If this prohibition is violated, human rationality requires reimbursement. Such reimbursement is meant to compensate for those losses which the rightful owner has suffered due to the offence. Again, Natural Right is not concerned with the details of property rights or with rules on unjust enrichment, but only with peace and order in human society. Once again the notion of expletive justice as restoring justice becomes apparent.

The natural rationality of human beings entails the necessity to honour one's promises as the third principle of expletive justice.[117] In this respect, Grotius' quotation of Simonides deserves particular attention: justice not only includes the return of what had been received, but also speaking the truth. This illustrates the importance of human language as means of communication. Truth in the use of language therefore means faithfulness towards one's promises, to live up to one's words, and in the end compliance with natural rationality. Truth of words is implemented, and if necessary restored, by deeds.

The compensation for damages is the fourth principle of expletive justice: damages imply a violation of the legal position accorded to individuals. The idea of compensation relies on the idea that the violator has to restore the

115 Cf. M. Kaser, *Römisches Privatrecht*, pp. 3 et seq.

116 Cf. IBP, I.I.x.4.

117 Cf. ibid., II.XI.i.4.

original state of his victim's legal position. Indeed, damages and their compensation present one of the major issues of Grotius' concern in *De Iure Belli ac Pacis*.[118]

The fifth and last principle of expletive justice requires punishment for misdeeds. Punishment is an alternative to compensation as restoration of justice. For Grotius, punishment is a certain evil that is inflicted on someone because of his wrongdoings.[119] He conceives punishment as something which is permitted by nature because it is not prohibited.[120] Grotius does not explicitly claim that there is a commandment to punish, or a commandment to suffer punishment. Punishment belongs to Natural Right in a reductive sense. The infliction of just punishment does not result in an obligation to compensate for damages or in any other obligation of the punishing instance towards the punished offender. Therefore, punishment satisfies the underlying obligation. The implementation of expletive justice by way of punishment is, however, more central to Grotius' interest than the above-quoted lines from *De Iure Belli ac Pacis* might seem to suggest. It is indeed the central topic to Grotius' treatise on atonement, *De Satisfactione*, in which he presents his views on the implementation of divine justice with respect to the sins of mankind by God inflicting the punishment deserved by man upon his own innocent son. By this mankind could be spared from the rightful but disastrous punishment of death, and still justice could be upheld.[121]

The principles of expletive justice listed by Grotius are endorsed by nearly all concepts of restorative justice, by the medieval Christian understanding of justice as well as by liberal ideas of justice, or by Muslim theories of justice. The acceptance of the idea that moral wrongs have to be remedied requires no particular divine revelation or any supernatural act of legislation. Grotius presents this code of principles of expletive justice simply as a minimum requirement for the functioning of a human society founded on the grounds of rational morality.

4.2. Attributive justice

While Grotius' remarks on expletive justice more or less follow the traditional approach to Artistotle's concept of commutative justice, except for the taxonomy applied, the principle of attributive justice introduced by Grotius in this context presents more than a terminological step away from Aristotle's idea of distributive justice.

---

118 Cf. ibid., II.XVII.
119 Cf. ibid., II.XX.i.1.
120 Cf. ibid., II.XX.i.2.
121 Cf. H. Grotius, *De Satisfactione*, I. § 2.

In contrast to expletive justice, attributive justice is for Grotius the subject of a wider sense of Right, other than Right properly so called. This wider sense of justice is alluded to in Prolegomena 9 and 10: Here Grotius states that another sense of Right had been derived from the strict sense of law as presented in Prolegomena 8, which is again closely tied to the nature of human beings. Human beings are distinguished from animals by a specific capacity to judge: they can distinguish between the pleasant and the harmful, not only for the time being, but also for the future. Moreover, human beings have the capacity to judge upon the means by which the pleasant can be achieved and the harmful be avoided. Human nature gives guidance to human beings through insights into what is right, regardless of fear or temporary temptations by lust and passions; anything which contradicts such insights into what is right contravenes the Right of human nature.[122]

With his distinction between expletive justice and attributive justice Grotius parts company with Aristotle's famous distinction between distributive justice and commutative justice, which had also been adopted by Thomas Aquinas and his disciples in the School of Salamanca[123]: Aristotle had proposed two concepts of justice: One concept understands justice generally as a primary virtue comprising all others. The second concept views justice particularly as a specific kind of virtue amongst other virtues; this second type of justice may be labelled "particular justice"[124]: commutative justice and distributive justice are the two phenotypes of this particular justice in the Aristotelian sense. Aristotle links distributive justice as justice regarding the distribution of what is common with geometric proportionality, and relates commutative justice as justice in transactions to arithmetic proportionality.[125]

In expounding his theory of justice in *De Iure Belli ac Pacis*, Grotius finds this Aristotelian account of particular justice deficient, not only with respect to the taxonomy applied: for Grotius, Aristotle treated justice merely as mathematical exercise, and could not explain how particular justice was to relate to other virtues. Grotius insists that the second sense of justice to be added to expletive justice is not about geometrical proportions between two different pairs of reference. Instead, this wider sense of justice concerns the just relationship between a certain subject and an object, e.g. a certain candidate with certain qualifications to a certain post.

Grotius describes attributive justice as companion to those virtues that entail the usefulness of a human being to other human beings, such as

---

122 Cf. IBP, *Prolegomena* 9.

123 Cf. O. M. T. O'Donovan, J. Lockwood O'Donovan, *From Irenaeus to Grotius: A Sourcebook in Christian Political Thought*, pp. 790 et. seq.

124 Cf. Aristoteles, *Ηθικα ικομαχεια*, V. 1 et seq., 6 et seq.

125 Cf. ibid., V. 7.

generosity, pity, or guidance.[126] Attributive justice hence includes a "para-legal" principle of equity and virtue which adds to the strict Right in terms of what is equitable rather than in terms of what is due. It is a justice of judgement: while expletive justice primarily has a backward-looking perspective, as it is designed to rectify unjust situations that already have occurred, attributive justice directs the judgement about what is going to happen. Attributive justice hence may be labelled "forward-looking".

This wider sense of Right firstly directs the method of allocating abilities and properties. Thus, a wiser man has precedence over a man who is less wise, a relative has precedence over a stranger, etc., each according to the circumstances of facts and nature. Grotius' idea of attributive justice is not focusing exclusively on the acting party, but also takes an interest in the status of the passive party involved in an action: fitness pertains to the suitability of a person for a certain office, or honours to be conferred are dependent upon the dignity of the recipient, which is a notion which had already been present in Calvin's concept of Natural Right.[127] From this we may infer that equality is not something that is inherent in Natural Right. Grotius seems very willing to acknowledge natural inequality.[128] Yet, on the other hand the wider sense of justice as attributive justice also includes virtues, such as generosity, mercy and a careful guidance, and thus is related to virtuous human conduct in a more general sense.

Secondly, according to Prolegomena 9, human beings have the power of judgement to distinguish between the beneficial and the harmful, and of what is and what is not in compliance with human nature.[129] Attributive justice therefore also includes virtues which direct the conduct of human beings in relation to other human beings beyond what already falls into the category of expletive justice. Human beings possess this ability not only with regard to the present, but also to the future. Human beings are thus more far-sighted than animals, having the potential to judge undisturbed by present passions and fears. Any contradictions to or impediments against such judgement are contrary to human nature. We can identify those virtues that are to be looked upon as part of Natural Right from Grotius' remarks on the characteristics of human judgement: these virtues include fortitude, as human judgement may not be influenced by fear. Another virtue included in attributive justice is temperance, as human judgement shall not be corrupted by any momentary lust. Furthermore, human judgement has to rely on prudence, for it shall be independent of any passionate outbreaks.

---

126 Cf. IBP, I.I.viii.1.

127 Cf. J. Calvin, *In quinque libros Mosis, commentarii*, 41.38.

128 Cf. K. Nabulsi, *Traditions of War*, p. 145.

129 Cf. IBP, "Prolegomena" 9.

This inclusion of virtues in the concept of attributive justice can be illustrated by Grotius' elaboration on the restrictions to the killing of aggressors in chapter 1 of the second book of *De Iure Belli ac Pacis*: An invader who is useful for the lives of many may not be killed under Natural Right, for this is not only forbidden by expletive justice, but also by other virtues, such as temperance, fortitude, and prudence. The implementation of such virtues is not only good and praiseworthy, but also obligatory.[130] Virtues such as prudence, fortitude, and temperance are thus rules of moral acts which oblige us to do what is right in the sense of Grotius' third definition of Right as law.[131] These virtues as part of attributive justice are to be drawn upon when we judge the question of whether we may take advantage of a permission under expletive justice. This can be furthermore exemplified by Grotius' comments on the Right in War: For example, Grotius believes that in a just war there is a relatively far-reaching licence for the war-faring party which allows the destruction of the enemy's property under the Human Right of Nations. Under this licence, everything that belongs to the enemy may be spoiled and sacked.[132] However, Grotius then adds certain restrictions: the commandment of prudence prohibits the destruction of the enemy's property if such destruction is not useful to the justified party but merely motivated by wrath or lust for revenge.[133]

We may again illustrate Grotius' account of attributive justice by applying its principles to the contemporary law of the seas. Basically every state, coastal or land-locked, has the right to fish in the high seas. This right of fishing is only limited in a practical sense by the fish present in the high seas, but not by the rights of other states that wish to fish in a particular region of the high seas. Nevertheless, it would be unwise to exhaust the fish stocks to the extent that they could not recover out of their own strength. Hence, it is a matter of prudence and thus of attributive justice not to over-exploit fish stocks. This problem is solved in practice by the relevant states agreeing on the total allowable catch. The modern law of the seas, in particular the 1982 United Nations Convention on the Law of the Seas, even provides one example of attributive justice in the sense of an allocation of goods: if a coastal state is not able to exploit the total allowable catch in its Exclusive Economic Zone, this state shall admit other neighbouring states to fish in this area according to Section 62 of the United Nations Convention on the Law of the Sea. In determining the relevant allowable catch for all other states, the coastal state shall take into account, *inter alia*, the respective economic needs of other states in the same region.

---

130 Cf. ibid., II.I.ix.1. Cf. Also D. M. Sprackling, "Divine and Human Law in Hugo Grotius", p. 159.

131 Cf. IBP, I.I.ix.1.; cf. Sprackling, "Divine and Human Law in Hugo Grotius", p. 160.

132 Cf. IBP, III.V.i. et seq.

133 Cf. ibid., III.XII.i. et seq.

While in Grotius' system of Right, certain virtues have more than a suggestive influence this is not necessarily the case for all virtues. The crucial term to be drawn upon for the decision on whether virtues beyond pure expletive justice are part of Natural Right as part of attributive justice is Grotius' phrase *obligans ad id quod rectum est*[134]: the mere relatively higher moral quality of a certain act does not suffice to cause an obligatory effect as long as there is no absolute necessity to adhere to such a moral standard. Indeed, virtuous conduct may be praiseworthy without being obligatory. It is therefore legally irrelevant what nature deems to be appropriate and better than its opposite as long as it is not deemed legally binding.[135] In the context of his treatment on unjust reasons of war Grotius himself states that one cannot with the assistance of arms demand something which is only subject to a moral obligation but not to a legal obligation in the strict sense. Grotius here means that certain virtues may create moral obligations to do something which is better than any other alternative, but which at the same time is not the only admissible alternative from a legal point of view. Hence Grotius excludes a violent enforcement of moral obligations rooted in virtues like generosity (*liberalitas*), gratitude (*gratia*), mercy (*misericordia*), and affection (*dilectio*), as such moral obligations cannot be enforced as Natural Right.[136] However, Grotius does not offer any general guideline for distinguishing true legal obligations from merely moral obligations or from relative counsels.

The importance of Grotius' concept of attributive justice lies in the connection between a wider sense of justice and the relevant situation in which a certain judgement is to be made. It refrains from offering one criterion for a variety of undertakings, but rather requires a prudence of judgement appropriate to the undertaking to be judged upon. This Grotian idea of attributive justice in prudence of judgement thus might indeed be a supplement to a modern concept of justice in international relations which too often narrows down its attention to justice in transactions, and thus merely prescribes standard equivalents for the exchange of goods. However,

134 Cf. ibid., I.I.ix.1.

135 Cf. ibid., I.I.x.3.

136 Cf. ibid., II.XXII.xvi. In relation to this D. M. Sprackling, "Divine and Human Law in Hugo Grotius", p. 160, comments that the virtues of attributive justice could not give rise to rights and therefore not present just causes for war; he appears to draw this conclusion from Grotius' comments in IBP, II.I.ix.1. At the same time Sprackling argues that Grotius applied his third definion of *Ius* as *lex* to the virtues of attributive justice (ibid., p. 160). In the light of Grotius' statement according to which virtues in general can be given legal force by *leges divinae et humanae* it appears to be questionable whether Sprackling's equating of the virtues of fortitude, temperance, and prudence can be sustained. It seems doubtful whether one could ever construe debts out of virtues like fortitude, temperance, and prudence. Hence this problem seems to be a mere theoretical and abstract one. The obligatory effect of attributive justice is supported by Sprackling in any case (ibid., pp. 160 et seq.).

in some sense attributive justice as viewed by Grotius resembles the modern idea of procedural justice as described by Rawls in his justice as fairness[137]: the modern idea of a "just judgement" relies on the adherence of the decision-maker to certain procedural standards which come close to the Grotian attributive justice.

This can be illustrated by the procedure of a judicial review of administrative decisions. While both common law and civil law jurisdictions follow concepts of administrative law which are fundamentally different in their respective approach, there is a common understanding in both traditions of law that the judicative power must have the competence to remedy defective decisions of the executive power: both common law and civil law jurisdictions grant the executive power relative discretion in making its decisions; because of the division of powers, this freedom of discretion may be interfered with not even by the courts. In consequence, the scope for judicial review of administrative decisions which have been made in exercising the executive power's discretion is limited to procedural mistakes: the courts may nullify discretionary decisions only if the executive power had considered the wrong factors in its decision-making, e.g. by not considering anything at all, or by ignoring certain factors which should have been considered, or by considering certain factors which it should have ignored. Yet, the courts may not replace the executive power's exercise of discretion by its own exercise of discretion. One could well argue that Grotius' idea of attributive justice is a doctrine on the proper consideration of relevant factors in the decision-making and in passing judgement. Attributive justice is not restricted to the methodology of decision-making, however; it goes beyond procedural standards by including virtues into the decision-making itself. In this sense, it is not fully compatible with a modern consensual approach, which is only interested in proper procedures in international law, as attributive justice in the Grotian sense also refers to the moral quality of decisions and judgements.

4.3. Natural Religion

In the introductory sentence to his remarks on Natural Religion Grotius claims that the principles of expletive justice and of attributive justice could be upheld even if one admitted that there is no god or at least only a god who does not attend to human affairs. The phrase *etiamsi daremus Deum non esse* has become the magic formula of generations of scholars who regarded Grotius as the first lawyer who "secularised" natural law and freed it from its

137 Cf. J. Rawls, *A Theory of Justice*, pp. 47 et seq., 73 et seq.

theological chains[138] – and in doing so hyperbolised its meaning for Grotius' more general argument, just as much as the Papal authorities, which found this bone (although it had been chewed on long enough by Scholastics preceding Grotius) too hard to digest and consequently put *De Iure Belli ac Pacis* on the Index Librorum Prohibitorum.[139] Magic formulas tend to go hand in hand with superstition; users of magic formulas too often ignore rational considerations, and thus move away from reality. Indeed, the assumption that Grotius secularised natural law is rather the result of an incomplete reading of this single sentence and of Grotius' works than of careful scholarly analysis. Those who endorse this assumption confidently ignore the theological foundation of Grotius' treatises, letting the wish to find a starting point for the secularisation of natural law prevail over the content of Grotius' actual comments. A full account of those Grotian interpreters who could not be convinced by Grotius' text does not seem in place; rather, we shall proceed immediately to the source itself, and we will endeavour to refute the secularist interpretations of Grotius on the spot.

After the afore-mentioned remark Grotius states that rationality, as well as tradition, have confirmed that there is a divine being and that God attends to the world. Grotius here alludes to rational evidence as well as to miracles for the existence of God; moreover he states that the existence of God has been proved throughout the centuries.[140] Richard Tuck has speculated whether certain additions by Grotius to this statement as well as to other parts of *De Iure Belli ac Pacis* for the second edition in 1631, in particular the direct reference to "divine laws" in the later editions, can be explained by Grotius' wish to stress God's role in Natural Right, about which he allegedly had been rather "dismissive" in the first edition of *De Iure Belli ac Pacis* in 1626.[141] Tuck asserts that, while the relevant passages in the former version had been more in line with *De Iure Praedae Commentarius*, Grotius, for example, now added in Prolegomena 11 a longer sentence by which the fact that God exists is confirmed. Finally, Tuck concludes: "It is clear that the alterations to the text of *De Iure Belli ac Pacis* were part of a campaign to make Grotius' views appear more acceptable to the Aristotelian, Calvinist culture of his opponents within the United Provinces". However, there is no evidence to prove that the alterations between the first and the second edition present more than a shift in emphasis. As explanation for these rather "conspicuous" additions, Tuck suggests that Grotius had hoped the new

138 See for example Graf Vitzthum, "Begriff, Geschichte und Quellen des Völkerrechts", p. 56.

139 Cf. O. M. T. O'Donovan, J. Lockwood O'Donovan, *From Irenaeus to Grotius*, p. 788, and D. M. Sprackling, "Divine and Human Law in Hugo Grotius", pp. 1 et passim for a critique of this tradition.

140 Cf. IBP, "Prolegomena" 11.

141 Cf. R. Tuck, *The Rights of War and Peace*, pp. 99 et seq.

version of *De Iure Belli ac Pacis* to prove more acceptable to his opponents in the Netherlands, as Grotius had at this stage wished to return to his home country.[142] It may be conceded that the 1631 edition is certainly more detailed and perhaps even more emphatic about God's role in shaping Natural Right. Yet, this does not represent a shift in Grotius' views on God as author of Natural Right and on the obligations of human beings to believe in him. He had already claimed this in earlier works, yet using a leaner wording: given Grotius' elaborations in the *Meletius* and in *De Veritate Religionis Christianae*, both of which were written quite early, there could not have been any doubts on Grotius' views on God's authorship of Natural Right. Therefore, we should resist the temptation to exaggerate the respective amendments by interpreting them as a change of mind on the part of Grotius, or even for taking them as evidence to support the suggestion that Grotius had solely been driven by a wish to please his opponents when re-editing *De Iure Belli ac Pacis*. Homesickness for the Netherlands may well have gripped Grotius already when he was writing the 1625 edition; but to believe that he earnestly had regarded additions to *De Iure Belli ac Pacis* as a remedy to cure it would probably overstate the case.

From the existence of God Grotius concludes that God is the creator. From God's position as creator Grotius derives an obligation for human beings to be grateful for their existence, and in consequence an obligation of obedience towards God. For Christians this has been confirmed by explicit divine words. Nevertheless, these principles can also be accessed by purely using rational reason. One does not have to be a Christian in order to believe in God; nor are only Christians obliged to be grateful and obedient to God.

The natural rationality of human beings can recognise that God is a rewarding legislator. We have already seen how Grotius undertook to prove this on logical grounds in *Meletius*; he did so similarly in *De Veritate Religionis Christianae*, where he undertook to demonstrate that God exists, that there is but one God, that all perfection is in God, that God is eternal, omnipotent, omniscient, and absolutely good, and that God is the cause of all things.[143]

Grotius names four principles (*praecepta*) of Natural Religion in the context of his considerations on potential punishment for disbelief.[144] Firstly, God exists and there is only one God. Secondly, God is invisible and a sublime being. Thirdly, God directs human affairs and decides on the grounds of equity. Finally, God has created all things except himself. While these principles constitute for Grotius the common religion which has been

142 On Grotius' attempt to return to the Netherlands cf. C. G. Roelofsen, "Grotius and the International Politics of the Seventeenth Century", in: H. Bull, B. Kingsbury, A. Roberts (eds.), *Hugo Grotius and International Relations*, pp. 126 et seq.

143 H. Grotius, *De Veritate*, I.1–3.

144 Cf. IBP, II.XX.xlv.

true throughout the ages, not all of them are clear to everyone to the same extent. Yet, in Grotius' views it is obvious that God is a uniform being in the sense of the first principle and that according to the second principle he is an invisible being, whence it is prohibited to make images of God. God directs human affairs, as we can see from the third principle, and therefore we have to conclude that he knows our thoughts and deeds. The fourth principle, according to which God has created the world leads to the conclusion that we have to honour him; if we do not honour God, then we deny the fact of the divine creation, as Grotius illustrates with the harsh punishments provided by Jewish law for the violation of Sabbatical rules.[145] Moreover, in the first book of *De Veritate Religionis Christianae,* Grotius also elaborates on the soul, which lives on after death. Thus, according to Natural Religion man's destination is to be found in the happiness expected for the next world.[146]

Grotius believes his views on these four principles to be confirmed by the witness of ancient authorities; it is explained by the Decalogue in the Old Testament, but also by Christian and Jewish sources, as well as by Greek philosophers.[147] He thus conceives these principles as religious standards of Natural Right which have to be adhered to by all human beings, Christians and non-Christians alike. Yet even though these principles have been true throughout the ages, they and their consequences are not all clear and obvious to the same degree.[148] They constitute Natural Religion, but they are not identical with Christianity, which added certain elements to the aforementioned principles of Natural Religion.

From these principles Grotius draws further conclusions: God is to be honoured, to be loved, to be worshipped, and to be obeyed. Grotius bases these conclusions not only on traditions, but also on rational considerations. Our senses teach us that all things created hint to something that has not been created. But even if one's senses are too weak to realise this, it is in Grotius' opinion sufficient that human beings of all ages and all countries, with very few exceptions, have agreed upon the truth of these principles. The fact that they have never been proved wrong through time lends further evidence for their truthfulness.[149] Grotius here refers to a quotation of Dio of Prusa, who had summarised this in a statement according to which faith in God is partly innate, and partly delivered to us by tradition.[150] Hence,

145 Cf. ibid., II.XX.xlv.

146 Cf. H. Grotius, *De Veritate* I.20, 22; cf. also J. P. Heering, "Hugo Grotius' De Veritate Religionis Christianae", in: H. Nellen, E. Rabbie (eds.), *Hugo Grotius, theologian: Essays in Honour of G. H. M. Posthumus Meyjes*, pp. 42–52.

147 Cf. IBP, II.XX.xlv.2 et seq.

148 Cf. also Grotius' comments upon pagan belief after faith in God had been replaced by alternative objects of worship in *De Veritate* IV.1 et seq.

149 Cf. IBP, II.XX.xlv.3.

150 Cf. ibid., II.XX.xlv.4.

tradition supplements reason as assistance to faith in God. As the aforementioned principles are deemed obvious by Grotius, ignorance of them cannot be excused. Whether ignorance with respect to these principles can or must be punished, is a different question. We will return to it when we deal with the possibility of enforcing Natural Right.

It should have become clear, however, that for Grotius Natural Religion as part of Natural Right is more than a rather obscure concept of natural piety. It contains a quite elaborate idea of God's essence, his appearance, and his origin as part of Natural Right. Furthermore, faith in God, gratitude, and resulting from this, obedience to God are obligations under Natural Right and therefore independent from the above-described two fields of expletive justice and attributive justice. These obligations can be deduced from the rational nature of human beings and are therefore already implied in creation. Rationality suffices for discerning a natural sort of religion, a religion Grotius calls the primary Natural Religion in *Meletius*. The independence of Natural Religion from Christianity is merely a matter of quantity of religious precepts and of the quality of their source. This is not to say that primary Natural Religion is altogether different from Christianity in substance. The primary Natural Religion is existent due to Natural Right, whereas Christianity is a combination of the religious contents of Natural Right and the revealed Arbitrary Divine Right.[151]

We can find additional evidence for an inter-relation between Natural Religion and other religions in Grotius' treatment of the issue of just punishment. When examining how to handle wars which are only waged against nations because of their refusal to adopt Christianity in chapter 20 of the second book of *De Iure Belli ac Pacis*, Grotius refrains from giving a precise answer. Yet he emphasises that even if one acknowledged this as a just cause, or in other words, as a breach of a corresponding legal obligation from Arbitrary Divine Right, the use of violence would not be admissible in this case. Christianity has added a great deal to the natural and primitive religion; these additions could not be approached by natural reason alone, but also greatly rely on the resurrection of Christ and on the miracles effected by him and his apostles. Though for Grotius these have been attested to by creditable witnesses, they nevertheless happened a long time ago, which is why one needs the secret assistance of God in order to accept these principles faithfully.[152] Consequently, Grotius believes it to be inadmissible to punish nations or individuals for their refusal to accept the Christian faith. We shall

151 Cf. D. Wolf, *Die Irenik des Hugo Grotius*, pp. 23 et seq., regarding Grotius' dependence upon Nicolaus of Kues and Erasmus of Rotterdam as regards the reduction of religions or Christian confessions to common principles; cf. also J. Lagréé, "Grotius, Stoïcisme et Religion Naturelle", *Grotiana*, 10 (1989), pp. 80–96.

152 Cf. IBP, II.XX.xlviii.1.

penetrate this field more deeply later when examining Arbitrary Divine Right. In our present context it suffices to note that Grotius believes Christianity to have built its doctrine on the fundament of Natural Religion, adding further peculiar Christian precepts to it. Following Thomas Aquinas[153], Grotius argues against any punishment for the refusal to accept the Christian faith.

Nevertheless, Grotius takes a remarkably strong line against other forms of impiety. Only a few paragraphs after his treatment on the inadmissibility of Christian missionary wars Grotius turns to the punishment of those who do not worship their own gods, stating that the infliction of punishment on the impious of any religion is more just than a missionary war against infidels who refuse to adopt Christianity. Grotius here mainly argues by quoting ancient sources and authorities that use a variety of different arguments in a multitude of historic contexts. He does not at all refer explicitly to Natural Right in general or Natural Religion in particular in this context.[154] One might be surprised by his relatively harsh position towards impiety in general, given his leniency towards the offence of rejecting the adoption of Christianity. Yet, given his concept of Natural Right and Natural Religion, his conclusion is fully coherent: while there is no obligation under Natural Right to adopt the specific Christian faith, there is a general obligation to be pious. From this we can infer Grotius' general willingness to acknowledge a resemblance of Natural Religion in other religions. Natural Right consequently obliges to adhere to a faith. Impiety or even atheism is a breach of this natural obligation which warrants punishment. But even here Grotius acknowledges that there is only relatively more justification to punish impiety with respect to other religions; the identification of the principles of Natural Religion may sometimes have been aggravated by a corrupt tradition, and thus acts of impiety may have to be excused.

Grotius' view of a Natural Religion as primary legitimate form of the Christian religion has an interesting parallel in the Islamic law of nations. The perspective taken by the Islamic conception on other, non-Islamic religions depends on whether their central teachings have been codified in a holy scripture. If such a codex exists, the religion is accorded a relatively higher tolerance than other religions. Thus, Christians, Jews, Zoroastrians, and other religions have been accepted as subjects by Islamic rulers on the condition of the payment of a poll tax, while other unbelievers who worshipped by other means or atheists met with fundamental intolerance.[155] In this sense, the Grotian idea of Natural Religion might indeed possess a

153 Thomas Aquinas, *Summa Theologica*, II, ii, Q. 10. Art. 8.

154 Cf. IBP, II.XX.li.

155 Khadduri, *The Islamic Law of Nations*, pp. 47, 53 et seq.

limited compatibility with the Islamic view of foreign religions in international relations.

We may note another interesting aspect regarding the actual content of Natural Religion: As the difference between Christianity and Natural Religions in Grotius' opinion mainly consists of additional elements of Christianity that have been revealed by God in the redemption of Christ, in particular, in the answer to the question of how a sinful man can be restored, one might suspect that Natural Religion is simply Judaism as a kind of transitional stage of religion before the coming of Christ. There is, of course, a difference between Grotius' respective perceptions of Natural Religion and of Judaism in that the scope of Judaism is narrowed to the Jewish people only, while the picture Grotius paints of Natural Religion is more universal. Furthermore, Grotius acknowledges that there have been particular positive Jewish laws, given by God specifically to the Jews as his chosen people, while the respective regulations of such additional Arbitrary Divine Laws are naturally absent from Natural Religion. Moreover, it remains unclear whether Grotius actually assumes that Natural Religion had been in practice anywhere during any stage of history, or whether it is simply an abstract ideal of a virtual religion. However, these differences between Judaism and Natural Religion regarding historicity and the narrower applicability of Judaism do not necessarily provide enough reason to refute the suggestion that Grotius was actually thinking of Judaism, in particular its religious doctrines, when talking about Natural Religion. Hence, Judaism may be viewed as a specific regional instance of the universal Natural Religion.

In *Meletius* Grotius presents Judaism in line with Natural Religion as being true but less perfect than Christianity.[156] Interestingly, this statement provoked the criticism of Antonius Walaeus[157], who reasserted Jean Calvin's thesis that Judaism was perfect in its own kind.[158] Grotius' view of Judaism and its relation to Christianity may therefore also illustrate his move away from orthodox Calvinism that took Judaism and Jewish law as an important role model for the moral standards of Christians, and thus accorded relatively less importance to the perfection of the Jewish heritage through the revelation in Christ. In this respect we also have to note that Grotius probably did not make any deeper inquiries into contemporary or older Jewish literature. In particular, it is unlikely that Grotius, at the time he was working on *Meletius,* had any sort of extensive first-hand knowledge of Rabbinic literature, or even a sufficient command of Hebrew[159]; rather, it

156 H. Grotius, *Meletius*, § 12.

157 Cf. E. Rabbie' s comment in H. Grotius, *Meletius,* § 12.59–60.

158 Cf. J. Calvin, *Institutio Religionis Christianae,* 2.11.

159 Cf. the extensive examination by E. Rabbie, "Grotius and Judaism", in Henk J. M. Nellen, Edwin Rabbie (eds.), *Hugo Grotius, theologian*, pp. 108–111.

seems that he based his observations on scholarly commonplaces about Judaism.

Though there are certainly a number of differences between Natural Religion and Judaism, the doctrinal nucleus of Natural Religion is identical to what Grotius takes as doctrinal substance of Judaism. Judaism holds that God exists and that there is only one God, that God is invisible and a sublime being, that God directs human affairs and decides on the grounds of equity, and that God has created all things except himself. Moreover, as we shall see later in more detail, Grotius believes that the first sets of Arbitrary Divine Right granted to the entirety of mankind or to the Jewish people prior to the promulgation of the Law of the Gospel in the redemption by Christ very much resembled the creational Natural Right; in fact, Grotius presents a large portion of Jewish law essentially as a restatement of and reminder to what has already been prescribed by Natural Right. There are certainly a number of Jewish regulations regarding rites, the *Caeremonalia,* which Grotius holds to be an exclusive part of the Mosaic law and which had been granted as particular set of Arbitrary Divine Right to the Jewish people only. However, these ritual regulations hardly affect doctrinal principles of Judaism, and thus such regulations do not contradict the material equivalence between Judaism and Natural Religion. Finally, in Grotius' opinion Jewish law also entails the same defects as Natural Religion, in particular, the lack of any satisfactory and reasonable solution to the question of how sins can be redeemed, which plays a major role in Grotius' theological understanding of International Right.

5. Natural Rights as Subjective Natural Rights?

In comparing the modern understanding of international law to Grotius' theological approach, one question of particular relevance is whether there are any subjective rights in Grotius' concept of Natural Right, i.e. individual and subjective legal positions of human beings against other human beings or against human society in general. Subjective human rights receive increasing attention by the modern international legal science: Though the current system of international law as viewed by the "classical" modern theory of international law exclusively acknowledges states and state-like entities as legal subjects of public international law, there are increasing tendencies to rethink this focus on states so as to accommodate humanitarian concerns in public international law effectively.[160] There are also notions of subjective legal positions in the religious traditions of Right: while Gerson

160 Cf. Keene, *Beyond the Anarchical Society. Grotius, Colonialism and Order in World Politics,* pp. 13 et seq.

had probably been the first to talk about subjective rights explicitly, canon lawyers had already acknowledged a personal freedom of the individual within the framework of ecclesiastical law, and similarly, Muslim legal scholars of classic Islamic jurisprudence had discussed individual subjective positions under Divine Right.

As has already been indicated above, individual subjective rights only play a minor role in the definitions of Right used by Grotius. While there is a certain but slight notion of individual rights in Grotius' second definition of Right, such a subjective dimension appears to be completely absent from his other definitions. Yet Grotius mainly uses the third definition for explaining his understanding of Natural Right, while the second definition is less often referred to in this context. However, a concept of subjective liberty shines through Grotius' treatment on the relationship between nature and Natural Right: when dealing with the relationship between natural impulses and the Right of Nature, Grotius speaks of life, limbs, and freedom that are the property of the respective individuals. Human society is designed to protect these as well as property, whether this is private property (*dominium*) or common property.[161] Moreover, Grotius states that it does not contradict the nature of society to care and to cater for oneself as far as the right of others (*ius alienum*) is not impaired.[162] Therefore, even the use of violence is not unjust as long as there is no counter-indication because of the right of others (*ius alterius*).

Do we have to understand individual property as a legal position, amounting to a right to avert any intrusion by others, resulting e.g. in a subjective and individual right to self-defence? Or are the individual property of life, one's own body, and personal liberty rather a kind of individual realm of personal freedom which is assigned to the individual human being under Natural Right, with the result that any intrusion into it is objectively unlawful under Natural Right allowing anyone to avert the intrusion? The use of the terms *ius alienum* and *ius alterius* as rights of others indicates an application of Grotius' second definition of Right, which includes the power over oneself and powers over others. This would indeed suggest an individual right under the framework of Natural Right. However, it should be helpful first to ask another question: Does the attacked party that wishes not to be defended have a right to prohibit the defence by others on its behalf? Or, to put it more precisely, is self-defence subject to a specific subjective right subject to the sole disposition of the individual holder? If so, it would suggest the existence of subjective natural rights. If not, we can presume that Grotius, when talking about the rights of others or about alien

161 Cf. IBP, I.II.i.5.
162 Cf. ibid., I.II.i.6.

rights, thinks of a personal realm, into which no one may intrude, and which may be defended by anyone.

To answer this question we have to make deeper enquiries into Grotius' position on self-defence. We have seen that the use of violence does not necessarily contradict Natural Right; nor is there any absolute prohibition of self-defence under Natural Right: as Natural Right either commands or prohibits positively, but is silent otherwise, self-defence is allowed in principle. However, this does not say anything about whether there is an individual subjective right to self-defence. The fact that Natural Right is silent on matters of self-defence allows the Gospel law to restrict it: though Grotius states that we are allowed to kill an innocent third party in order to preserve our lives, he nevertheless stresses that the Gospel law counsels against it. This becomes clear from Grotius' treatment of the just causes of war[163]: first of all it seems that only nature would allow the killing of an innocent third party, while the respect for society (*societatis respectus*) which determines the actual application of Natural Right, does not necessarily approve of this. Yet Gospel law clearly prohibits the killing of innocent third parties. Hence there is at least no obligation to self-preservation regardless of the expense.

Now there remains the question of whether there is any individual right to self-defence that must be distinguished from the general admissibility to defend any other party against attacks or injuries. Grotius arrives at this question in chapter 5 of the first book of *De Iure Belli ac Pacis,* in which he is concerned with the authority to wage war, and then returns to it in chapter 25 of the second book. He states that according to nature everyone is his own protector; to this end we have received our own hands.[164] Nevertheless, this is only a practical observation and not a rule. Grotius does not say that rendering assistance to others is prohibited; he even claims that help is due, not only to friends or neighbours, but to any member of the entire human society.[165] This is a consequence of the harm that any breach of Right committed in relation to an individual inflicts on human society as a whole.

Grotius returns to this issue when examining causes for waging war on behalf of others. He claims that under Natural Right one cannot only enforce one's own "rights", but also alien "rights". If any measure may be taken in self-defence by the violated party, the same is also true for any third party that wishes to assist the violated party.[166] Grotius here presents a hierarchy for the rendering of assistance according to the degree of relationship between the attacked and the assisting parties: A primary position within this hierarchy is taken by the ruler's own subjects that are attacked and whom the

163 Cf. ibid., II.I.iv.1.
164 Cf. ibid., I.V.i.
165 Cf. ibid., I.V.ii.
166 Cf. ibid., II.XXV.i.1.

ruler should help against the attacker.[167] The second rank is accorded to allies.[168] The third position is given to friends, even if they have not been guaranteed any help, as far as this help is owed due to the friendship and can be given easily.[169] Finally Grotius includes in this hierarchy all other members of human society; he even regards help by human beings to other human beings to whom they are merely connected by their common membership in human society to be the wisest case for granting assistance in defence against attacks.[170]

Hence, defence is not necessarily a right of the attacked, but in any case a duty for any other member of society. Not only the party actually attacked suffers from an unlawful attack, but also human society in its entirety, as its rules – which are not subject to the disposition of individual members – are violated by the attack. Grotius even offers one example for circumstances in which third parties are more likely to defend attacked persons than the attacked persons themselves[171]: the defence of the honour of women, which Grotius thinks more likely to be defended by a man than by the attacked woman. He hints to various examples where offenders attempting rape were killed by other men, whereas there are only few incidents of women killing attackers.

As a consequence, the individual property of life, one's body, and one's liberty merely presents a borderline to mark the individual space of freedom, which stands in the disposition of the owner; it is he who has the "power" (*potestas*) over it. Yet this personal power does not present a specific personal right to the defence of one's own legal position: indeed, anyone may defend an individual human being's life, his property, and his freedom. Such defence does not require any specific legal title.

Yet, we still have to ask whether one can abandon one's own property with no third party being permitted to lawfully help in case of an attack. Grotius does not answer this question explicitly, though he notes that if a creditor waives his claim against the debtor, it is the claim that ceases to exist, but not Natural Right, which still upholds that existing claims have to be fulfilled.[172] Thus it is certainly possible under Natural Right to relinquish one's own property. Here the Roman law principle of *volenti non fit iniuria* applies. In some cases the consent of the party concerned might even exclude any breach of law, e.g. it is impossible to steal something in a legal sense if the owner is relinquishing property voluntarily. Thus, any infringement of

---

167 Cf. ibid., II.XXV.i.2.
168 Cf. ibid., II.XXV.iii.1.
169 Cf. ibid., II.XXV.v.
170 Cf. ibid., II.XXV.vi.
171 Cf. ibid., II.I.vii.
172 Cf. ibid., I.I.x.6.

individual liberty presupposes the individual to make use of this liberty. Otherwise, an action restricting individual liberty cannot result in an infringement of individual property. Yet, if there is no infringement of individual property or of the individual realm, then there is nothing to be defended by a third party. Instead, any interference by a third party would result in an infringement of the former proprietor's freedom. On the other hand there are, according to Grotius, some aspects of individual property over which no disposition may be made. These are, in particular, life and limbs of an individual. According to Grotius, every human being has received life from God and therefore no human being may make any free decision as to whether or not he wishes to live. Consequently, suicide is prohibited due to Natural Right, save for few exceptions.[173]

There is then hardly any evidence for a specific natural rights theory in Grotius' concept of Natural Right. Thus, attempts to view Grotius as a protagonist in this respect are problematic.[174] Though proprietary Right to life, physical immunity, and liberty are important features of the position of individuals within Natural Right, this does not amount to an exclusive, subjective, and individual right in the "modern" sense. It is merely a personal realm of individual immunity, containing a borderline of Natural Right between the public sphere and the individual sphere. The violation of this borderline, however, does not affect the individual more than human society as a whole. Though the individual sphere is without doubt an exclusive one, it is only exclusive with respect to the classification of being related to the individual human being; it is not exclusive with respect to its susceptibility of defence against attacks: attacks not only affect the individual realm, but also the public realm of society. Consequently, there are no subjective rights that correspond to respective obligations of one's counterparts under Natural Right. The obligation of a man not to kill someone else does not necessarily correspond to a right of this other man not to be killed.

The conclusion that Grotius' concept of Right does not consider subjective elements in its definition of Right is certainly not to say that Grotius completely ignored the fact that subjective rights could be acquired under Human Right, e.g. by way of a contract. Private rights had even become dominant features of the medieval political landscape, when contractual theories provided the basis for feudalist concepts of power.[175] However, such personal subjective rights are then foremost human in character rather than part of Natural Right. Moreover, such rights are acquired by voluntary acts; they are not innate elements of man.

---

173 Cf. ibid., II.XIX; though Grotius here deals with aspects of Jewish law, it becomes clear from the context that the prohibition of suicide is part of *ius naturale*.

174 Cf. e.g. R. Tuck, *Natural Rights Theories*, pp. 58–81.

175 Cf. J. N. Figgis, *Studies of Political Thought from Gerson to Grotius: 1414–1625*, pp. 10–13.

Notwithstanding this, expletive justice as principle of Natural Right certainly may consider such subjective rights for determining what is due to someone.

Overall, Grotius here again places himself in the religious tradition of Christian jurisprudence in emphasising the individual subjective obligations for anyone to render assistance to any other fellow human being. This also likens the position of classic Islamic jurisprudence vis-à-vis subjective rights. Grotius does not advocate subjective human rights in the modern sense, and thus cannot serve as point of reference for those who argue in favour of a transformation of modern public international law to accommodate such subjective human rights. However, it will certainly be possible to lean on Grotius in order to reason for a personal responsibility of the individual in international relations. Thus, Grotius' arguments regarding the assistance of human beings for the defence of their fellow human beings might be employed to justify humanitarian interventions. Likewise, Grotius' concept of personal responsibility in international relations could be drawn upon for the establishment of a system of international criminal law, as for Grotius an attack launched on the freedom of the individual is at the same time an attack on human society as a whole.

6. Enforcement of Natural Right

Modern theories of law are only willing to acknowledge those principles as law in a true sense which are enforceable.[176] This is most obvious for the modern category of "soft law", in which certain institutions or other legal subjects express their wishes for the further development of public international law, but which does not entail any obligatory effect in the strict sense. Merely moral obligations which are deemed as an ethical standard in the inter-relations amongst human beings, but which cannot be implemented through the use of force, thus do not qualify as law, and consequently a breach of such moral obligations cannot be punished.

In our modern understanding of punishment as the most important means to enforce the validity of legal obligations, we normally take a positivist outlook: the principle of *nulla poena sine lege* requires for punishment a positive law which sanctions a certain offence. This principle has been described as one of the great achievements of human rights endeavours against arbitrary tyranny, but until the recent adoption of the International Convention on Criminal Law it has given rise to numerous problems in practice: how can this principle of *nulla poena sine lege* be reconciled with the need to sanction human forms of such outrageous conduct as genocide,

---

176 On this see Graf Vitzthum, "Begriff, Geschichte und Quellen des Völkerrechts", pp. 6 et seq.

massacres of civilians, and similar acts, if they were previously not codified as criminal offences under public international law? Until the Rome Statute of the International Criminal Court took effect in 2002, the punishment of war criminals had been justified in practice mainly with the recourse to a rather vague concept of natural law, which can be summarised briefly as follows: There are certain offences which are so manifestly contrary to the common understanding of justice in the international society that they warrant punishment even though there is no positive sanction provided for under national or international law.

Enforceability is a relatively modern requirement for the acknowledgement of legal principles. Neither the Christian legal tradition nor classic Islamic jurisprudence questioned the legal quality of principles because of a lack of enforceability. In an understanding of law as metaphysics and of metaphysics as law, the effective implementation of legal principles into reality naturally plays a much less important role than in modern jurisprudence, which measures legal principles according to their efficacy. Moreover, these traditional approaches did not require any positive regulations for the punishment of violations against the Divine Right: the mere breach of Divine Right sufficed to justify punishment.

As to Grotius' position in this respect, we have already seen that he does not consider enforceability a necessary element of his definition of Right. Yet, it still remains to be asked whether Grotius believes that Natural Right can be enforced through punishment. In the following we shall first turn to his views on the punishment of offences against Natural Right in general, before we turn to offences against Natural Religion.

6.1. Punishment of Offences against Natural Right in General

Grotius discusses the enforcement of principles of Natural Right through punishment in the context of penal wars. As a consequence of the establishment of states, rulers are competent to punish not only offences which affect themselves and their subjects, but also violations against Natural Right and the Right of Nations by other rulers and nations.[177] Therefore Grotius agrees with Innocent and contradicts the late Spanish Scholastics Vitoria and Vasquez in confirming that a violation of "nature" presents sufficient cause to wage war against the offender: he interprets Vitoria and Vasquez to have claimed that any war could only be justified by a violation of one's own rights, or of the rights of one's subjects, or if one had jurisdiction over the offender – by which he fails to acknowledge that in particular for Vitoria the waging of war was a means of safeguarding the

177 Cf. ibid., II.XX.xl.1.

common good by avenging and punishing wrongdoing even beyond a pure violation of individual rights.[178] Yet, according to Grotius the power to punish is not to be derived from civil jurisdiction, but from Natural Right. Civil jurisdiction and the exclusive power of punishment of states in the domestic realm are the result of the establishment of states, whereas Natural Right still grants the power to punish in the aforementioned limits to anyone if no superior power has been established.[179]

What Grotius appears to have granted here is partly taken away in the next paragraph, where he applies several qualifications to the enforcement of principles of Natural Right – as well as to the question of whether there can be innocent ignorance about Natural Right. First of all he argues in favour of a strict distinction between Natural Right and what he calls "civil customs".[180] Though these civil customs of nations do not emerge arbitrarily, they do not possess the same legal authority as Natural Right. These civil customs may be similar to Natural Right, yet they are not necessarily completely equal in content and in force. We may add that potentially such customs might develop in contrast to Natural Right, e.g. in the case of licences from Natural Right, as we shall see later when concentrating on Grotius' concept of a just war.

Secondly, Grotius warns not to jump to the conclusion that something is prohibited by Natural Right if it is either obscure whether such prohibition exists or if something is prohibited by God's will rather than by nature as God's creation.[181] In this context, Grotius gives examples like sexual intercourse amongst the unmarried, certain types of incest, and usury, which he takes to be prohibited by Arbitrary Divine Right and not by Natural Right. Here we can note an important distinction between Natural Right and Arbitrary Divine Right in relation to their respective susceptibility of enforcement: Natural Right thus is in principle more apt to be enforced than Arbitrary Divine Right, as the latter often prescribes moral rules without allowing for earthly sanctions against their transgression.

Thirdly, we have to distinguish according to the discernibility of necessary principles. Some principles can be recognised as necessary and applied easily, e.g. that one shall live in an honest way and may therefore not rob others. The same is true for obvious consequences, e.g. the prohibition of adultery after the introduction of marriage. The necessity of certain other principles is not as easy to discern and apply, such as the prohibition of taking revenge.[182]

178 Cf. F. de Vitoria, *De indis recenter inventis et de iure belli Hispanorum in barbaros. Relectiones*, q. 1 a. 4.
179 Cf. IBP, II.XX.xl.
180 Cf. ibid., II.XX.xl.1.
181 Cf. ibid., II.XX.xl.2.
182 Cf. ibid., II.XX.xliii.1.

Grotius compares this to mathematics: while there are some proofs that are true and obvious, others are also true, but less easy to understand. If there is innocent ignorance, e.g. due to weakness of senses or deficient education, respective violations of Natural Right are to be excused. Grotius here applies the same principles as in civil law: even if ignorance is caused by negligence and therefore avoidable, it nevertheless diminishes the offence.[183] Thus the punishing of offences against Natural Right depends very much on the appearance of the respective rule which has been breached: punishment requires guilt on the part of the offender, which will be hard to establish if the violated rule is obscure.

6.2. Punishment of Offences against Natural Religion

This leads to one of the most interesting features of Grotius' concept of Natural Right, namely the punishment of offences against Natural Religion. We have seen above that Grotius regards Natural Religion to be a part of Natural Right. Under Natural Right, human beings are obliged to recognise God as existing being, as one being, as creator, and as director of human affairs. Can these principles of Natural Religion be enforced as part of Natural Right? One might doubt that the impiety of an individual or of a group directly or indirectly affects other human beings. Is it not rather a question for God to judge? Grotius himself realises these difficulties. Nevertheless he argues in favour of the possibility to punish offences against God, even to the extent that he justifies wars against impious human beings.[184] Firstly, there is the general possibility to punish offences which do not affect other human beings directly, but indirectly, such as suicide, sodomy, and the like. Though God's power to punish such offences is not disputed, they also can be punished legitimately by human beings, as has been demonstrated in history.[185] In a second step Grotius asks whether offences against God also affect human beings. In his opinion, religion not only appeals to the grace of God, but also has major implications for human society. Religion produces the bond of human fellowship and provides protection of law and authority, as well as a framework of moral discipline in general.[186]

Natural Religion therefore is for Grotius' concept of Natural Right more than a mere compliment to the religious emotions of his contemporaries: it presents the essence of a general and universal moral fellowship amongst human beings, whether in the domestic or the international realm. It is, in

183 Cf. ibid., II.XX.xliii.2.
184 Cf. ibid., II.XX.xliv.1.
185 Cf. ibid., II.XX.xliv.2.
186 Cf. ibid., II.XX.xliv.3.

other words, at the centre of the rational and social nature of human beings. Grotius thus points out the relevance of religion, not only for the human community within a state, but also for the international community.[187] While in a state the function of religion can be partly supplemented by domestic laws which support their own enforcement, any enforcement of Right is considerably more difficult in the international context, where enforcement normally requires the use of force in war. Therefore Grotius stresses that offenders against the Right of Nations are often regarded as violators of divine law; the Roman emperors had deemed violations of religion acts of injustice against all.

Yet punishment requires guilt on the side of the offender. Guilt requires sufficient knowledge regarding the norms violated. Therefore one still needs to ask: When is an offender guilty of violating a legally relevant principle of Natural Religion? We have seen that Grotius holds four principles of Natural Religion to be essential, namely that God exists and that there is only one God; that God is invisible and a sublime being; that God directs human affairs and decides on the grounds of equity; and that God has created all things except himself. But though all of these principles, including the obligation to honour, love, worship, and obey God, are part of Natural Right, they are not all discernible and intelligible to the same degree. Grotius distinguishes between principles of Natural Religion according to their susceptibility to proof: those principles according to which God exists and directs human affairs are the highest principles of Natural Religion that have always been known and recognised by man. In this context it is irrelevant for Grotius whether the notion of God's existence has always been applied to only one God or eventually to several divine beings. The principles of God as an existing being and of God as director of human affairs are indispensable for judging the truth of any religion.[188] Consequently, the contravention of these two doctrines may be punished as breach of Natural Right according to the principles of punishment described above.

The other principles of Natural Religion – that there is only one God, that God is invisible and that God created everything except himself – are less obvious in Grotius' opinion. This may be seen from history, for these principles were forgotten repeatedly throughout the ages. Therefore, those to whom the divine law has not been made known must be excused; they cannot be punished by human beings.[189] Here Grotius contradicts what he had claimed in *Meletius*: that polytheism cannot be excused.[190] In this respect, a shift of Grotius' emphasis is to be noted: in *De Iure Belli ac Pacis* he hesitates

187 Cf. ibid., II.XX.xliv.6.
188 Cf. ibid., II.XX.xlvi.
189 Cf. ibid., II.XX.xlvii.
190 Cf. H. Grotius, *Meletius*, 20.

to ignore widespread polytheistic traditions in history. In *Meletius* Grotius is solely concerned with rational reasoning, which for him could only lead to the principle of monotheism.

IV. Conclusion

From this analysis of Grotius' perception of Natural Right we may conclude that the role of Natural Right in his theology of international law is that of an overarching set of legal principles which embraces mankind in its entirety. Natural Right provides the rule of justice between all human beings; at the same time Natural Right entails Natural Religion as fundamental creed which determines the basic category of a universal religious standard in that it presupposes God as single, personified, and omnipotent being acting as legislator in creation. For Grotius, Natural Right is therefore by no means a minimalist least common denominator for international relations; it entails relatively high moral standards for human conduct.

In his universal perspective of Natural Right, Grotius stands in the Christian Scholastic tradition of a universal fellowship of mankind. It should suffice in this context to liken his concept of the fellowship of human beings to that of Dante Alighieri as presented in *De Monarchia*[191]: Dante as well as Grotius argue in favour of an all-encompassing order as guarantee for the peaceful striving of human beings on earth, which presupposes the use of human intellect as a means to recognise the legal order entailed in divine creation. The major difference between the concepts of Dante and Grotius is that the former identifies the universal order with the historical Roman Empire by referring to the natural virtue of the Romans and to their divine designation, whereas Grotius conceives of a global bond through universally applicable principles of Natural Right without any particular institutional set-up in the shape of a universal rule. For Grotius, the international relations between all nations are dominated by a universal equality in freedom under Natural Right, even though Roman law had to a great extent embodied principles of Natural Right.

The Grotian concept of a theology of Natural Right entails certain fundamental differences to the Islamic concept of a law of nations. While Grotius' concept is designed for universal application, regardless of the acceptance of a divine revelation by individuals, classic Islamic jurisprudence primarily relied on the divine revelation of all-encompassing legal rules and thus restricted its scope of justice to the realm of Islam. While Grotius offers a concept of Natural Right which reaches beyond the traditional scope of the

191 Cf. Dante Alighieri, *De Monarchia*, I.iii., v. et seq.

respublica Christiana, the classic doctrine of Islamic law adhered to the traditional distinction between the realm of Islam and the realm of war, with the consequence that Islamic law was only fully applicable in the realm of Islam, while only natural equity was expected to govern legal relations in the realm of war. Nevertheless, in general the Islamic concept of justice was accessible to anyone who wished to avail himself of it, regardless of his individual belief. Furthermore, the classic doctrine of the Islamic law of nations acknowledged the legitimacy of a co-operation between Muslims and unbelievers; it displayed a limited tolerance to followers of other codified revelations. There are further similarities between Grotius and the Islamic concept in their respective religious orientation: God is accepted as legislator and thus as ultimate ground for the validity of Right. The identification between law and metaphysics results in a focus of both concepts on the individual as legal subject of the respective systems of Right, without mediating the individual from the international level through the state.

Yet we still must ask in how far the Grotian idea of Natural Right may already have anticipated similar patterns in modern concepts of international law. In this respect we first have to return to the fundamental difference in the approaches between typical "Western" concepts of international law and the theologically orientated ideas of Grotius: Grotius seeks to delineate universally applicable principles, in particular the principles of expletive justice and of attributive justice, from divine legislation in creation. Yet while Grotius' ontology of Natural Right is essentially theological in character, the epistemological approach is shaped by the necessities of a legal system, thus taking into account the requirements of practical legal efficacy. This becomes most apparent in Grotius' explanation on how rules of Natural Right can be recognised, for which he offers an empirical alternative in addition to his inductive method.

While modern liberal theories of international law endeavour to open ways for a peaceful cohabitation of a diversity of cultures, they could not adopt Grotius' distinct theological approach. While a truly pluralist approach certainly could live with a distinct theological concept in the pre-legal realm of any legal subject's motivation, it would concentrate on modes of ensuring a peaceful co-existence between different theological standpoints rather than identifying itself with any particular religious position. Still, the principles of natural justice introduced by Grotius would seem to be compatible even without full acceptance of their theological roots. Moreover, given the focus on the individual as legal subject of Natural Right, it would be well conceivable that modern theories of international law welcome the assistance of the Grotian conception in order to overcome the existing focus on states as sole legal entities of public international law, which so far hinders the recognition of the rights and responsibilities of individuals.

Chapter 2

Arbitrary Divine Right

I. Introduction

To the category of Natural Right Grotius adds Arbitrary Divine Right as a second category of Divine Right. As its name indicates, Arbitrary Divine Right consists of legal rules that are not already entailed in the design of the divine creation of the world but owe their existence to an explicit expression of the will of God. The revelation of God's will adds to the Right that God has given in creation.[1]

In viewing the revealed Divine Right as a category of International relevance, Grotius again follows a long-standing Christian tradition of International Right. Various canon lawyers had argued that the Right of Nations was divine in nature, and consequently any acts undertaken by human beings in the international arena were measured by prescripts of the Gospel.[2] However, at the same time Grotius' idea of Arbitrary Divine Right may claim originality, as he strictly distinguishes it from the creational Natural Right. While Grotius presents a rather detailed set of legal principles under Natural Right, which is applicable to all human beings regardless of their individual religious allegiance, the role of Arbitrary Divine Right mainly adds to Natural Right in expressing certain legal principles in greater clarity and in more detail.

For Grotius Arbitrary Divine Right is mainly important for Christians, as it contains various clear and detailed prescripts for human conduct. Yet Natural Right already entails similar principles as Arbitrary Divine Right, and thus the legal framework of both Arbitrary Divine Right and Natural Right are also nearly identical. The most important material addition of Arbitrary Divine Right is the demonstration of a way human beings will be able to lead a blameless life.

Grotius' concept of Arbitrary Divine Right also resembles classical Islamic concepts of international law, which stress the relevance of a revealed Divine Right. For the classic Islamic lawyers the revelation of the Divine Right through Mohammed as chief prophet was not merely an additional

1 Cf. IBP, I.I.xv.1.

2 J. A. Brundage, *Medieval Canon Law*, pp. 23 et seq.

category of Divine Right.[3] Instead, the revealed Divine Right in the Quran is in Islamic law the primary and decisive category of Right, which claims precedence over all other shapes of law. Though there has been a tradition of rational jurisprudence in the Shi'ism, this view has never gained much prominence in the wider field of Islamic legal thought. While Islamic law is, in principle, a code of good conduct for Muslims, this function is already taken in Grotius' concept by Natural Right in relation to Christians and non-Christians. Arbitrary Divine Right on the other hand demonstrates in Grotius' concept how Christians can adhere to God's will despite the fallibility of human nature.

Obviously, modern pluralist systems of international law of the "Western" tradition will not be compatible with a distinct set of Arbitrary Divine Right which draws on divine revelation as act of legislation. Though liberal jurisprudence certainly takes into account the individual belief in divine revelation, and acknowledges the importance of the religious allegiance of individuals in the shaping of their conduct in the international arena, the decisive factor for liberal concepts of international law is the acceptance of legal rules by legal subjects, regardless of whether or not these rules are compatible with any divine revelation.[4] Nevertheless, the function which Arbitrary Divine Right performs in the Grotian system of International Right in creating a strong bond between Christian states, peoples, and nations is not completely alien to modern theories: very often modern theories also recognise stronger connections amongst states that have a liberal constitution and acknowledge basic human rights than between other states, as can be seen in John Rawls' theory of a "Law of Peoples".[5]

We shall now first take a closer look at the various subcategories of Arbitrary Divine Right presented by Grotius before we move on to examine the relationship between Arbitrary Divine Right and Natural Right, the question of how rules of Arbitrary Divine Right can be discerned, the basic principles of Arbitrary Divine Right, and finally the enforceability of Arbitrary Divine Right.

---

3 Cf. B. Krawietz, *Hierarchie der Rechtsquellen im tradierten sunnitischen Islam*, pp. 88 et seq.

4 Cf. A. Hurrell, "International Law and the Making and Unmaking of Boundaries", in A. Buchanan, M. Moore (eds.), *States, Nations, and Borders: The Ethics of Making Boundaries*, pp. 276-278.

5 Cf. J. Rawls, *The Law of Peoples*, pp. 4 et seq.

II. Subcategories of Arbitrary Divine Right

Grotius distinguishes two subspecies of Arbitrary Divine Right, differentiated according to their addressees: Arbitrary Divine Right has sometimes been given to the entirety of mankind, but sometimes only to one particular people. The most important set of Arbitrary Divine Right is Gospel law, which represents the third revelation of God's law to mankind in its entirety. The other sets of Arbitrary Divine Right are far less important for Grotius: while the older revelations of God's law to mankind remain rather cryptic in Grotius' treatment, the revelation of the Mosaic law to the Jewish people serves Grotius mainly as an illustration of minimum standards for Christians, as he believes God to require a higher standard of conduct from Christians than from Jews.

1. Arbitrary Divine Right Given to Entire Mankind

According to Grotius, God gave three different sets of Arbitrary Divine Right to all of mankind in the course of history: first, immediately after creation; a second time, after restoring mankind after the Great Flood; and finally, in the course of the higher redemption of mankind through Christ.[6] Though these three sets of Arbitrary Divine Right had been given to mankind in its entirety, these rules are in Grotius' opinion only obligatory to those human beings to whom they have been made known. We shall see later how this phrase *notitiam pervenerunt* is to be understood, when we examine the ways of how rules of Arbitrary Divine Right can be identified.

In relation to the three subcategories of Arbitrary Divine Right Grotius spends most of his attention to the law granted by God with the redemption of mankind by Christ. This is Gospel law (*lex evangelica*), which Grotius even calls the "more perfect divine voluntary law".[7] The other subcategories are hardly mentioned in the course of *De Iure Belli ac Pacis*. As far as they are dealt with by Grotius at all, they are merely presented as rather cryptic sets of Right which reconfirm Natural Right through divine revelation—for example, in chapter 2 of the second book of *De Iure Belli ac Pacis*, where Grotius examines the position of war under Arbitrary Divine Right in general terms before proceeding to Gospel law in particular. Here Grotius asks whether the law given by God to Noah prohibits war:[8] "And surely your blood of your lives I will require; at the hand of every beast will I require it, and at the hand of man; at the hand of every man's brother will I require the

6 Cf. IBP, I.I.xv.2.
7 Cf. ibid., I.III.iii.1.
8 Cf. ibid., I.II.v.

life of man. Who sheddeth man's blood, by man shall his blood be shed: For in the image of God made he man".[9] Grotius discusses whether this speech of God must either be interpreted as a general statement or as a general warning without serving as an approval of the killing of murderers. Finally Grotius brings forward an interpretation of his own: These words of God are merely to be taken as an explanation and clarification of the commandments and prohibitions of Natural Right that had been forgotten by the time of Noah. God now calls this back to memory. Nevertheless, the prohibition to kill another human being exclusively refers to the intentional killing of innocent people. Thus the pre-Christian Arbitrary Divine Right here serves just as means of clarifying the content of Natural Right as positive restatement; it does, however, not have any distinctive content of its own which differs from the prohibitions and commandments that have already been set out by Natural Right.

Another example of Grotius' account of pre-Christian Arbitrary Divine Right can be found in his comments on alliances that are formed with infidels, in chapter 25 of the second book of *De Iure Belli ac Pacis*. After having stated that Natural Right is "indifferent" with respect to the religion of human beings participating in alliances – very likely because it merely endorses Natural Religion and does not have anything to say about more developed creeds – and therefore does not prohibit any alliances between followers of different religions[10], Grotius moves on to look upon this question first from the aspect of the ancient Divine Right (*Ius divinum veterum*) and then from the aspect of the new Divine Right (*Ius divinum novum*). Yet, in so doing, Grotius again comments not upon those pre-Christian sets of Arbitrary Divine Right that address all of mankind, but instead deals with the laws of Moses (which only address Jews, but not all of mankind). Those examples of Right that are taken from the Old Testament refer to Jewish law after Moses; they deal with the conquest of the Holy Land, with the wars that are undertaken by the kings of Israel, and with certain incidents that were commented upon by the prophets after Moses. Again the rules of the universal pre-Christian Arbitrary Divine Right do not receive any further attention. Thus, for Grotius the pre-Christian rules of Arbitrary Divine Right appear only to have reinstated principles of Natural Right, or are too obscure to uphold any practical relevance.

While pre-Christian Arbitrary Divine Right mainly serves as reconfirmation of Natural Right in Grotius' exposition, his interest centres on Gospel law. In the first book of *De Iure Belli ac Pacis* Gospel law provides Grotius' point of reference to most restrictions that are imposed upon the freedom of war under Natural Right. It does not forbid war altogether though. Grotius

9 Gen. 9: 5–6.
10 Cf. IBP, II.XV.viii.

uses Gospel law in order to show that war has not been prohibited by Christ; he demonstrates that self-defence is not categorically prohibited to Christians, but that acts performed as self-defence are only severely restricted in their scope, their direction, and their prerequisites.[11]

When focusing on the question of waging war against superiors, Gospel law is examined as one of the layers of law next to Natural Right.[12] In the treatment of just causes of war, the examination is structured by considerations of Natural Right, as most causes are derived from it; however, Grotius in turn again views every just cause from every layer of Right, and it is mainly Gospel law that limits the justification of wars and is to shape the conduct of belligerent parties in the course of a war.[13]

It is thus Gospel law that we have to pay special attention to when dealing with the content of Arbitrary Divine Right. Though Gospel law is only a subcategory of Arbitrary Divine Right, it is indeed the most important component for Grotius, as it is the most recent version of Arbitrary Divine Right.

2. Arbitrary Divine Right Given to a Single Nation

In the context of Arbitrary Divine Right Grotius also addresses Jewish law as a special sort of Arbitrary Divine Right given only to a single nation. While he believes Jewish law to have lost its obligatory force, he still finds it useful to identify principles of Natural Right and minimum standards of Arbitrary Divine Right.

Grotius claims that Jewish law was given to the Jewish people exclusively, and that God had thereby dignified the Jews.[14] However, because Jewish law was given only to the Jews, there is no obligation for outsiders to "take its yoke unto themselves".[15] Yet Grotius also states that some foreigners who had lived amongst the Jews had obtained a quasi-legal position under Jewish law; however, such exceptions could not prove that the Jewish law was designed to apply beyond the Jewish people.[16] Jewish law is mainly Mosaic

11 Cf. ibid., I.II.viii, 3, 7; IBP, I.III.iii.3, 8.

12 Cf. ibid., I.IV.vii.

13 Cf. ibid., II.I.iv-vii, xi-xiii – limitations of the cause of defence against certain injuries; cf. ibid., II.V.ix – restrictions on marriage and divorce; cf. ibid., II.X.x-xii, xvi, xx-xxiv, xxxiv – limitation of punishment; finally, cf. ibid., III.XXV.iii – exhortation to faith and peace; cf. also D. M. Sprackling, "Divine Law and Human Law in Hugo Grotius", pp. 173 et seq.

14 Cf. IBP, I.II.xvi.1.

15 Cf. ibid., I.II.xvi.2.

16 The restrictions of the Jewish religion, its ethical precepts as well as its view on salvation, to the chosen Jewish people is something that Grotius frequently contrasts

law, given by God to the Jewish people through Moses. Therefore, Jewish law does not include circumcision, as this is ordered by God to all descendants of Abraham. The order of circumcision was not limited to the descendants of Jews as descendants of Jacob, and consequently, this was obligatory also to people other than the Jews as old Arbitrary Divine Right.[17]

The applicability of Jewish law is not a prerequisite for the salvation of every human being: those heathens to whom Jewish law was not explicitly applicable could still be rewarded with the same merits as the Jews, if they complied with what has been described as "law of the heart". Though formally Jewish law was limited to Jews, the moral law of Israel in Grotius' opinion merely resembles in its greater part what has already been prescribed by nature, as becomes apparent from the tradition of the ancestors; however, this certainly does not extend to the ceremonial law or procedural law of Israel. Grotius here refers to Paul, who suggested in Romans 2: 14–15 that Gentiles might comply with the requirements of the Torah instinctively, and thus adhere to what may be described as a "common-sense knowledge of the one Law of God".[18] In this sense the prescripts that are complied with by the Gentiles are not part of a Natural Right parallel to the Jewish law; rather, Jewish law restates what is already entailed by Natural Right. It seems quite probable that Grotius here may have been influenced indirectly by Vossius' works on paganism.[19]

Ultimately Grotius comes close to Calvin regarding the continuing relevance of Jewish law to Christians: like Calvin, he dismisses the assertion that Jewish law had lost all its relevance with the coming of Christ; like Calvin, he only regards the procedural and ceremonial laws to be completely abrogated, while the moral laws still retain their importance.[20] However,

---

to the "universal" approach of Christianity; cf. H. Grotius, *Meletius*, §§ 16, 56, 64, 79; it seems quite probable that Grotius here refers to the popular commonplaces regarding Jewish religion and ethics that were wideley known by that time, cf. P. T. van Rooden, *Theology, Biblical Scholarship and Rabbinical Studies in the Seventeenth Century*, pp. 91–93; P. de Mornay, *De la verité de la religion chrestiene: Contre les Athées, Epicuriens, Payens, Juifs, Mahumedistes, et autres Infideles*, pp. 768–770. However, it is unlikely that Grotius undertook thorough research of the respective Jewish literature, in particular the Talmud, of his own; cf. E. Rabbie, "Grotius and Judaism", in J. J. M Nellen, E. Rabbie (eds.), *Hugo Grotius, theologian: Essays in Honour of G. H. M. Posthumus Meyjes*, pp. 106–107.

17 Cf. IBP, I.I.xvi.3, 4 and ibid., I.I.xvi.5.

18 M. Bockmuehl, *Jewish Law in Gentile Churches: Halakhah and the Beginning of Christian Public Ethics*, pp. 131–132.

19 Cf. F. Laplanche, "Grotius et les religions du paganisme dans les Annotationes in Vetum Testamentum", pp. 54–56, in: H. Nellen, E. Rabbie (eds.), *Hugo Grotius, theologian*, pp. 53–63.

20 Cf. Calvin, *Institutio Religionis Christianae*, 4.20.14–15.

Grotius states more clearly than Calvin that this importance does not spring from the promulgation of the relevant Jewish law, but instead from the fact that Jewish law merely restates principles of Natural Right and therefore, though they have become legally inapplicable, help to identify the content of Natural Right. Hence, Grotius is far more reluctant than other Reformed theologians to still attribute importance to Jewish law. John Knox, for example, regarded the Old Testament as a legal code with full applicability, and sought to have the Mosaic Law acknowledged as binding authority on the governance of Christian rulers.[21]

How does Jewish law relate to other species of the Arbitrary Divine Right, in particular to Gospel law? Is it still binding at least for the Jews? To this Grotius answers no. The ritual regulations of Jewish law lost their binding force with the appearance of Christ, his act of redemption, and the promulgation of his new Law of the Gospel. The rest of Jewish law (in particular those regulations not immediately connected to the ritual of the Mosaic religion), however, lost its obligatory force when the Jews' community was destroyed and the Jews were dispersed all over the earth without any hope of becoming reunited again. We may take it that Grotius here refers to the ultimate destruction of the Jewish community in A.D. 135. In other words, Jewish law became devoid of its object of reference. As there was no addressee left, the law itself was abandoned.[22]

Moreover, before the arrival of Christ, non-Jews had already had a legitimate – if weak – hope of gaining salvation outside the Jewish community. Since the arrival of Christ, Christians are explicitly protected by a new covenant. According to Grotius, Christians could now, after the abolishment of Jewish law, amalgamate with the descendants of the Jewish people in one common Church.[23] Here Grotius subtly alludes to the notion of the Gospel as freeing from the burden of the law – a traditional theme of the Reformation. However, he is still quite reluctant to take up this theme fully; he conceives the relevance of Jewish law to be limited to its addressees. It has thus not been of great importance to any Christians other than those who had been Jews before the advent of Christ. For all others, the burden of the Jewish law did not have to be lifted by the Gospel, because it had never applied to them. In this Grotius' emphasis is different from Ockham's, who praised the Gospel as the law of freedom in relation to the Jewish *caeremonialia*.[24] Grotius

---

21 Cf. J. Knox, *The First Blast of the Trumpet: Against the Monstrous Regiment of Women*, I.iii. et seq.

22 IBP, I.I.xvi.7.

23 Cf. ibid., I.I.xvi.7.

24 Cf. William of Ockham, *Breviloquium de potestate papae*, II.iii.; id., *Dialogus inter militem et clericum*, I.III.i. et seq.

believes that the Law of the Gospel has certainly been a law of freedom for Jews; however, it was simply a new divine law for others.

As already explained above, Grotius thinks that Jewish law still has some relevance for Christians as well, in serving as an indicator to assist Christians in finding out about true Right, Natural Right as well as Gospel law. Firstly, as Arbitrary Divine Right cannot contradict Natural Right, one may conclude that all prescriptions contained in the Old Testament at least do not contradict Natural Right. Therefore Jewish law may help to find the borderlines drawn by Natural Right for the admissibility of human behaviour.[25] This function is especially relevant where Jewish law commands something, or grants a full permission in the sense of a right to do something in contrast to a mere licence. However, where Jewish law only grants an imperfect permission – a permission to do something unimpeded and without punishment – it is not as helpful. Yet, Grotius points out that one will rarely be able to apply this function of Jewish law with respect to permissions, as one frequently will need Natural Right in order to interpret permissions of the Jewish law. Hence, it is more difficult to draw inferences in the opposite direction.

Secondly, we may conclude from Jewish law that Christian rulers may enact similar legal regulations through human legislation, except for regulations that refer exclusively to the time before Christ's arrival and the revelation of the Gospel, or are in contrast to Christ's explicit orders.[26]

Thirdly, we may, according to Grotius, conceive Jewish law as a minimum standard for what is prescribed by Gospel law: any virtue that has been commanded according to Jewish law can be deemed to be commanded in at least the same degree by Gospel law. According to Grotius, this is because the heavenly promises given to mankind in Gospel law are given more clearly. Hence, where Jewish law had ordered that one seventh of one's time be spent in worship, Christians must worship for no less than a seventh of their time; the same applies to the share of income that must be spent for the maintenance of ministers and the like.[27] Grotius thus refers to Jewish law also as an instrument for the interpretation of Gospel law: Wherever Jewish law commands the exercise of virtue, Gospel law orders at least the exercise of the same degree of virtue. Wherever Jewish law speaks in commandments of virtues, Gospel law says at least the same.

25 Cf. IBP, I.I.xvii.2.
26 Cf. ibid., I.I.xvii.3.
27 Cf. ibid., I.I.xvii.4.

III. The Relationship between Natural Right and Arbitrary Divine Right

In distinguishing between Natural Right as Right of creation and Arbitrary Divine Right as Right of revelation, Grotius follows an established tradition of Christian legal thought. However, for him much of the revealed Arbitrary Divine Right is simply a reconfirmation of principles of Natural Right. Thus in Grotius' views, God has time and again brought certain Natural Right principles back to memory by stating them in revealed sets of Right. Though Grotius certainly conceives of certain additions of Arbitrary Divine Right to Natural Right, the latter still takes the primary position in Grotius' system of Right. Natural Right thus is a quite detailed system of legal principles which is supplemented in some respect by subsequent divine acts of will. In the following we shall investigate the relationship between Natural Right and Arbitrary Divine Right in Grotius' concept of Right in greater detail. Yet, before embarking on this investigation we need to look at the alternative legal traditions of reason and revelation.

Though the concept of a Natural Right entailed in the reason of creation was already firmly rooted in the Christian legal tradition, it is fair to say that the revealed Divine Right had frequently been held to be more important for Christians. The idea of Natural Right thus had often been used to fill those legal loopholes where no precise legal principles from the Gospel could be found. Thus, for example, some authors had thought that Natural Right had had relevance in governing the legal relationships between human beings prior to the revelation of the Gospel and of other pieces of divine legislation, or that Natural Right still mainly applied to non-Christians who had not heard about the Gospel.[28] Yet, as regards the legal obligations pertaining to Christians, divine law had been thought to play the primary role.

A similar distinction between a law of reason and a law of revelation had also been discussed in classic Islamic jurisprudence. While some of the early Muslim jurists had taken an intense interest in a law of reason as an addition to the revealed law of the Sharia, the dominant position taken in classic Islamic jurisprudence can be described as an interpretation of the revealed law as revealed divine reason.[29] Hence, the Quran was taken as God's own explanation of his reason, which consequently also had to be interpreted with

28 C. A. Stumpf, "Völkerrecht unter Kreuz und Halbmond: Muhammad al-Shaybani und Hugo Grotius als Exponenten religiöser Völkerrechtstradition", *Archiv des Völkerrechts*, 41 (2003/1), pp. 86–100.

29 One notable example of an Arab jurist and philosopher who had been one of the most prolific writers on reason and justice was Avorroës, also known in Arabia as Abu al-Walid Ibn Rushd. Cf. Ibn Abi Usaybi'ah, *Uyun al-Anba' fi Tabaqat al-Atibba*; see also Khadduri, *The Islamic Conception of Justice*, pp. 93 et seq.

a methodology relying on this reason: for example, when using the method of analogy the lawyers used revealed principles pertaining to certain facts to determine what God's reason prescribed in relation to different, but similar, facts.[30] Nonetheless, all principles of Right stemmed from the divine expression of will through his last and most important prophet. A separate set of Right which merely relied on reason but was not rooted in divine revelation could not be sustained.

The modern liberal theory of Right takes a completely different approach to Right than the religious legal tradition. While various authors, such as John Rawls with his theory of justice as fairness, display inclinations to accept certain core principles of Natural Right as Right of reason which obligate all and any human beings[31], an understanding of Right as divinely instituted principles is completely absent from their concepts[32]: most liberal theorists would certainly be willing to accept religious allegiances of the individual members of domestic and international societies as a legitimate driving force to seek the common good within a legal framework.[33] However, a liberal theory will not accept legal regulations which cannot at least to some degree be explained by reason. At the same time, any form of conduct of an individual which is driven by religious motivations will not be recognised under a liberal theory of jurisprudence as far as it is detrimental to what is commonly accepted as reasonable. Society's law of reason thus limits the role which revelation may play for an individual.

Grotius follows the Christian tradition in adding Arbitrary Divine Right as Right of revelation next to Natural Right as Right of creation. However, Grotius overall places greater relevance than the major part of the Christian legal tradition on Natural Right as reasonable creational Right. This raises the question of how Grotius believes the divine legislation through revelation to relate to the Divine Right entailed in creation. In particular, it has to be asked whether God has amended and altered his initial Right of creation through revelation. The answer is no: though Grotius confirms that God is omnipotent, God cannot contradict himself by amending the natural order as given in creation. Arbitrary Divine Right therefore may not contradict Natural Right in the sense that the former prohibits something that the latter commands, or that the former commands something that the latter prohibits. Yet we have already seen that Natural Right only provides a general legal framework without regulating human behaviour in every detail. It only contains obligations as commandments and prohibitions; it does not contain

30 B. Krawietz, *Hierarchie der Rechtsquellen im tradierten sunnitischen Islam*, pp. 203 et seq.

31 Cf. J. Rawls, *A Theory of Justice*, pp. 209 et seq.

32 Cf. J. Rawls, *The Law of Peoples*, pp. 149 et seq.

33 For a more detailed analysis of the interrelation between reason and revelation in the public life of a liberal society see R. Song, *Christianity and Liberal Society*, pp. 220 et seq.

any subjective rights in the strict sense; it never expressly allows certain human behaviour, but only permits certain modes of conduct by being silent. Arbitrary Divine Right may regulate matters which are left open by Natural Right: Where Natural Right is silent, Arbitrary Divine Right may speak. Where Natural Right speaks, Arbitrary Divine Right may say the same, perhaps in clearer words, more precisely, and more loudly, or it may have something additional to say. If something is declared praiseworthy but not obligatory by Natural Right, it may be made binding by Arbitrary Divine Right, as Grotius points out when dealing with the legitimacy of war.[34] What is part of the "Right not properly so called" may be made obligatory by proper law under Arbitrary Divine Right. Yet even within Arbitrary Divine Right there may be different degrees of demands: thus it is possible that Gospel law has higher legal standards than both the preceding sets of Arbitrary Divine Right and Natural Right.[35]

This may be illustrated firstly by the example of self-defence: Natural Right does not clearly forbid self-defence, but is silent about it. Even after the establishment of courts, self-defence is still not prohibited by Natural Right as far as courts are not available.[36] Moreover, under Natural Right it is not even prohibited to kill an innocent person in order to save one's own life even though this might not necessarily be compliant with social respect (*societatis respectus*). This (implicit) permission to use force in self-defence according to Natural Right is, however, partly removed by Arbitrary Divine Right, in particular by Gospel law: though Grotius admits that the admissibility of self-defence under Gospel law is a rather difficult and ambiguous issue – given the divinely imposed duty of patience under Arbitrary Divine Right[37] – he does not recognise its total prohibition. While Gospel law commands human beings to love one another, it does not command one to love others more than oneself.[38] Yet self-defence at the expense of third parties is completely prohibited under Arbitrary Divine Right, and it is the silence of Natural Right on this issue which allows Gospel law (as part of Arbitrary Divine Right) to prohibit it.[39] This presents an example where Natural Right is silent, while Arbitrary Divine Right speaks.

God may reinforce Natural Right through explicit laws as part of Arbitrary Divine Right.[40] Such divine laws are to be qualified as Arbitrary Divine Right, though they do not differ in content from Natural Right. The only difference between the otherwise identical legal principles may then be

34 Cf. IBP, I.II.v.1.
35 Cf. ibid., I.II.vi.2.
36 Cf. ibid., I.III.ii.1.
37 Cf. ibid., I.III.iii.1.
38 Cf. ibid., I.III.iii.3.
39 Cf. ibid., II.I.iv.1.
40 Cf. ibid., Prolegomena 13.

their respective enforcement: if the respective principle of Natural Right has been obscured in history, any human being who is ignorant of it may be excused for contravening it. However, a Christian who is not only bound by the Right of reason but also by that of revelation should normally be aware of it. This raises the question of how principles of Arbitrary Divine Right can be discerned, which is also relevant for determining the applicability of the Right of revelation.

IV. Discernibility of Norms of Arbitrary Divine Right

The discernibility of norms of Divine Right has always been a matter of controversy amongst Christian theologians and lawyers. While quite often lawyers as well as theologians had believed certain principles of the revealed Divine Right to be identified quite easily, they frequently disagreed upon what these principles were. However, most authors agreed that ultimately the revealed Divine Right was only obligatory to those individuals to whom it had been made known, whether through revelation itself or through reports by other human beings. Further controversy arose in connection with the question of whether the plain learning of certain principles of the revealed Divine Right was sufficient to make them obligatory, or whether some additional assistance, such as the working of the Holy Ghost, was required. The controversy became relevant, for example, in connection with missionary wars: some medieval canon lawyers held that pagans had to be taught about the contents of the Gospels; if however they rejected Christianity afterwards or if they altogether refused to hear about Christ's message, a just war could be waged against them.[41]

Similar problems had also been discussed in classic Islamic jurisprudence.[42] Yet most scholars of classic Islamic jurisprudence agreed that the divine revelation was the most important source of Divine Right, and that the spreading of Islam was one of the most important obligations of any faithful Muslim. However, the confidence that the mere learning of God's revelation through his Prophet sufficed to be obligated to accept Islam or at least its rule was developed more strongly in classic Islamic jurisprudence than in medieval canon law. Consequently, the doctrine of Jihad ultimately required a peaceful request of Muslims to their opponents to submit to Islamic rule.

41 C. A. Stumpf, "Völkerrecht unter Kreuz und Halbmond: Muhammad al-Shaybani und Hugo Grotius als Exponenten religiöser Völkerrechtstradition", *Archiv des Völkerrechts*, 41 (2003/1), pp. 86–100.

42 Ibid.

Only if the opponents declined to comply with such a request could a legitimate military Jihad be waged against them.

As modern liberal theories of jurisprudence do not accept Divine Right as a fully valid category of Right, they do not possess any distinct concept of identifying such principles of Divine Right. The notion of a divine revelation as a source of legal principles obviously is not compatible with the secular idea of liberal jurisprudence, which views consensus amongst human beings as the most important source of Right. Likewise, modern theologians treat the Holy Scripture as an expression of divine experiences made by human beings, and thus analyse it using a historical-critical methodology. Nonetheless, in modern liberal jurisprudence as well as in modern Christian theology there is a willingness to acknowledge the individual's belief that God wants a certain conduct from human beings. How God's wishes are made known to man – by a kind of direct revelation or through other human beings' divine experience – is only of secondary importance. In any case, the divine will is at least acknowledged as a legitimate motivation of the individual as regards his participation in the legal discourse in society.[43]

With respect to the discernibility of principles of Arbitrary Divine Right, Grotius in general follows the medieval Christian tradition, but with certain qualifications: he accepts that God reveals himself immediately through the Holy Scripture, but in doing so already uses a rather modern critical methodology. For Grotius the plain understanding of the Holy Scripture suffices in order to grasp the relevant principles of Arbitrary Divine Right. This also bears relevance for the principles that can be identified as Arbitrary Divine Right: Grotius believes God's revelation has made clear the principles of Arbitrary Divine Right so that they can be easily identified by human beings. Only those principles that have been made clear by God can be deemed to constitute a legal obligation. On the other hand, if something is left obscure in divine revelation, then one can be sure that it is legally irrelevant. However, the plain learning about the content of the Gospel is still not sufficient to create enforceable obligations to adhere to its law, which for Grotius still requires the assistance of the Holy Ghost

Grotius holds that Arbitrary Divine Right constitutes an obligatory nature only in so far as human beings have received notice of it.[44] This does not mean that those who are ignorant of it are all victims of a corrupt tradition: infidels remain in the natural state in relation to knowledge concerning the remission of sins; it means that they are not aware of their redemption through Jesus Christ offering satisfaction for the sins of mankind by taking them upon himself and suffering on the cross.

---

43 See for example the approach taken by D. Fergusson, *Community, Liberalism and Christian Ethics*, pp. 1-9.

44 Cf. IBP, I.I.xv.2.

How do human beings receive notice of the divine will and of the revelation of the divine truth? Moreover, even if human beings receive notice of the divine revelation, do they instantly have to acknowledge this divine revelation as divine truth? Grotius seems to deal with this question rather ambiguously: On the one hand, the condition of *notitiam pervenerunt*, of receiving notice of the contents of the divine revelation, suggests that the plain reading of the Holy Scripture is sufficient to subject the reader to Arbitrary Divine Right.[45] On the other hand, Grotius is quite hesitant about allowing human beings to be punished because of their refusal to accept Christianity, because no one could accept Christianity without the secret assistance of God through the Holy Ghost, as Grotius explains in *De Iure Belli ac Pacis*[46] (1625) as well as in *De Iure Praedae Commentarius*[47] (1609) and in *Meletius*[48] (1611).

This raises the question of whether Grotius distinguishes between obligation on the one hand and punishment on the other. In chapter 1 of the first book of *De Iure Belli ac Pacis* Grotius deals with Right, the obligatory nature of Right, and different legal categories. He is not concerned in this context with the enforcement of law, punishment, or whether force may be employed in order to force someone to fulfil his obligations. Grotius here simply asks what one has to do under different categories of law, who is addressed by which category of law, and why and how such obligations arise. Guilt and possible excuses for misdoings are not issues that attract Grotius' attention at this level.

From this we may conclude that Arbitrary Divine Right becomes obligatory to people as soon as they receive notice of it; further assistance by God through the Holy Ghost is not required for the applicability of these norms. If, however, the Holy Ghost does not seize the hearts of human beings, they cannot be held guilty of misdeeds against Arbitrary Divine Right according to Grotius. A similar distinction between the mere obligation to accept the Christian faith and the impermissibility to punish someone had already been brought forward by Vitoria in his lectures *De Indis recenter* in taking up the Thomist views regarding the obligation to believe: Vitoria held that the individual had no duty to believe the Christian dogmas if he was not familiar with them. Even giving infidels the mere information that Christ has come and redeemed mankind will not result in obliging anyone to accept Christianity; only a full explanation of the Christian Gospel will suffice. Moreover, infidels are under an obligation to hear what is told them about Christianity. Nevertheless, even if they still refuse to accept Christianity and

45 Cf. H. Grotius, *Meletius*, 52 et seq.

46 Cf. IBP, II.XX.xlviii.1.

47 Cf. H. Grotius, De iure praedae commentarius, XII.

48 Cf. H. Grotius, *Meletius*, 52 et seq.

subsequently breach their obligation to do so, they may not be punished, as Christianity may not be spread by violence.[49]

However, this raises additional questions: How does revelation work? How do we receive knowledge of the divine truth? Grotius seems to be quite confident about the self-explanatory nature of the Holy Scripture in *Meletius*. This becomes evident from his praise of the simplicity of the Holy Scripture[50]; hence even uneducated people are able to understand the divine revelation as it is plainly presented in the Holy Scripture. In fact, neither age nor gender, nor education, nor intelligence can make any difference with respect to the capacity to understand those words that describe the forgiveness granted by God. The only faculty required to understand God's word is the capability of using reason.

In *De Iure Belli ac Pacis* Grotius places more weight on tradition as a means of learning about Arbitrary Divine Right than in *Meletius*: the faith of people in all ages and all places throughout history proves the existence of God as much as miracles do.[51] Even if man should not be susceptible to reason, he at least can – and is in Grotius' view obliged to – trust in the accuracy of beliefs of earlier generations. Therefore, Grotius seems to imply that the rules of Arbitrary Divine Right are as easy to understand as those of Natural Right. Moreover, the dogmas and precepts of Gospel law are not ambiguous for Grotius. It may be noted that Grotius himself wrote his booklet *De Veritate Christianae religionis* for the purpose of facilitating missionary attempts undertaken by the Dutch in the East Indies: here he treated the dogmas and precepts of Christianity as clear commandments by God, which follow logical considerations.

Nonetheless, Grotius admits that the principles of Natural Right and of Arbitrary Divine Right are to some extent a matter of interpretation. In his views on the accessibility of the Christian religion, the same epistemological progression is in operation as in the accessibility of Natural Right precepts. There are not simply a random number of items of knowledge that can and must be known, but rather a hierarchal structure, starting with those pieces of knowledge that can be clearly identified by using reason, and ultimately leading to the mystery of things which can only be grasped by approximation to the truth. Grotius here takes an epistemological approach to Arbitrary Divine Right which is quite similar to his respective views in relation to Natural Right.

49 Cf. F. de Vitoria, *De indis recenter inventis et de iure belli Hispanorum in barbaros: Relectiones*, q.2 a.4.

50 Cf. H. Grotius, *Meletius*, 54–55.

51 Cf. IBP, "Prolegomena" 11.

V. Basic Principles of Arbitrary Divine Right

We have seen above that for Grotius the most important category of Arbitrary Divine Right is Gospel law. The two other types of Arbitrary Divine Right that are addressed to the entirety of mankind remain rather obscure in Grotius' treatment of the subject, probably because Gospel law is the most recent as well as the most detailed source of Arbitrary Divine Right. When dealing with the principles of Arbitrary Divine Right within the Grotian categories of law, we may hence restrict our examination to Gospel law.

The first thing we should note in this context is the use of the term law (*lex*) which hints at Grotius' third definition for Right. Hence the Law of the Gospel can be viewed as rules of moral actions which oblige human beings to do what is right.

Grotius frequently uses aspects of Gospel law in *De Iure Belli ac Pacis*, for example the twofold love commandment, in order to explain particular features of the laws of war. Nevertheless, *De Iure Belli ac Pacis* does not contain a carefully worked-out description of the contents of the Law of the Gospel. In order to find out about the principles of Gospel law we have to turn to other works of Grotius. The obvious place to look for is *Meletius*. While *Meletius* is primarily a theological work dealing with the rational foundation of Christianity, it is also of legal relevance, because Grotius holds that Christian religious principles are legal principles as part of Arbitrary Divine Right. In fact, Grotius does not strictly distinguish between theological reasoning and legal principles. Both are closely connected with each other: theological content may be contained by a legal vessel; yet the theological content of legal regulations must be accessible to rationality. At the same time Grotius strictly distinguishes between the content of legal regulations – be it theological or a-theological – and their enforceability: law obliges the addressee to do what is right. However, whether the addressee can be forced to do this by other human beings is to be distinguished from the obligation itself. Therefore Grotius can coherently perceive religious faith and ethical precepts as subject to Right, in particular to Arbitrary Divine Right and to Gospel law, and at the same time admit that doctrinal precepts are not necessarily enforceable.

In relation to the theological content of Arbitrary Divine Right, Grotius holds that Christianity follows the same theological principles as Natural Religion under Natural Right: there is one God, who is invisible; he is a sublime being; he attends to human affairs and directs them; he decides on the grounds of equity; and he has created all things except himself. The difference between Natural Religion as entailed in Natural Right and Christianity as entailed in the Law of the Gospel is not one of quality, but one of quantity: Christianity is distinct from Natural Religion not because it is different in substance, but because Arbitrary Divine Right adds certain doctrines and precepts to Natural Religion under Natural Right.

Therefore, it will now be necessary to identify the additions that Christianity makes to Natural Religion. For Grotius, religion consists of a theoretical and a practical part. The theoretical part is made up of dogmas (*decreta*), the practical part of ethical precepts (*praecepta*). In this context Grotius stresses that any practical science may not ignore principles, but that principles should incite an action or at least offer some practical applicability. This is due to the intermediary function of religion between God and human beings. Hence, religious principles pertain both to God and things divine as well as to human beings and things human.[52] In the following we shall enquire first into the dogmas and then the precepts under Gospel law.

1. Dogmas

In *Meletius*, Grotius mentions some of the dogmas explicitly, others become obvious from his comments. In the following we will list those dogmas that Grotius directly or indirectly holds to be constituent elements of Christian doctrine and therefore to be part of Arbitrary Divine Right.

The most distinguished dogma of Christianity is that there is only one God, which in Grotius' view is already proved by the fact that God exists.[53] There is no excuse for believing in polytheistic religions. However, we have already seen that Grotius is willing to excuse followers of polytheistic religions in *De Iure Belli ac Pacis* on the grounds of tradition. That God is most simple, infinite, and best[54] is a dogma which Grotius asserts rather than proves.[55] From this dogma he derives God's omniscience, omnipotence, and benevolence.[56]

Focusing on the relationship between God and the world, Grotius states that God is the creator of everything, for God is the primary cause.[57] God created everything for man's sake, but man for God's own sake.[58] God is the attentive ruler of everything he created. In dealing with God's position as ruler of everything, Grotius discusses the question of whether man can exercise free choice. Grotius answers yes: God rules everything for the preservation of the natural order, and guarantees free choice, which he granted to the rational mind of human beings. If God refrains from

52 Cf. H. Grotius, *Meletius*, 19.
53 Cf. ibid., 20.
54 Cf. ibid., 21.
55 Cf. D. M. Sprackling, "Divine and Human Law in Hugo Grotius", p. 54.
56 Cf. H. Grotius, *Meletius*, 22 et seq.
57 Cf. ibid., 26.
58 Cf. ibid., 28.

intervening in negative events, he does so because he wishes to preserve free choice, of which intervention would deprive his creation.[59] Nevertheless, as we shall see, Grotius still allows for divine providence and for God interfering with human affairs. Grotius does not explain the reason why God interferes in some cases and abstains from interference in others; we may assume that Grotius considers this a matter of God's secret discretion.

Now there follow dogmas that are concerned with the quality of human beings: Man consists of body and soul. Man has free choice. Man is the finest and worthiest of all things visible. God made man good.[60] As God made man good, man owes honour to God; to honour God means loving, admiring, revering God, the desire to please him, and the fear to displease him, and more generally the aversion to things that are contrary to God's laws.[61]

Furthermore, man should value his fellow man, for all human beings have been created as the living image of God; if we are thankful, we are not only to love God, but also our fellow man as image of God.

Then there follow the dogmas that define what man actually is: he is sinful and breaks the law, as he is ungrateful and far from what he ought to be. Though God created man as the best of all things living, in exercising the free choice and discretion accorded to him, man more often than not chooses a way of behaviour that is contrary to the laws of God.[62]

Man loses his free choice by doing bad things repeatedly. Grotius is firmly convinced that repeated practices of bad deeds weaken man's freedom to act well; consequently man is increasingly bound to behave unlawful. Citing Aristotle, Grotius states that vice leads to decline. Those who are initially free cease to be so by becoming slaves of their sins.[63] From this it follows that man is liable to punishment, because he breaks the law.[64] God's justice demands both punishment and the amendment of the human character.

This is where inductive reasoning ends for Grotius: while all the preceding dogmas could be established solely by reasoning, the dilemma of how to exercise punishment as remission of sins, and the problem of the correction of human vices as reparation for sins, cannot be solved by reasoning alone. The rational mind of human beings can go this far; beyond this point man needs external guidance towards the way of how sins can be remitted and repaired. This thought had already been used by Augustine to demonstrate the defects of Platonism.[65] For Grotius any religion that does not

59 Cf. ibid., 29.
60 Cf. ibid., 30.
61 Cf. ibid., 33.
62 Cf. ibid., 34.
63 Cf. ibid., 36 et 39.
64 Cf. ibid., 41 et 43.
65 Cf. A. Augustinus, *Confessiones*, 7.

offer a solution for the redemption of mankind is obsolete; yet only Christianity can do so both satisfactorily and reasonably. The revelation of the redemption of mankind as presented in the Holy Scripture is perfectly consistent with rationality.[66]

At the heart of this problem is the fact that, according to Grotius, man deserves no less a penalty than death. Moreover, he is in need of a mediator between himself and God.[67] Christianity brings these elements together, establishing the following dogmas: God has sent his son Jesus Christ as mediator. Jesus Christ is both God and man, as he was born as human beings are born.[68] Moreover, Christ as god and man died for the remission of the sins of man. God can illustrate the gravity of man's sins by sacrificing his only son. Additionally, the price paid by God matches that gravity without doubt. Man can therefore be confident that his debts are paid for.

Christianity, according to Grotius, is the only religion that teaches a satisfactory explanation of forgiveness. Yet the question remains of who has access to this forgiveness. Forgiveness is in principle attainable for all mankind, but requires penitence and belief. Penitence requires the acknowledgement that one's doings were wrong. Belief is the firm confidence that God has actually forgiven one's sins through the redemption granted in the sacrifice of Christ.[69] Beside the remission of sins, man is also in need of restoration. There are three remedies that help to restore man, the first of which is to remove ignorance. This is done by the teaching of the Holy Scripture, as well as by the clear recognition of these dogmas as divine truth.[70]

Though these dogmas are revealed by God in the Holy Scripture, they receive rational support by the fact that nothing taught in them is unworthy of God and that nothing is contained in them that is not conducive to the best conduct of life. Moreover, the writings of the Holy Scripture are coherent in themselves.[71] Finally, the authority of these writings is also established by their antiquity[72] and by a combination of simplicity and majesty.[73] Therefore man may trust in the authority of the Holy Scripture and have his ignorance removed.

The second remedy for the restoration of man's former strength is the example set by Christ, who is a perfect image of how man should behave.

---

66 Cf. H. Grotius, *Meletius* 43 et seq.
67 Cf. ibid., 45–46.
68 Cf. ibid., 47.
69 Cf. ibid., 50 et seq.
70 Cf. ibid., 51.
71 Cf. ibid., 52.
72 Cf. ibid., 53.
73 Cf. ibid., 54–55.

Christ led a blameless, virtuous life, accepted suffering for the sins of others, and gave his life for mankind.[74]

The third and, according to Grotius, most important remedy for the restoration of man is God's secret power, the Holy Ghost. The Holy Ghost incites the human heart to live a good and virtuous life. Grotius acknowledges that man cannot receive divine grace unwillingly, but only willingly. Man has to urge God to grant divine favour by sending this Holy Ghost to enable him to conduct a truly Christian life.[75]

Though Grotius mentions the Holy Ghost as an important remedy, his entire doctrine of the Trinity and in particular his perception of the function of the Holy Ghost remains somewhat obscure: can the work of the Holy Ghost be accessed by reason? How should we understand the secrecy of God's assistance in the Holy Ghost? These issues are not discussed by Grotius exhaustively. In Grotius' rational concept of Christian doctrine the Holy Ghost presents a factor that transcends rationality.

2. Precepts

After having established in the dogmas the abstract principles of Christian doctrine Grotius turns to their ethical consequences, which are contained in the precepts. He distinguishes between precepts that contain obligations to God, to humanity, to one's neighbours, and to oneself. Moreover, he distinguishes precepts that refer to internal acts from those that refer to external acts.

The following precepts are the most important obligations towards God with respect to internal acts. Firstly, to believe in God presupposes that we know God's word. Otherwise this precept would be difficult to comply with.[76] From there follows the precept to invoke God. Grotius counts prayer as an internal act towards God, which he also sees as a difficult necessity, but nevertheless as obligatory. Christians therefore must learn how to pray.[77] External acts towards God can be either commanded or prohibited. Thus it is forbidden to speak about God in a profane, rash, or irreverent way, and to make images of God.[78] Moreover it is forbidden to worship God with laborious rites.[79] This latter prohibition can be explained by the assumption that such rites are contrary to God's wishes and contrary to the principle that the worshipping of God takes place in the mind rather than in the visible

74 Cf. ibid., 56.
75 Cf. ibid., 57.
76 Cf. ibid., 61.
77 Cf. ibid., 61–62.
78 Cf. ibid., 63.
79 Cf. ibid., 63–64.

sphere. Furthermore, according to Grotius it is commanded to worship God in gatherings. In such gatherings God's word is to be proclaimed, people are to be stimulated religiously, and collective prayers are to be said.[80] Moreover, appropriate signs are to be used in worship. The signs used in worshipping God are to be few but effective. Grotius delineates from this the sacraments of the cleansing with water in baptism and of the Holy Eucharist.[81]

Then there are precepts that refer to the obligations of human beings to other human beings and to themselves. Obligations to others can be obligations to humanity or to institutions of society. The following two precepts are the most important: First, man owes friendship to humanity on the ground that man is a natural kinsman of all human beings, as they are the image of God.[82] This may be equated with the commandment to love one's neighbour as oneself. This friendship is regardless of the religious conviction of the neighbour, though Grotius admits that the ties amongst Christians are stronger than those between Christians and non-Christians.[83] From this precept Grotius develops the second precept, according to which man has to treat his fellow man as he himself wishes to be treated by God, a precept with special relevance for forgiveness: as man is in need of forgiveness by God he shall forgive his neighbour that trespassed against him.[84]

The next precepts refer to institutions of society, of which Grotius conceives two: family and state. Marriage is a sacred institution. This precept also entails the prohibition of sexual intercourse between the unmarried, of promiscuous relationships, of polygamy, and of the marriage of near relatives.[85] Moreover, Christians must take care of their children. Marriage is indissoluble due to this precept. Furthermore, Grotius names as another precept the nature of authority as a sacred institution. Because of the sacred character of authority, Christians are commanded to be good and loyal citizens. Christians must be tolerant of rulers who are difficult to bear and must accept their orders unless these are in contradiction to divine commandments.[86] We shall see later in greater detail how this sacred character of authority can be reconciled with Grotius' perception of the state as a human institution.

Finally, there are precepts under Gospel law as obligations of man to himself, which can either concern man directly or concern matters that are connected with him. With respect to the former man is obliged to preserve himself as best he can. The precept of self-preservation results in man's

80 Cf. ibid., 65.
81 Cf. ibid., 66.
82 Cf. ibid., 68.
83 Cf. ibid., 69.
84 Cf. ibid., 70.
85 Cf. ibid., 71.
86 Cf. ibid., 74.

obligation to preserve his own life, safety, and health.[87] This includes a prohibition to commit suicide, for man has received his life from God, and may not overrule the divine decision of when to end his life. Moreover, man may not consider death a greater evil than the sin of which he is guilty, nor may he prefer the preservation of his life to the maintenance of virtue. As a consequence man may not try to escape the fate God has designed for him. Grotius explains this by stating that only Christians have a true consolation for death, which is the forgiveness of sins granted by God.[88]

Connected with man are, in Grotius' view, matters, actions, words, and thoughts. This entails additional precepts: man has to be suspicious of the struggle for honour, wealth, and pleasure. Therefore man is prohibited to value honour, wealth, and pleasure more than God. If he is by chance favoured with such things, he is obliged to render due reverence for this to God.[89] Man has to acknowledge gratefully pleasures like food and drink as divine gifts. He may neither reject such gifts in ingratitude to God, nor exalt immodestly in these.[90] Sexual intercourse between the unmarried is prohibited. According to Grotius, intercourse was instituted for the sake of progeny. Children should not be begotten unintentionally; moreover, children should be well educated by both parents.[91] This is also due to the aforementioned precept according to which marriage is a sacred institution. Deeds which are neither commanded nor prohibited shall be done or left undone under consideration of the effects such deeds have on the virtues of others. If others can be induced to vicious behaviour due to one's own doings, these doings should be omitted.[92] Obviously, this is also a direct application of attributive justice. Moreover, man may not lie and must keep his promises. This is because God, according to Grotius, has given speech to man in order to strengthen human kinship. Lying or breaking promises results in disorder amongst the human community, which is contrary to the divine will.[93] We have seen that the keeping of promises also follows from expletive justice, as we have to live up to the words we use.

The next precept states that what is wrong to do is wrong to think. According to Grotius, thoughts are the roots of deeds. Therefore deeds and thoughts are equated by God.[94] What is commanded has to be done, because it is commanded. The fulfilment of obligations must be accompanied by a corresponding intention and not by second thoughts, e.g. the achievement of

87 Cf. ibid., 75.
88 Cf. ibid., 76.
89 Cf. ibid., 77.
90 Cf. ibid., 79.
91 Cf. ibid., 81.
92 Cf. ibid., 82.
93 Cf. ibid., 83–84.
94 Cf. ibid.,85.

honour and the like.[95] Here Grotius follows the long-standing tradition of pure love of God, which is not to be stained with selfish motives.

According to a further precept, man must let himself be guided by repentance and ask for forgiveness, as even after the remission of his sins, he is still in danger of falling back into vicious habits, and the dangers for a good and virtuous life are never fully conquered.[96]

What Grotius outlines in these dogmas and precepts is what he regards to be the essence of the Christian religion. His concept of the Christian religion and of Gospel law is by no means minimal and even less minimalist[97], it is not a limitation of religion to a natural nucleus. Rather it is a fully developed code of belief and of behaviour for human beings under Gospel law. The precepts cover nearly every aspect of human life and furnish human beings with principles of behaviour, though Grotius does not go into detail on any single aspect. The religious essence he proclaims is, however, restricted to what is accessible by reason. What cannot be proved by reason may be true nevertheless, but it is neither part of the essence of Christianity nor a true part of Gospel law. Otherwise it would have been made clear by God and not been left in doubt. In a rather Erastian fashion, Grotius believes that every relevant part of Christianity and of Gospel law is clear of the mist of uncertainty.[98] However, Gospel law can claim obedience as a legal norm only insofar as it has been revealed clearly.

What is quite remarkable about this presentation of dogmas and precepts is the nearly complete absence of biblical references in *Meletius*. Instead Grotius frequently discusses ancient philosophers and certain theologians, either to find support from them or to refute them as erroneous. While Grotius is keen on proving the accessibility of the revelation by rationality, he does not use a particularly biblical form of illustration, let alone argumentation. Rather, he presents Christianity as a distinctly revealed religious philosophy fully consistent with reason. Arguably, his motivation was to elevate the discussion about doctrines and ethics from the level of biblical interpretation to that of rational reasoning, which he probably regarded as a more convincing way of proving theological principles than blunt references to the Bible. It would be wrong, however, to suggest that all of his rational arguments are indisputable and avoid decisionism at all levels. In fact, some of his deductions actually move from one assertion to another. For example, the statement of God's perfection is asserted rather than

95 Cf. ibid., 86.

96 Cf. ibid., 87.

97 This is in contrast to what R. Tuck, "Grotius, Carneades, and Hobbes", *Grotiana*, 4 (1983) pp. 43–62, would have us believe.

98 Cf. J. Trapman, "Grotius and Erasmus", in: H. J. M. Nellen, E. Rabbie (eds.), *Hugo Grotius, theologian*, pp. 77 et seq.

proved; furthermore, Grotius' thesis that repeated behaviour leads necessarily to a loss of free choice is far from indisputable.

We may further note that Grotius presents these legal principles of Gospel law as an objective system of regulations, mainly consisting of obligations to do or not to do something in relation to God, to other human beings, or to oneself. Like his concept of Natural Right, Gospel law contains no subjective rights of human beings against others that might correspond to respective obligations.

VI. Enforcement of Arbitrary Divine Right

We have already seen that Grotius does not include the enforcement of regulations as prerequisite for their acknowledgement as Right, which complies with the older tradition of Christian legal thought. In their analysis of legal ethics, the Patristic as well as the canon law authors were mostly concerned with the quality of legal principles as directives for human conduct.[99] While this quality also implied at least to some extent the potential of such principles for enforcement through human beings, this is not to say that legal principles always had to be enforceable through human beings by means of force. Nevertheless, in many cases an implementation of the divine will through human measures was held possible. Thus, for example, numerous canon lawyers regarded it admissible to wage war against pagans who refused to accept Christianity, or to punish heretics. Still, the definition of Right, including Divine Right, and its actualisation through enforcement were kept strictly separate.

The Christian tradition corresponds to the views of classic Islamic jurists on this issue. However, early Islamic jurisprudence clearly presupposed that any kind of revealed Divine Right could be implemented through human acts, which also included the use of force, for example in punishment or in waging war against human beings who refused to comply with divine orders.[100] Yet, again Divine Right received its legal quality and its obligatory force merely by the revelation of the divine will through the Prophet, not because of its potential to be put into action by human beings.

Here again modern liberal jurisprudence deviates from the respective religious tradition. Numerous legal theorists include the potential for enforcement in the definition of Right, and consequently a principle which restricts its obligatory force to a mere appellation to human beings for

99 Cf. J. A. Brundage, *Medieval Canon Law*, pp. 62 et seq.
100 Khadduri, *The Islamic Law of Nations*, pp. 38 et seq.

compliance will not normally be acknowledged as Right in the strict sense.[101] This approach has also raised the question of whether public international law could be deemed as proper Right, given the lack of a central authority for enforcing its rules in the international arena. This problem can be overcome by viewing such measures like international sanctions as enforcement of international regulations: then the definition of force is extended to cover non-violent measures. However, the definition of Right including the requirement of enforceability remains the same.

In this respect, Grotius again follows the Christian tradition, but again also brings forward an original outlook on the subject. While he clearly views the enforceability of Right as irrelevant for its quality, he is nevertheless willing to allow for the enforcement of principles of Divine as well as of Human Right. Yet, as we shall see in the following, he is less supportive of the enforcement of the Law of the Gospel than of other categories of Right. It may even be suggested that Arbitrary Divine Right and Gospel law contain rules which contradict their execution by forceful means. This may be illustrated by the commandment to love one's neighbour: Is it possible to punish someone because he has not loved his neighbour enough?

Generally, Grotius holds that offences against Arbitrary Divine Right are indeed as punishable as offences against Natural Right or against any other types of Right as far as such offences are committed against other human beings. This becomes clear from his example of the punishment of different kinds of theft in Jewish law, which is regarded as Arbitrary Divine Right[102], while there is no order of Gospel law mentioned to the contrary. Hence, Grotius holds it admissible for human beings to punish offences under Arbitrary Divine Right by other human beings at least to a certain extent.[103]

Yet, Grotius also conceives of some severe restrictions for the punishment of offences against God. There are two instances in which the offender is to be deemed innocent of an offence against God. The first instance is if the violated rule of Arbitrary Divine Right was unknown to the offender, provided that a corresponding rule under Natural Right was also unclear, e.g. because it was obscured by a corrupt tradition. No punishment is due if human beings have not received any notice of Arbitrary Divine Right and consequently are at variance with it, e.g. by worshipping the stars, natural powers, or the like. The principle of Natural Right according to which Natural Religion is monotheistic is in Grotius' views true, but not as clear as

101 Cf. H. Neuhold, W. Hummer, Christoph Schreuer (eds.), "Grundlagen und Rahmenbedingungen des heutigen Völkerrechts", in H. Neuhold, W. Hummer, C. Schrummer, *Österreichisches Handbuch des Völkerrechts*, pp. 11 et seq.; W. Graf Vitzthum, "Begriff, Geschichte und Quellen des Völkerrechts", in W. Graf Vitzthum (ed.), *Völkerrecht*, pp. 6 et seq.

102 Cf. IBP, II.XX.xxxv.

103 Cf. ibid., II.XX.xliv.1.

other principles, such as the existence of God.[104] The same applies to Christians who acknowledge the truth of Gospel law, but err with respect to some principles of the Christian faith, provided that these principles are not essential and therefore either not part of Gospel law or ambiguous in their meaning. Offences of this kind are then committed innocently.

A second case of innocence is the refusal of infidels to accept the Christian religion. Grotius has no doubt that infidels who have received notice of the revelation of the divine truth and, consequently, of Gospel law are under an obligation to accept Christianity as the true religion. Yet in his opinion infidels are not necessarily guilty if they refuse to accept Christianity: however convincingly the Gospel is preached to infidels and whatever miracles and witnesses may prove the truth of Christianity, still Christianity cannot be accepted without the secret assistance of God in the Holy Ghost.[105] God may have his reasons for refusing such assistance, yet these reasons are beyond human understanding and therefore cannot be subject to human judgement and punishment.

This presents one of the few instances where Grotius' general optimism regarding the susceptibility of human beings to reason is limited: he hesitates to assert the obligations of Arbitrary Divine Right forcefully. The work and the effects of the Holy Ghost form an element of uncertainty within Grotius' concept of law and its enforcement. Yet this does not contradict his overall concept – Grotius does not regard the Holy Ghost as an essentially irrational factor, but claims that it is rather a matter of God's superior reason, which surpasses human understanding. Still the assistance by the Holy Ghost is no prerequisite for the applicability of Gospel law, and its lacking does not suspend the validity of Gospel law. Absence of the Holy Ghost's assistance merely removes guilt in relation to offences against Gospel law.

It would certainly go too far to contend that Grotius here paved the way for the modern distinction between law and morals in denying the enforceability of the Law of the Gospel in its entirety. Grotius still adheres to the older tradition of Christian legal thought in regarding the Law of the Gospel as true Right. However, he endeavours to differentiate between such aspects of Arbitrary Divine Right which are to be implemented by means of human acts on earth and those aspects of Gospel law which are indeed Right in a true sense, but nevertheless would not be compatible with an implementation through force. Thus, Grotius in this respect can be regarded as an intermediary between preceding religious lawyers, who had treated all Divine and Human Right in a similar way and thus also argued in favour of the enforceability of both types of Right, and subsequent modern secular lawyers, who concentrated their attention to Human Right as only true

104 Cf. ibid., II.XX.xlvii.4.
105 Cf. ibid., II.XX.xlviii.1.

category of Right, while neglecting any divine legal principles as legally irrelevant.

VII. Conclusion

We have seen that in relation to Arbitrary Divine Right Grotius may be seen as an intermediary between the older Christian legal tradition, which saw the revealed Divine Right as proper Right, and the modern secular tradition of liberal jurisprudence, which concentrates on the mere consensus in human society as the exclusive source of Right, while viewing the religious allegiance of the members of society as relevant only for their internal motivation in participating in finding a consensus.

At the end of the previous chapter, the principle underlying the international relations between all nations was described as universal equality in freedom under Natural Right. Consequently, Natural Right provides a common legal standard valid for all nations in their international conduct, whereas it does not prescribe a hierarchy amongst nations in their international relations. This should now be the place to enquire about the difference that Arbitrary Divine Right makes for international relations in comparison to Natural Right. It has been demonstrated above that Arbitrary Divine Right does not accord more rights or powers to its addressees than Natural Right does. Rather the opposite is true: Arbitrary Divine Right provides additional obligations and, in particular, more precise obligations than does Natural Right. In particular the Law of the Gospel does not give Christians a higher power or an enhanced legal position than it does to heathens. Instead, the Law of the Gospel requires a higher moral standard from Christians than Natural Right requires from anyone.

However, the higher moral standards which Grotius sees imposed on Christians on the one hand correspond to a more specified promise of redemption given by God to Christians on the other. Natural Right as Right entailed in creation is content with addressing matters relevant for this world only. Such matters are earthly affairs, human inter-relation, and a general natural faith in God as legislator in creation. Arbitrary Divine Right as a divinely revealed set of legal rules goes beyond that: in Grotius' system it opens the way for a celestial dimension of legal obligations and a corresponding heavenly reward for obedience. In so doing, Arbitrary Divine Right assists Christians in escaping from the vicious circle of moral transgressions. Arbitrary Divine Right not only prescribes moral standards to human beings, but also explains how these moral standards can be adhered to effectively by reconciling divine justice with divine grace in the death and resurrection of Christ.

As a conclusion to the previous chapter, a comparison was drawn between Grotius' system of Natural Right and the universal legal order envisioned by Dante Alighieri in his *Monarchia*. In relation to Grotius' views on Arbitrary Divine Right and its position in relation to Natural Right it should be interesting to confront his concept with the system described by Marsilius of Padua in his *Defensor pacis*.

In *Defensor pacis* Marsilius examines, *inter alia*, the relationship between the striving of human beings in this world and the hope of human beings to be rewarded in heaven[106]: Summarising Marsilius' thoughts very briefly, he is quite optimistic about the conduciveness of Christian expectations from the next world to their conduct as citizens of this world: Christians are held in awe before eternal punishments and rewards.[107] Thus the moral virtues of Christians contribute to their behaviour in society; however, the same may also be true for followers of other creeds.[108]

Grotius would not totally disagree with this conclusion. However, compared to Marsilius' elaboration one will find a shift of emphasis in Grotius' attention to the motivation of Christians when adhering to the Law of the Gospel. It is not simply the fear of punishment and the hope for rewards in eternity which induce man to adhere to God's laws. It would not even be possible to adhere to God's law if God had not opened the way to this by the atonement for the sins of mankind through the sacrifice of his son. As Grotius repeatedly points out, the fallibility of man results in his inclination to remain in sinful habits. Man is therefore in need of external help in order to be rescued from the vicious circle of perpetual sin.

As for the place of Christians in the international arena, Grotius would not expect to find them elevated completely from the rest of mankind. Nevertheless, in addition to their high standard of moral obligations, Christians are distinct from others because their justified trust in their redemption from sin enables them to comply with this very standard.

While Grotius certainly follows the Christian tradition in taking Divine Right as a general framework for international relations amongst all states, he deviates from the tradition considerably by distinguishing between the divine Natural Right as entailed in creation, which is applicable to mankind in its entirety, and Arbitrary Divine Right, which is a revealed set of dogmas and ethical precepts, binding only for those who have received notice of it and are supported by the assistance of the Holy Ghost. The importance of Arbitrary Divine Right for Christians in their international relations lies not so much in the provision of an alternative set of regulations, but in the

---

106 Cf. Marsilius of Pada, *Defensor pacis*, I.v.2. et seq.

107 Cf. O. M. T. O'Donovan, J. Lockwood O'Donovan, *From Irenaeus to Grotius: A Sourcebook in Christian Political Thought*, p. 424.

108 Cf. Marsilius of Pada, *Defensor pacis*, I.v.12, 14.

enhanced moral standard which it prescribes. The ground on which this enhanced moral standard rests is the redemption from perpetual sin of those who accept the divine revelation. Those who become aware of the redemption and the way to attain it, are now free to break out of the perpetual circle of failing in adhering to the divine commandments.

If we once more draw a comparison with the Islamic theory of international law, we are bound to notice the dogmatic differences between the functions of laws in Islam and Christianity: while in Islam the redemption of man from evil happens simply through adherence to the law that is revealed in the Quran, the redemption according to the Christian faith is effected through the acceptance of the sacrifice of God's son as an act of liberation from sin, from which an adherence to the divine will follows. Nevertheless, the role of the revealed law is essentially the same in the Christian concept as presented by Grotius as it is in the classical Islamic legal concept: the moral standards revealed by God tie the believers together in their international affairs just as much as they provide a bond amongst them in every other respect as well.

Surely, modern pluralist theories of international law would regard much of the contents of the Arbitrary Divine Right as envisioned by Grotius as part of an ethical concept beyond the scope of what Right in a modern strict sense is concerned with. Such a traditional Christian ethical concept would certainly not be incompatible with pluralist concepts, as it would not provide any obstacle to the peaceful living-together of Christians with followers of other religions. If taken seriously, such a Christian concept of moral standards in the international arena might even well enhance the moral foundations of an international order, which is something a pluralist, value-neutral concept of Right obviously will hardly be able to achieve.

Chapter 3

Human Right and Human Rule

I. Introduction

In the foregoing chapters it has been argued that for Grotius both Natural Right and Arbitrary Divine Right provide a framework for all human social life on the international as well as on the domestic level. Natural Right as well as Arbitrary Divine Right obligate human beings directly and individually. Thus, Grotius regards human beings as personally responsible agents in international relations. This opens the way for the question in how far Grotius also acknowledges a purely human category of Right in addition to the sets of Divine Right. Furthermore we need to ask how Grotius perceives the nature, function, and organisation of human rule.

In the history of Christian legal thought prior to Grotius, there had only been limited space for a genuine Human Right within the system of international relations. According to many authors, such as the canon lawyers or the Scholastics of the School of Salamanca, International Right was mainly dominated by a framework of divinely devised principles.[1] Consequently, Human Right could only have limited relevance to determine matters of international relations. This traditional approach by Christian theologians and lawyers corresponds to an understanding of the Church as the only true international institution, apart from the Roman Empire, which sometimes had been regarded as a Christian world state in the sense of the *respublica Christiana*.[2] In consequence, the Roman Emperor and the Pope could claim, for example, the position of temporal and spiritual lords of the world to which all other political institutions are subordinated.[3] Furthermore, as the International Right of the Middle Ages was mainly thought to be divine in nature, ecclesiastical measures of penitence were regarded as most effective means to sanction of-

---

1 H. F. Köck, *Der Beitrag der Schule von Salamanca zur Entwicklung der Lehre von den Grundrechten*, pp. 29 et seq.

2 Cf. H. Dreier, "Kanonistik und Konfessionalisierung: Meilensteine auf dem Weg zum Staat", *Juristenzeitung*, 57 (2002), pp. 3 et seq.

3 Cf. C. A. Stumpf, "Völkerrecht unter Kreuz und Halbmond: Muhammad al-Shaybani und Hugo Grotius als Exponenten religiöser Völkerrechtstradition", *Archiv des Völkerrechts*, 41 (2003/1), pp. 90 et seq.

fences against International Right, which again granted the Church an important role in international relations.

In the Christian medieval tradition of international relations, the temporal rulers of people were the only relevant actors in International Right, whereas the concept of states as legal subjects had not yet fully emerged.[4] The idea of sovereign states as legal subjects of international law developed very slowly: while originally the Emperor had been accorded the status as temporal ruler of the *respublica Christiana*, the canon lawyers helped other temporal rulers to emancipate themselves vis-à-vis the Emperor first *de facto*, and later even *de iure*, until finally every perfect society, including the Church itself, was regarded as sovereign for the purpose of International Right.[5] Nevertheless, even when the sovereignty of rulers had finally been acknowledged, International Right still applied directly to the individual. The impermeability of states as exclusive legal subjects of public international law only came up in the 17th and 18th centuries.[6] Furthermore, a number of moral theologians as well as temporal and canon lawyers continued to maintain that only Christians could establish rightful authority, whereas pagan communities could not be acknowledged from the perspective of Christian International Right.[7]

If we compare the aforementioned traditional Christian concept of Right and of rule with Islamic jurisprudence, we can discern certain similarities: in Islamic jurisprudence, the role of human law is essentially the implementation of divine commandments.[8] Likewise, the traditional Christian view of a common *respublica Christiana* as political manifestation of Christianity finds an Islamic parallel in the realm of Islam which is institutionalised in the *umma* as global Islamic community; the realm of Islam hence is a political as well as religious entity. Classic Islamic jurisprudence does not acknowledge any sovereign states apart from the *umma* itself. This perception only changed subsequently through a decentralisation of power within the realm of Islam and the increasing power of local rulers.[9] Furthermore, the Islamic legal distinction between the realm of Islam and the realm of war, which consisted of communities of unbelievers, entails the refusal of Islamic law to fully acknowledge the respective authority of unbelievers. Consequently, the

4 Cf. C. A. Stumpf, "Der Westfälische Frieden und die Wiedervereinigung der Konfessionen in verfassungshistorischer Perspektive", in H. Klueting (ed.), *Irenik und Antikonfessionalismus im 17. und 18. Jahrhundert*, pp. 39 et seq.

5 Cf. C. A. Stumpf, P. R. Melot de Beauregard, "Die Entwicklung der staatlichen Souveränität im Spiegel der kanonistischen Völkerrechtslehre", *Der Staat*, 42 (2003), pp. 459 et seq.

6 Cf. C. A. Stumpf, "Völkerrecht unter Kreuz und Halbmond", pp. 90 et seq.

7 Cf. H. Dreier, "Kanonistik und Konfessionalisierung", pp. 3 et seq.

8 B. Krawietz, *Hierarchie der Rechtsquellen im tradierten sunnitischen Islam*, pp. 182 et seq.

9 Cf. C. A. Stumpf, "Völkerrecht unter Kreuz und Halbmond", pp. 85 et seq.

siyar as traditional Islamic law of nations only prescribes the conduct of Muslims vis-à-vis unbelievers, whereas it does not account for legal relationships between Muslims and unbelievers on equal terms.[10]

From the 17th century onwards the Christian tradition of international legal thought described above was supplanted by a secular, "enlightened" approach.[11] This development is mainly characterised by the separation of Right from ethics and metaphysics, which finally resulted in the modern positivist approach, according to which law is essentially what is agreed to be law amongst human beings. Consequently, the modern liberal theory of international law presented by John Rawls in his *Law of Peoples* follows the approach of modern public international law in that it regards consensus as the origin of any rule of international law.[12] At the heart of Rawls' idea of a Law of Peoples is the concept of justice as fairness, which can be characterised briefly as an identification of legal rules through a discourse between human beings on the common good.[13] Yet Rawls criticises the exclusive focus of modern public international law on states and counters this with his own concept of a Law of Peoples in which the liberal and "decent" societies join together to agree on mutually binding rules. For this concept, the internal organisation of states will be of particular relevance: only "well ordered societies", meaning either liberal societies, each of which establishes a liberal organisation of government, or "decent societies" which at least provide for a "decent consultation hierarchy" within their states' organisation, are accepted as full members of the international society which will identify international legal rules through a social contract.[14] International law can then only be human law which is accepted on the basis of a consensus.

Grotius pursues a *via media* between these traditions in following the Christian tradition insofar as he still views Divine Right as decisive legal framework for any human legislation on the one hand, and as he acknowledges an important role for Human Right on the other by accepting that any establishment of authority and its internal organisation is rooted in a purely human act of will. Furthermore, the Grotian theology of international law focuses on personal obligations under Divine Right and under Human Right, which obligate every individual human being in his status as moral agent – in contrast to modern public international law, the Grotian system of

10 Khadduri, *The Islamic Law of Nations*, pp. 60 et seq.

11 Cf. H. Dreier, "Kanonistik und Konfessionalisierung", pp. 3 et seq.; cf. C. A. Stumpf, "Der Westfälische Frieden und die Wiedervereinigung der Konfessionen in verfassungshistorischer Perspektive", pp. 39 et seq.

12 A consensus provides the fundament for the "international" social contract envisioned by J. Rawls, *The Law of Peoples*, pp. 58 et seq.

13 Cf. ibid., pp. 88 et seq.

14 Cf. ibid., pp. 4–5, 89 et seq.

Right is not that of a Right between states, but between individuals as members of human society. Nonetheless, Grotius displays willingness to accord greater importance to Human Right and to human political institutions than the early Christian tradition did. For him, rule and sovereignty are essentially human categories: while Divine Right necessarily binds all human beings directly, it still leaves much room for the self-organisation of human beings in states autonomously of divine prescriptions.

An elaborate account of Grotius' views on the nature of Human Right can be found in his treatment of the various types of Right in the first chapter of *De Iure Belli ac Pacis*. Regarding human rule, Grotius does not present us with a general treatise devoted exclusively to the topic of his doctrine of states, or to rule and authority as such. Nevertheless, he takes up this issue several times in his legal works, in particular in *De Iure Belli ac Pacis*, where he distinguishes between private wars and public wars; moreover, we find some remarks on the coming into existence of the rights and powers of rulers in relation to their subjects in Grotius' treatment of the original acquisition of rights within associations and commonwealths in the same work. In addition to this, Grotius examines the applicability of Divine Right to states and rulers, and deals with the exercise of authority by states in spiritual matters in both *De Imperio Summarum Potestatum circa sacra* and *Ordinum Hollandiae ac Westfrisiae Pietas vindicata*.

In the following we shall first examine Grotius' terminology in relation to Human Right and human rule, before we analyse his views on the origin and nature of Human Right as well as of human rule. Furthermore, we will investigate the relationship between Human Right and human rule on the one hand and Divine Right on the other. This will lead us to an examination of the internal organisation of human rule and of the relationship between the ruler and the citizens.

II. Categories of Human Right and of Human Rule

A few remarks on Grotius' terminology for Human Right and human rule are in place, as this terminology is decisive for a proper understanding of his perception of International Right.

1. Categories of Human Right

The location of Grotius' treatment of Human Right, which is to be found in *De Iure Belli ac Pacis* after his exposition of Natural Right and before his analysis of Arbitrary Divine Right, seems *prima facie* rather odd at its outset:

given Human Right's obvious subordination to both categories of Divine Right, Natural Right and Arbitrary Divine Right, one might expect it to be the last category of Right to be dealt with, to demonstrate how the superior categories of Divine Right shape the content of Human Right, or alternatively, to be the first category, so as to delineate Human Right in its practical application from the superior principles of a divine legal framework.

However, Grotius explains that he follows this sequence because Human Right is better known to his readers than Arbitrary Divine Right. We may sense Grotius' pursuit of a twofold aim here when writing *De Iure Belli ac Pacis*. This work is surely a legal treatment on the Right of War and Peace, but not in the sense of a series of supposedly detached observations by a neutral spectator of legal practice: in addition to the presentation to the legal practice of war and peace, *De Iure Belli ac Pacis* is also an exhortation addressed to Grotius' contemporaries to adhere to Christian ethical principles in international relations in situations of peace as well as of war. In the third book of *De Iure Belli ac Pacis* this notion is revealed more clearly than elsewhere in Grotius' work: here Grotius approaches the Right in War, firstly by a rather detached presentation of current practice of warfare under the Human Right of Nations, before he secondly criticises it by declaring most of it to contradict Natural Right or Arbitrary Divine Right. His legal analysis of the Right in War thus follows his general exposition of the three categories of Right: Natural Right in War may allow for a variety of alternative human conducts; then there follows the current position under the Human Right of Nations, before finally nearly all of what has apparently been admitted under the aforementioned categories of Human Right is taken away by severe restrictions – the *temperamentia* – under Natural Right and Arbitrary Divine Right, in particular under Gospel law. We shall return to this later, when dealing with Grotius' views on warfare.

As to the subcategories of Human Right, Grotius firstly distinguishes between "National Right" (*Ius civilis*) and the "Right of Nations" (*Ius gentium*). National Right is Human Right restricted in its force to one nation, or only parts of it; it comprises private law as well as public law, including criminal law, in the modern taxonomy. The Right of Nations denotes that Human Right which governs international relations between states, including both public international law and private international law in the modern sense.[15]

The former type of Right, National Right, is enacted by the superiors in a state. Here a primary feature of Grotius' views on the origin of the human state is to be noted: the state is an association of free human beings that join together in order to enjoy legal security and the utility of sociability. Next to that Human Right which is enacted by superiors, there is also a domestic

15 Cf. IBP, I.I.xiv.

type of Human Right in the sense of household regulations, which have a more restricted applicability. Such domestic Human Right comprises the authority of a father or of an overlord over his children, servants, and the like. This kind of Right is again dependent upon the general Right of the state in the sense that the former is shaped by the latter, though it is not granted by the state. We may liken it to modern family law, which, for example, leaves it to the decision of individual family members how they support their relations in want of financial aid, though minimum support may be made obligatory by the general laws of the state.

International Human Right is the Right of Nations. The principles of the Right of Nations receive their obligatory force from an act of will of all or of several nations, and thus – like modern public international law[16] – rely on the consensus of the legal subjects. Yet, the legal subjects are – contrary to modern public international law[17], but quite in line with the liberal concept of John Rawls' Law of Peoples[18] – not states, but peoples or even individuals; this again confirms Grotius' position on the personal responsibility of the individual as moral agent in international relations. In this context, Grotius points out that hardly any rule of the Right of Nations is regarded as obligatory in every part of the world; most rules of the Right of Nations are only of regional relevance. European nations will employ other paradigms when agreeing on a particular set of principles governing the relationships with their respective neighbours than princely states in India. Differences in climate and geographical design may also require distinct regulations: in the densely populated lands of Europe, the Human Right of Nations is more likely to produce detailed provisions for the determination of borderlines than in scarcely populated deserts of Arabia or in the island-centred culture of Polynesia. In the end, the only true universally applicable type of Right is in Grotius' opinion Natural Right, while even the applicability of Arbitrary Divine Right is somewhat narrower, addressing only those who have received support by the Holy Ghost in accepting it, or who have at least been notified of its existence and content.

That there really are rules of such a Human Right of Nations is proved for Grotius in a similar way as the existence of customary law on the domestic level is identified, which is by the permanent exercise of rules and by the witness of experienced men. Grotius' legal epistemology here already presupposes what is acknowledged as sources for the Right of Nations under

---

16 Cf. W. Graf Vitzthum, "Begriff, Geschichte und Quellen des Völkerrechts", in W. Graf Vitzthum (ed.), *Völkerrecht*, pp. 72 et seq.

17 Cf. I. Seidl-Hohenveldern, "Die Staaten", in H. Neuhold, W. Hummer, C. Schrummer (eds.), *Österreichisches Handbuch des Völkerrechts*, p. 129; K. Hailbronner, "Der Staat und der Einzelne als Völkerrechtssubjekte", in W. Graf Vitzthum (ed.), *Völkerrecht*, pp. 169 et seq.

18 Cf. J. Rawls, *The Law of Peoples*, pp. 26 et seq.

modern public international law. For example, according to Article 38 of the Statute of the International Court of Justice, the Court shall apply, *inter alia*, "international custom, as evidence of a general practice accepted as law", "the general principles of law recognized by civilized nations", and "judicial decisions and the teachings of the most highly qualified publicists of the various nations, as subsidiary means for the determination of the rules of law".[19]

Furthermore, as regards Human Right we may add another distinction between two subcategories of Human Right, which are not explicitly mentioned by Grotius but are supposedly implied by him[20]: as far as the people of a state is Christian it will form its own legal regulations along the specific principles of Christianity, in particular the dogmas and precepts of Gospel Law. Consequently, it will have a particular Human Right peculiar to Christian people, a set of Human Right which is shaped by Christian moral ideas. Yet, as far as the people of a state is not Christian – regardless of whether it has not received notice of the divine revelation in the redemption through Christ, or has heard of it, but has remained untouched by the Holy Ghost – this people will not follow such specific Christian principles in formulating its law, but will endorse a non-Christian type of Human Right. The law of marriage may serve as an illustration for this distinction between Christian Human Right and non-Christian Right: According to Grotius polygamy is neither contrary to Natural Right, nor to the old Arbitrary Divine Right.[21] The same is true for a divorce, which is deemed permissible under both Natural Right and old Arbitrary Divine Right.[22] Consequently, most ancient nations admitted polygamy as well as divorce.[23] Likewise, contemporary non-Christians states too may establish a marriage law as part of their National Right which sets a certain procedure of divorce and entails certain legal consequences of divorce. Furthermore, a non-Christian state may have legal regulations admitting polygamy and determining the legal status of a wife in relation to her polygamous husband. However, Christ objected to divorce[24]; moreover, the Law of the Gospel explicitly prohibits polygamy.[25] Hence, a Christian state may not have polygamous laws or laws

19 *Statute of the International Court of Justice*, Art. 38.

20 Cf. M. Wight, *System of States*, p. 125 et seq.

21 In IBP, II.V.viii.2, Grotius observes that Natural Right requires that man and woman live together in a way that the wife is under the observation and the protection of her husband. In II.V.viii.1 he then adds that Arbitrary Divine Right, prior to the revelation of the Gospel, had not required anything further; it had been permissible for a man to have several wives.

22 Cf. ibid., II.V.ix.2.

23 Cf. ibid., II.V.ix.4.

24 Cf. ibid., II.V.ix.3.

25 Cf. ibid., II.V.xi.

admitting divorce: it will neither admit divorce (save for those cases in which the Gospel law allows divorce), let alone provide for a divorce procedure; nor will it allow polygamous connections, and consequently it will very likely treat the offspring from such connections as illegitimate children.

Hence, one may also distinguish between a specific Christian Human Right as National Right and Human Right of Nations amongst Christian states on the one hand, and a Human Right as National Right and Right of Nations which is at best marked by Natural Religion on the other. As already mentioned, Grotius does not expound upon this distinction explicitly. Nevertheless, we can infer from remarks made by him that he indeed presupposes such a distinction: thus, Jews and Christians have often referred private disputes amongst themselves to arbitration, so as to avoid seeking recourse to pagan courts. Grotius deems such arbitration most appropriate for the avoidance of an even greater evil – that of war.[26] Furthermore, the mutual relationship amongst Christians, informed by the commandment to love one's neighbour as oneself, is also accounted for in Grotius' treatment on the Right in War: though in history prisoners of war frequently have been enslaved by victorious infidels, this practice has never been made a principle of law amongst Christians.[27] Moreover, while Natural Right sometimes permits the sacking of cities as a consequence of warfare, the Gospel Law never does so, for the bond connecting Christians to each other is stronger than other, more natural, connections.[28] Extremely significant in this respect is Grotius' observation that there is a general obligation of Christians to join together to resist enemies of Christianity; Grotius believes this obligation to derive from the fact that all Christians belong to one body, individually and jointly, as nations. Therefore any Christian has to serve Christ not only with one's personal means, but also with the power entrusted to one.[29] More vividly than elsewhere, Grotius here paints the picture of a genuine Christian alliance of states which is united in resisting non-Christian threats.

2. Categories of Human Rule

When dealing with the distinction between private and public wars in *De Iure Belli ac Pacis,* Grotius sets out to explain his views on the tasks of the ruler regarding the government of a state by discussing the exercise of civil power and, in particular, of the highest civil power, which marks a ruler as sovereign. For Grotius this becomes relevant for his treatment of the Right to

26 Cf. ibid., II.XXIII.viii.3.

27 Cf. ibid., III.VII.ix.1.

28 Cf. ibid., III.XII.viii.4.

29 Cf. ibid., II.XV.xii.

War, as a just (public) war could in Grotius' opinion only be waged by a ruler vested with the highest power. Therefore Grotius ventures to expound the relevant terminology by defining the content of the power of the ruler in governing the state. The state is subject to rule and therefore subject to the exercise of power by the ruler. In the following we shall analyse Grotius' terminology in relation to civil power, and sovereignty.

2.1. The Definition of Civil Power

Grotius examines several ancient definitions of the moral power to govern the state, which also serve to draw conclusions regarding the definition of the state itself: Thucydides had asserted that the true state has its own laws, its own courts, and its own magistrates. Aristotle had distinguished between three different objects of state administration: the consultation on common matters, the election of magistrates, and courts. Dionysus of Halikarnas had listed the tasks of government: the right to appoint magistrates, the right to promulgate and abolish laws, and the right to decide on war and peace; to this he later added courts, the right to administer spiritual laws, and the right to convene public assemblies.[30]

Grotius himself describes civil power and its content by listing single aspects of it. One can govern a state either by oneself or through others, i.e. by way of delegating power. If one governs the state oneself, one can do this either generally, e.g. by setting up abstract rules or laws, or particularly, e.g. by making individual decisions in order to settle specific affairs. This distinction resembles the modern distinction between the establishment of abstract general rules through legislation on the one hand and the specific individual measures taken by the executive power of a state on the other.

General tasks of government for the civil power are in Grotius' opinion the promulgation and abolition of laws about things divine and about things temporal as far as the state is responsible for these; we shall return to this in due course. Particular tasks of government comprise matters that are either public or private. Public matters include the common affairs that affect the state as such and have immediate relevance to the state, e.g. matters of war, peace, alliances, taxes, and the eminent right of the state over its citizens and their property for public purposes.[31] Private matters that are subject to the government include disputes amongst individuals, as far as it is in the public interest to have such disputes settled authoritatively by the civil power – the civil power may decide that such disputes have to be resolved exclusively by

30 Cf. ibid., I.III.vi.1.
31 Cf. ibid., I.III.vi.2.

its courts.[32] Other tasks of the state are taken care of by magistrates or other civil servants, including legates.

We can see from these remarks that Grotius accords to the ruler a rather comprehensive power to order the public life of human society, as well as parts of the private life of citizens. The matters that are to be governed by the state therefore cover all areas that constitute the public order.

2.2. The Definition of the Sovereign Civil Power

Only a civil power which in its actions is not subject to any other power in a way that would allow that other power to decide upon the validity of this power's actions in its own free discretion is a "highest" civil power and therefore a sovereign power. The subject of the highest civil power is the state. The state is a perfect society in the sense of a kind of self-contained unit which has all means to achieve its ends. Grotius thus adopts the respective canon law tradition of the sovereign state as perfect society.[33] At the same time he parts with the more ancient understanding of a hierarchical structure within the *respublica Christiana,* with the Emperor and the Pope as respective temporal and spiritual heads to whom all other kings and princes as well as all other bishops and prelates are subordinated.[34] Grotius thus already paves the way for the modern idea of equality amongst sovereign states, whereas he still endorses a personal responsibility of every individual in international relations according to his respective position as ruler or subject.

A clarification of Grotius' terminology used in his treatment of states and rulers is requisite for a proper understanding. It may be suggested here to translate the expression *civitas* in the classical Roman legal sense as "state in the strict sense", comprising the institution of government and rule as administration of the state as legal entity. *Respublica,* on the other hand, a term comparatively rarely used by Grotius, seems rather to refer to the state in a wider sense, in particular the commonwealth commonly pursued by its members, and therefore presents the whole legal and social body which presents a nation organised within a state; sometimes it may, however, also refer to a particular liberal form of government; a republic is then a free state. That Grotius indeed uses these terms as suggested may become clear from the following examples: When elaborating upon the subject of the government of

32 Cf. ibid., I.III.i.2.–ii.1.

33 Cf. H. F. Köck, *Rechtliche und politische Aspekte von Konkordaten*, pp. 83 et seq.; U. Scheuner, "Die internationalen Beziehungen der Kirchen und das Recht auf freien Verkehr, in E. Friesenhahn, U. Scheuner, J. Listl (eds.), *Handbuch des Staatskirchenrechts*, vol. II, pp. 239 et seq., 323 et seq.

34 Cf. C. A. Stumpf and P. R. Melot de Beauregard, "Die Entwicklung der staatlichen Souveränität im Spiegel der kanonistischen Völkerrechtslehre", pp. 459 et seq.

the state, Grotius uses the term *civitas* as object of the rule exercised by the government; this is to be taken here as state in the strict sense.[35] Likewise, Grotius notes that Rome's dependent territories did not each form a state in the strict sense of *civitas*, but belonged to the greater Roman *civitas*.[36] When dealing with self-defence, Grotius remarks that self-defence is sometimes impermissible because of the commandment to love one's neighbour, and then adds that we seek the good for our state for our own sake as well as for the sake of others; the state is here referred to by the term *respublica*.[37] On other occasions, however, *respublica* refers to a particularly liberal constitution.[38] Nevertheless, one still has to be aware of a discrepancy that may exist between the respective English and Latin terms.

The decisive factor for sovereignty in Grotius' theory is thus the absence of subordination of a civil power to any other power. In order to be sovereign the highest civil power must be able to make decisions without having to defer to any external authority. However, the actual holder of this highest power may alter his own decisions; so may his successor, who has the same power.[39] At the same time Grotius also gives examples of what cannot be regarded as "sovereign", e.g. peoples that have submitted themselves to other peoples, such as the provinces of the Roman Empire: such peoples are to be regarded rather as dependent parts of a greater state, like servants who are members of the family of their masters.[40] If certain states, however, share a common head while remaining perfect societies of their own, this does not result in a loss of sovereignty of each single state. Several legal bodies may share one head, whereas natural bodies have to have one head each.[41] This can be illustrated by the constitutional framework of Grotius' home country, the Netherlands, which presented itself as the union of several provinces that remained separate legal entities with a unified institution of government, the *Stadthouder*, as ruler of the United Provinces.[42] Likewise it is possible that several states interrelate with each other, e.g. to shape an alliance, so that they constitute a system of states, each without losing its independence or its quality as individual sovereign state.

---

35 Cf. IBP, I.III.vii.2.

36 Cf. ibid., I.III.vii.2.

37 Cf. ibid., II.I.ix.2.

38 Cf. ibid., I.III.viii.6; III.XV.viii.

39 Cf. ibid., I.III.vii.1.

40 Cf. ibid., I.III.vii.2.

41 Cf. ibid., I.III.vii.2.

42 Cf. C. G. Roelofsen, "Grotius and the International Politics of the Seventh Century", in: H. Bull, B. Kingsbury, A. Roberts (eds.), *Hugo Grotius and International Relations*, pp. 95, 122 et seq.; H. Bull, "The Importance of Grotius in the Study of International Relations", ibid., p. 68.

Grotius does not acknowledge any limitation on the scope of the highest civil power: The highest civil power either must be a comprehensive one that covers all areas of public life within a state; otherwise it is not the highest civil power. Furthermore, the highest civil power is, in principle, indivisible.[43] Though it is possible that two or more institutions hold the highest civil power jointly, as was the case with the Roman Empire, which at times had two or three emperors, it is not possible to divide this highest civil power in a way that would separate and single out various aspects of it. The reason is that such a division of power could not be undertaken without creating a hierarchy amongst the institutions that hold parts of the power.

Implicitly, Grotius hereby discerns a qualitative difference between external and internal sovereignty, and thus already anticipates a modern understanding of sovereignty.[44] In so doing, Grotius refutes, without however mentioning him explicitly by name, Bodin's theory of sovereignty, which had equated sovereignty with the plenitude of power.[45] Sovereignty, according to Bodin, had to be absolute (*absolue*) meaning pure, simple, and perpetual; hand in hand with this perception of sovereignty goes the identification of holding and exercising sovereign power. Neither of these features is taken up by Grotius: he lets the simple holding of power suffice for sovereignty, without giving any importance to the question of whether this power can actually be exercised in full, perpetually, or in its plenitude. Grotius is willing to let a sovereign be bound by certain promises or obligations to his people without having doubts about the fact that a sovereign ruler who is bound by such internal restrictions still can be deemed sovereign externally. In fact, the sovereign ruler who is not omnipotent internally still may be regarded as the highest power externally. In this Grotius also contradicts Hobbes, who had claimed that any statement to the effect that the sovereign power could be limited internally was subversive.[46] In this sense Grotius can be regarded as sympathetic to constitutional arrangements.

---

43 Cf. IBP, I.III.xvii.

44 Cf. C. Link, *Hugo Grotius als Staatsdenker*, p. 28, and C. Link, "Die Staatstheorie des Christian Wolff", in W. Schneiders (ed.), *Christian Wolff 1679–1754: Interpretation zu seiner Philosophie und deren Wirkung*, p. 177, who argues that Christian Wolff had served as transmitter of the separation between internal sovereignty and external sovereignty to the later centuries, in particular to the constitutional disputes in 19th-century Germany; cf. also O. von Gierke, *Das deutsche Genossenschaftsrecht*, vol. IV: *Die Staats- und Kooperationslehre der Neuzeit: durchgeführt bis zur Mitte des 17, für das Naturrecht bis zum Beginn des 19. Jahrhunderts*, pp. 318 et seq.

45 J. Bodin, *Les six livres de la République*, liv. 1, chap. 8.

46 Cf. T. Hobbes, *Leviathan*, II., chap. 26; this indicates that R. Tuck, "Grotius, Carneades, and Hobbes", *Grotiana*, 4 (1983), p. 54, was probably not entirely correct when asserting a close relationship between Grotius and Hobbes.

Thus, a king's powers might be curtailed internally, in particular by respective constitutional arrangements which provide for a veto right of the parliament. Nevertheless, the ruler still may possess the highest civil power externally, without the parliament becoming seat of the state's sovereignty. This distinction between external sovereignty, in spite of internal curtailment of power, still exists in contemporary public international law regarding the conclusion of international treaties: in the case of most modern states, it is for the head of state to represent the sovereignty of his state in ratifying an international treaty by accepting it as obligatory for his state. Nevertheless, frequently the internal order of competence within the state will require the head of state to seek the approval of parliament before ratifying a treaty. Still, the treaty will obligate the state even if the approval to the ratification by the head of state has not been granted by parliament. It may be an outrageous political undertaking if the head of state does so; but the relevance of his acting without parliamentary approval is restricted to the internal constitutional affairs of this state, without rendering the ratified treaty void.[47]

It may be concluded that the idea of sovereignty and the conditions which have to be fulfilled by a state to be acknowledged as sovereign are, in fact, part of the Human Right of Nations. Sovereignty in the sense used here by Grotius, as independence from any other external – human – authority, is not of any decisive relevance for Natural Right, though sovereignty certainly has corollaries in Natural Right.[48] Natural Right as well as Arbitrary Divine Right imply that any human institution is always dependent upon God's will. Hence, no state can be so sovereign as to regard itself independent of divine interference.

If we compare Grotius' terminological approach to human rule with other concepts, we are bound to see that he is greatly indebted to the Christian tradition in that he accepts the canon law doctrine of the sovereign state as perfect society.[49] He furthermore adheres to the Christian tradition by regarding the individual human being as citizen of the state or as its ruler to be obligated directly by the principles of Natural Right and Arbitrary Divine Right, without taking Human Right as intermediary between the individual human being and the divine sets of Right. However, he parts with those representatives of the Christian tradition who still advocated a hierarchical order of the *respublica Christiana* with the Emperor and the Pope acting as

47 For this see W. Graf Vitzthum, "Begriff, Geschichte und Quellen des Völkerrechts", p. 64; however, in extreme cases an international treaty may be regarded as void; cf. *Vienna Convention on the Law of Treaties*, Article 46 para. 2.

48 Cf. IBP, Prolegomena 15.

49 Cf. H. de Wall, "Protestantische Theorien über die Beziehung zwischen Kirche und Staat im Heiligen Römischen Reich Deutscher Nation", in C. A. Stumpf, H. Zaborowski (eds.), *Church as Politeia: The Political Self-Understanding of Christianity*, pp. 177 et seq., 187 et seq.

supreme and exclusive sovereign rulers at its top. Grotius argues in favour of an equality of sovereign rulers, thus providing the basis for the modern understanding of the system of international relations between sovereign states. By combining the concept of a system of sovereign states which are all equally entitled to participate in the international discourse with the idea of international sets of Right which obligate every individual human being directly, Grotius already comes close to John Rawls' theory of the Law of Peoples. Yet, as we shall see, in Rawls' theory the peoples participate in the identification of just rules through agreeing on them in the context of an international social contract, whereas Grotius still accords greater importance to a set of Divine Right which is valid independently of its acknowledgement by human beings.

In relation to the classic understanding of international relations in Islamic legal theory, various differences are to be noted. While both classic Islam and Grotius accept a divine set of Right which is directly applicable to the individual human being, there is a difference between the Islamic concept of the political institutionalisation of the one realm of Islam in the Islamic community (*umma*) and Grotius' concept, which endorses a variety of equally sovereign states, Christian as well as non-Christian. The Islamic theory accords only limited legitimacy to the political authority of unbelievers, denying equality between the rule of Muslims and of infidels. For Grotius, however, the question of whether any rule is sovereign simply hinges upon its independence from any higher authority, whereas its religious quality is irrelevant.

III. The Origin of Human Right and of Human Rule

When examining Grotius' theory of the origin of states and his views on the justification for the exercise of power, a distinction between the state as legal institution on the one hand and human society as a natural association of human beings on the other is to be noted: Grotius believes the state, including the position of the ruler, to emerge out of the natural institution of human society. In so doing Grotius puts a strong emphasis on the role of human establishment of the state, which is not required under divine law but nevertheless perfectly legitimate. He thus rejects the notion of a divine establishment of the ruler's position through a divine act, which had been accepted in the greater part of medieval Christian jurisprudence.[50]

---

50 Cf. H. G. Walther, *Imperiales Königtum, Konziliarismus und Volkssouveränität: Studien zu den Grenzen des mittelalterlichen Souveränitätsgedankens*, pp. 29 et seq.

An approach similar to the medieval legal concepts of Christian lawyers had also existed in classic Islamic jurisprudence, which regarded the Islamic *umma* as the only legitimate public body as it had been directly devised by divine revelation, though some of the Muslim lawyers who dealt with the legal relationships with unbelievers had at least been willing to accord limited legitimacy to political and legal structures of unbelievers in their realm of war as well.[51] While Grotius views the appointment of rulers as an exclusively human act which is only derivatively acknowledged by God through divine providence, the early Islamic lawyers held the position of the ruler to stem directly from God's choice; the only problem arising in this respect was then the question of how God's choice was to be identified, namely whether God wished rulers to be near relatives of the Prophet Mohammed's family as represented in the Imamate of the Shi'i Muslims, or whether the wider allegiance of the ruler to the Prophet's house was sufficient, as it was required for the qualification of the Caliphs of the Sunni Muslims.[52]

In this respect Grotius is already closer to the modern liberal political theory as represented, for example, by John Rawls. Grotius and Rawls both accept that the state and its offices rest on a human act of establishment in society. Yet, for Grotius it is sufficient that the establishment be undertaken through a respective decision within human society, whereas Rawls here goes further, requiring an ongoing recourse of the established rule to the will of the people.[53] As we shall see, Grotius is perfectly willing to accept any form of government as legitimate, whether it be a democratic form of parliamentary government or an absolute monarchy, while Rawls derives additional requirements for a legitimate government out of the social contract which he perceives as the initial act of establishing government. The government thus at least has to consult its people in order to ensure an ongoing legitimacy of its power.

In the following we shall take a detailed look at Grotius' views on the origin of human rule and on his distinction between the state as legal institution on the one hand and human society as a natural association of human beings on the other.

---

51 See for example the respective comments on the obedience to be paid by Muslims in the realm of the unbelievers, Khadduri, *The Islamic Law of Nations: Shaybani's Siyar*, p. 52.

52 Khadduri, *The Islamic Conception of Justice*, pp. 51, 68.

53 Cf. J. Rawls, *The Law of Peoples*, pp. 71 et seq.

1. Human Society as Natural Association of Human Beings

The most striking observation regarding Grotius' views on the origin of the state is the absence of a strict necessity for any state to exist. The state is neither based on divine will nor on a divine purpose implemented in the political realm. Grotius' strict distinction between a natural state in which self-defence is permissible to anyone and anywhere under Natural Right, and the subsequent establishment of an order of competence by virtue of Human Right which severely curtails the former right of self-defence[54], already clearly implies that states are not presupposed by Natural Right; nor does Arbitrary Divine Right introduce the existence of states to mankind. Natural Right as well as Arbitrary Divine Right apply to all human beings directly, without there being any need for implementation or reinforcement of such legal principles by Human Right in order to bind individuals. Therefore states are of human making and present a historically contingent phenomenon in Grotius' exposition: the state is a purely human institution designed for organising the affairs of human societies[55]; man has the desire to live in a group together with his fellow men. This is also the starting point from which Grotius sets out to present his views on the origin of states, rule, and authority. However, this indicates that there is at least a root for states in Natural Right.

The purpose human beings pursue when establishing a state is the organisation of common affairs and the protection of the individuals.[56] Thus, the ruler is entrusted with the task of ordering human society within the state. In Grotius' view, human beings have a social appetite which incites them to live in groups, an appetite that is one of the core elements of human nature.[57] This natural instinct for sociality is also taught by "sacred history" according to which all human beings are descendants of one couple.[58] However, the association of human beings can only be described as human society; it does not yet constitute the state as a particular form of human order. This is not to say, however, that human society is unorganised.

First of all, Grotius conceives a principle of Natural Right according to which it is mandatory to be social, i.e. a duty to seek the company of other human beings.[59] From this we may conclude that it would be unnatural, and

---

54 Cf. IBP, I.III.i. and ii.

55 Cf. ibid., "Prolegomena" 6; on the Aristotelian notion of a natural impetus towards political life in Grotius, cf. C. F. Murphy, "The Grotian Vision", *American Journal of International Law*, 76 (1982), p. 497.

56 Cf. IBP, I.I.xiv.1.

57 Cf. ibid., Prolegomena 6, 14, 16.

58 Cf. ibid., Prolegomena 14.

59 Cf. ibid., Prolegomena 6, 14, 16.

consequently also contrary to Natural Right, to dissociate ourselves from our fellow men and to keep away from society.

Grotius elaborates upon this in greater detail in his examination of the original acquisition of rights, which can be effected either by generation, e.g. by appropriating something, or by consent, which may be by way of association, e.g. marriage, or of subjection, e.g. slavery, and as consequence to an offence, e.g. a violation of a right which originates a liability claim against the offender.[60] In this context Grotius presents us with a detailed account of various forms of personal relationships. He starts with the rights of parents over their offspring, which are generated by producing offspring[61], before dealing with the right of the husband over his wife and the law of marriage[62], a right acquired by the consent of husband and wife, which Grotius each examines in turn under aspects of Natural Right, Arbitrary Divine Right, and Human Right. After having analysed marriage as the most natural form of an association creating rights amongst human beings by way of consent, he moves on to further associations, which can either have a private or a public character.[63] The latter can consist in one single nation or be formed out of several nations. The expression Grotius uses in this respect is rather peculiar: "[A]ut in populum aut ex populis", and seems to suggest that a single nation may transform itself into a public association without losing its identity, while an association that is formed by various nations then creates a new entity which is beyond the entities the single nations had constituted. This corresponds to the idea that the association is to be deemed as a new entity because it is more than the sum of the nations forming its parts. Perhaps one can aptly describe this phenomenon by reference to the medieval German kingdom, which was made up of the tribal duchies of Bavaria, Franconia, Saxony, etc.: the inhabitants all became Germans without ceasing to be Bavarians, Franconians, Saxons, and so forth.

Grotius does not mention any explicit principle under Arbitrary Divine Right according to which man has to be social and to live together with his fellow men. Man's social appetite seems only to be determined by creation and thus by Natural Right. Nevertheless, the twofold love commandment of the Gospel Law clearly presupposes the living-together of human beings – charity can hardly be exercised in isolation.

There is one principle which is valid for all of these connections: in a common matter, all or the majority of the participants of such a connection can oblige all members personally.[64] Thus, the minority has to submit to the

60 Cf. ibid., II.V.i.
61 Cf. ibid., II.V.i.–vii.
62 Cf. ibid., II.V.viii–xvi.
63 Cf. ibid., II.V.xvii. et seq.
64 Cf. ibid., II.V.xvii.

will of the majority. This principle of majority decisions is rooted in Natural Right, while additional or more particular commandments by Arbitrary Divine Right are absent. It is to be noted in this context that Grotius traces this principle back to the consensual basis for human associations: those who join society promise explicitly or tacitly to accept those rules as binding upon which the majority of the fellow members of the association or those to whom power has been conferred decide.

Apart from this, human society is not yet legally differentiated.[65] Nor is there yet any legally relevant hierarchy within human society other than the natural hierarchy amongst family members.[66] Moreover, there is not yet any legitimate rule to be exercised by some members of society over others. An order that is legally more differentiated by establishing authority requires the establishment of states.

2. The Establishment of the State's Authority

The state is defined by Grotius as a particular connection of human beings which also entails particular rights of the state and of the ruler over the subjects.[67] Grotius presents these rights of the state as one particular type of rights of some persons to or over other persons which are acquired by way of subjection: according to Grotius, the pure gathering of human beings is not in itself sufficient to constitute a state. An additional act of establishing the state and, consequently, of establishing rule in order to legitimise and provide the foundation of the power exercised by the ruler is required. This is done by way of subjection of certain members of human society, the citizens, to the power of other members, the rulers, who thus obtain authority. The function of the state is to take charge of common affairs and to provide for the security of the citizens; it also sets out the laws for rule and imposes certain limitations on the freedom of the individual citizens.[68]

A brief comparison between the views of Thomas Hobbes and Hugo Grotius will help to see how distant Grotius still is from contractual concepts of statehood which shaped the mainstream thought of the 17th century, and which still influence modern social and legal theories, such as that of John Rawls' Law of Peoples. First of all, Grotius takes a more positive view towards the nature of human beings and the function of the state than

65 Cf. C. Link, *Hugo Grotius als Staatsdenker*, p. 22 et seq.

66 One exception is a hierarchy by virtue of the conversion to Christianity; thus, according to Grotius, those rulers that had adopted the Christian faith first, enjoyed precedence in the councils over those who had been converted later; cf. IBP II.V.xxi.

67 Cf. ibid., II.V.xxiii.–xxv.

68 D. Willoweit, *Rechtsgrundlagen der Territorialgewalt: Landesobrigkeit, Herrschaftsrechte und Territorium in der Rechtswissenschaft der Neuzeit*, pp. 248 et seq.

Hobbes: for Grotius it is not the curse of freedom which induces or even forces human beings to assemble in human society and to organise themselves in a state by way of submission, but a more positive desire for an intensified human fellowship to be secured and defended institutionally within a state. As we shall see, this also has an important impact on Grotius' perception of the state: in contrast to Hobbes, Grotius still holds the state to be bound by extrinsic legal rules, such as the natural rules on expletive justice and attributive justice, while Hobbes denied any such limitations to be applicable to his Leviathan.

A further important difference between Grotius and Hobbes can be seen in their different views on the impact that the states' establishment has in relation to the authority of rulers: while Hobbes thought of a social contract as a mutual vow of the citizens in relation to each other with respect to their unconditional submission to the state[69], Grotius claims that the ruler as well as the ruled can all be party to certain obligations that could be characterised as contractual.[70] The ruler can therefore accept obligations towards the ruled people in return for their submission.[71] In so doing, he is bound by Human Right as well as Natural Right to honour such obligations, for Natural Right requires the honouring of promises as part of expletive justice. We can already see here that the state in Grotius' concept of sovereignty is by no means the terrifying monster of the Hobbesian blend: it is no Leviathan that is to replace God[72], but rather an application of the universal fellowship of all human beings to a specifically defined group of people, subordinated in its entirety to God. Grotius' concept of sovereignty is therefore wholly embedded in and derived from his legal theory.

Grotius' remarks on the rights of the state over its subjects imply that not every member of society participates actively in the establishment of the state; rather it is the heads of families that join together in founding a state by way of submitting themselves and their families on their behalf to the authority of rulers.[73] The individual is represented in effect by the head of the family, who acts as intermediary between the individual and the state. Some authors have suggested that Grotius here demonstrates a certain preference for a patrimonial, aristocratic system, such as that of the Netherlands at that time.[74] Yet this conclusion may be rather an exaggerated speculation on Grotius' social conditioning, especially given the fact that the perception of an individualistic society was nearly totally absent from the political ideas of

69 Cf. T. Hobbes, *De Cive*, cap. V.
70 Cf. IBP, Prolegomena 15–16.
71 Cf. e.g. IBP, I.III.ix, xvi, xviii; I.IV.viii.
72 Cf. H. Welzel, *Naturrecht und materiale Gerechtigkeit*, p. 120.
73 Cf. IBP, II.V.xxiii.
74 Cf. L. Barschak, *Die Staatsauffassung des Hugo Grotius*, vol. III, p. 214 et seq., who refers to Grotius' early works.

Grotius' time: the only alternative that had been proposed by Grotius' contemporaries displayed a tendency towards more federalism, e.g. by Althusius, who had argued in favour of an organic, corporative organisation of society.[75] Yet, for our purposes it suffices to state that Grotius indeed acknowledges marriage and family to be the most natural coalitions amongst human beings. It is therefore a natural consequence that the heads of these families should be the ones that become involved in founding the state in representation of their relatives.

Next we can ask by which category of Right the establishment of the state is governed: though the gathering of human beings constituting human society is a result of respective implications of Natural Right, the establishment of the state out of human society results from a voluntary human act. It is effected by way of consensual submissions of the greater part of members of society, in particular of the heads of the families, to appointed rulers. Consequently, the establishment of the state belongs to the sphere of Human Right, though it is certainly covered by and dependent upon the principles of justice under Natural Right. Hence any obligations or rights which are conferred on or established by the founding of a state as aspects of the ruler's authority rely on a respective expression of human will. Such rights and obligations, of course, have to be in compliance with Natural Right and, where applicable, Arbitrary Divine Right, but are a consequence of neither. Therefore, the establishment of the state is merely a product of a human decision, but it is neither an explicit expression of the divine will, nor is it an implicit consequence of created nature that there always should be states. Grotius obviously can imagine an existence of human beings without states, as this had probably been the case in the early stage of human history, though he certainly cannot think of a complete dissolution of all human societies. Existing states do not have to remain in existence indefinitely; they may be conquered, dissolved, or otherwise abolished by an act of human will, in particular in the course of a just war. There are various remarks in *De Iure Belli ac Pacis* on a *status ante republicam conditam* as an abstract projection that illustrate the relationship between Natural Right and Human Right, as an exception in the case of political breakdown, or as a description for regions that are in principle uninhabited, such as the high seas.

Yet, Grotius' general idea that states are not part of the natural order becomes most obvious in his aforementioned claim that the courts are human institutions and that their introduction has limited the natural freedom that

75 See for instance J. Althusius, *Politica methodice digesta atque exemplis sacris et profanis illustrata*; E. Reibstein, *Johannes Althusius als Fortsetzer der Schule von Salamanca: Untersuchungen zur Ideengeschichte des Rechtsstaates und zur altprotestantischen Naturrechtslehre*, pp. 93 et seq.

had existed initially.[76] This implies that there might have been a time when no states existed, which would be unthinkable if states had already been provided in the natural order of creation. However, it may be doubted whether Grotius really took this idea of such a "state-less" stage as historical fact. At least it appears to be important to him that there is indeed the theoretical possibility of a society without states: Grotius uses the idea of a state-less society mainly as a device for uncovering the order of the different elements of Right.

In relation to the position of states and the rulers' authority under Arbitrary Divine Right, Grotius holds that Christians have a duty of obedience to their rulers, which is a consequence of their submission to the rulers' authority. However, he establishes no precept of the Law of the Gospel to the effect that a Christian society has in any case to appoint rulers and submit itself to them. Furthermore, it cannot be doubted that Grotius' theory allows for divine providence to direct the actions of human beings in the process of establishing the state. As Grotius explicitly states, St. Paul could call the state a divine institution in his letter to the Romans, because God approved of its establishment.[77] However, there is no immediate role that divine revelation plays in this context: the human establishment of the states is presented as perfectly acceptable under the aspect of Arbitrary Divine Right – this is made clear by Grotius when he claims that God approves of states as human institutions. While they are not required by Arbitrary Divine Right to exist, Arbitrary Divine Right will certainly shape the functioning of the state in general and the exercising of rule in particular. We will return to this in due course.

A brief comparison between Grotius' views on Human Right and Human Rule on the one hand and two contrasting concepts by contemporaries on the other is helpful here: As we have seen, Grotius understands the state, or any forms of temporal rule, to have been instituted by human beings, but in compliance with Natural Right as well as with Arbitrary Divine Right. Theoretically, states are not necessary institutions; however, human society will have the (natural) tendency to establish institutions of government for the administration of common affairs. Yet, the rulers thus appointed are, in principle, not divinely appointed. They remain human beings appointed by human beings to rule over them. Moreover, as we shall see, Grotius holds that the authority of such rulers comprises the administration of things temporal and things spiritual. Without exercising any priestly functions, rulers nevertheless have the competence to decide upon spiritual matters, such as the right doctrine to be followed, or the form of worship to be publicly fostered.

76 Cf. IBP, I.III.i.2–ii.1.

77 Cf. ibid., I.IV.vii.3.

The Spanish moral theologian Suarez, who belonged to the School of Salamanca, and the Convocation Book issued by the House of Convocation during the reign of King James I represent alternative positions to Grotius from the Roman-Catholic and the Anglican side respectively: Suarez takes a voluntarist approach to government, similar to that of Grotius, in the third book of his work *De legibus ac Deo legislatore*, in which he refutes the popular Spanish doctrine of dominion by grace, which was designed to exclude pagans or non-Christians in general from legitimate government and thus could be used to justify the Spanish conquest in the Americas; yet his line of argumentation differs from Grotius' exposition of the origin of government significantly: Suarez stresses the inherent necessity for human beings to join together to form human society, and, at the same time, to appoint an authority of government and submit themselves to it. He argues that a human community lacking government would lack morality, as such a community would be bound to persist in anarchy. Yet, the government thus appointed by the people derives its power directly from God: though there may be various types of government – democracy, aristocracy, and monarchy – and though government may be established either by the community to be governed, or in the course of a just war by the victorious party, it is not in man's authority to confer those powers, which are necessary to govern, upon the ruler: "Men, as it were, provide the material, producing a candidate; God imparts the form and confers it".[78] Grotius, by contrast, subsumes the entire Right of government primarily under the category of the Human Right of Nations; only in a second step do Natural Right and Arbitrary Divine Right attach certain consequences to the establishment of government, such as the duty to obey the government, certain limitations to the right of resistance against the government, etc. However, in Grotius' concept government always remains a substantially human institution.

The Convocation Book is also at variance with Grotius as regards the nature of government. In presenting a genealogy of priestly powers and regal powers it claims that there never had been or even could have been any time when there was no government. Rather, government had already been established shortly after creation.[79] First Adam had been vested by God with priestly and royal functions. The same had been the case with Noah in the aftermath of the Great Flood. This approach contradicts Grotius' position with respect to the origin of government in that it assumes a divine appointment to government, which is a precondition for its legitimacy. However, in effect it resembles Grotius' views on the scope of the government's powers by also

78 F. Suarez, *Tractatus De legibus, ac Deo legislatore*, III. iii.

79 On the Convocation Book see O. M. T. O'Donovan, J. Lockwood O'Donovan, *From Irenaeus to Grotius: A Sourcebook in Christian Political Thought*, p. 778–786.

allowing an administration of spiritual matters by government, as we shall see now.

IV. Human Right and Human Rule in the Framework of Divine Right

Human Right and human rule are for Grotius subject to and dependent upon Divine Right, i.e. Natural Right and Arbitrary Divine Right. Human right as well as any other human act, such as ruling, can only be legitimate as far as it does not contradict the divine will. In so far, Grotius follows the traditional approach of medieval Christian jurisprudence in tying human law to a divine legal framework. Yet, while the Christian legal tradition overall adhered to a sharp distinction between temporal and spiritual law and a corresponding separation between spiritual legislation in particular within the Church on the one hand and temporal legislation through temporal authorities on the other, Grotius takes a more uniform approach to Human Right and human rule in spiritual as well as in temporal matters: as we will see, Grotius regards temporal and spiritual aspects of human life as a unity which requires both a uniform legal regime and a uniform administration. Thereby he implicitly parts with the Gelasian tradition of the doctrine of the two swords or the Lutheran doctrine of the two realms, which are ordered to a temporal and a spiritual authority respectively, both of which are designed only to exercise their powers in their own field of responsibility. Still, the papal version of the doctrine of the two swords gave precedence to the spiritual sword, which meant *inter alia* that the Church could also intervene in temporal affairs *ratione peccati*, through judging on the moral conduct of temporal authorities. Yet, Grotius here aligns himself more with the Calvinist tradition, which was willing to combine temporal and spiritual authorities in a uniform government under a uniform framework of Right.

If we compare this approach to classic Islamic jurisprudence we will find various parallels to Grotius as well as important differences. Islamic law does not provide for any strict distinction between temporal affairs and spiritual affairs. Instead, from the emergence of Islam onwards the Islamic rulers had exercised temporal functions as rulers of their people and as military leaders, as well as spiritual functions in ruling on the orthodoxy of the religious teaching and in passing judgements on moral questions.[80] As will be shown in the following, Grotius appears to accord similar functions to rulers in his own concept, in entrusting the rulers with the pursuit of the common good of the people, which includes the care for the religious welfare of the state, and

80 Cf. C. A. Stumpf, "Völkerrecht unter Kreuz und Halbmond", pp. 85 et seq.

in charging the rulers with decision-making powers in matters of identifying the right religious doctrine to be followed in public worship. Nonetheless, Grotius is willing to accept human autonomy under the framework of divine law, while Islamic jurisprudence seeks to identify the divine will in the human acts of the rulers, and thus accepts the acts of rulers as implementation of the divine will. In principle, classic Islamic jurisprudence focuses on the legitimacy of the ruler in order to accept his acts as legitimate, whereas Grotius sees the legitimacy of the ruler in the rightful establishment of rule through an act of will of the people, but then still requires that each act of rule be in compliance with the abstract principles of Divine Right.

In contrast to Grotius, modern liberal theories of government, such as that of John Rawls, restrict their attention to a much narrower scope of political affairs, in laying greater emphasis on modes of procedure than on the material substance of affairs. Thus, Rawls would concede that it is a government's task to promote the common good of a state. However, he would not be willing to include any religious substance in this common good, as he regards this as a matter of individual taste and choice which may not be politicised.[81] Instead, Rawls, following his concept of justice as fairness, puts greater emphasis on the legal framework a state has to provide in order to assist a peaceful discourse of its people on the common good[82] Thus, the individual citizen might have his own religious views on which he bases his preference.[83] However, it cannot be expected that such specific religious positions will also be accepted by other citizens, and thus in the forum of the state the citizens have the opportunity to discuss their individual preferences in order to identify common preferences which then are to be pursued as common good. The government's task is then the organisation and moderation of this discussion process and the implementation of its results. However, it will not be for the government to promote the individual religious welfare of the citizens beyond that. Here Grotius is still closer to the older medieval Christian tradition, which does not separate law from morals and thus also entrusts the ruler with various religious and spiritual responsibilities, which he has to take charge of as an individual who is bound by Divine Right as well as by Human Right.

---

81 Cf. J. Rawls, *The Law of Peoples*, pp. 127 et seq.

82 Cf. ibid., pp. 71 et seq.

83 This is very aptly illustrated in Robert Song's comparison between Rawls and Jacques Maritain: while Maritian follows a Thomist approach to natural law as basis for the specification of constitutionally recognised human rights, Rawls sees the principles of justice specified by derivation from the very terms on which citizens will co-operate, without any reference to an antecedent moral law, although Christians are welcome to provide for themselves a justification based on natural law; cf. R. Song, *Christianity and Liberal Society*, pp. 234 et seq.

In the following we shall firstly examine how Human Right and the two categories of Divine Right pertain to each other in Grotius' concept. Thereafter we shall approach the scope of human rule by analysing its relationship with Divine Right.

1. Interrelations between Human Right and Divine Right

There are, in principle, three major fields in which Natural Right and Arbitrary Divine Right on the one hand and Human Right on the other interrelate:

Firstly, according to Grotius, Human Right is necessarily subject to restrictions by Natural Right and Arbitrary Divine Right. Human Right may neither contradict the rational and social nature of human beings, nor may it contravene the divine will. This means that Human Right may regulate issues that have been left open by one or both of the other two categories of Right. Moreover, Human Right may regulate particular details under the general principles of Natural Right and Arbitrary Divine Right.

There are, secondly, corollaries and effects of Human Right which follow from it by virtue of Natural Right. For example, while private property is not something that is provided for by Natural Right but has only been introduced by Human Right, Natural Right forbids offences against private property in its own specific understanding of justice.[84] It is not necessary under Natural Right to have private property; if, however, private property exists because Human Right devises thus, it is to be respected under Natural Right. Consequently, it is a breach of Natural Right not to render alien property to the person to whom it is due. If Human Right provides a law of loans, it is against Natural Right not to perform the obligation under a loan.

Thirdly, Human Right may regulate those areas where Natural Right and Arbitrary Divine Right are either silent or at least do not imply any detailed regulation of their own. In consequence, an order of competence may be established under Human Right so as to limit the exercise of certain powers to special institutions, whereas such powers can be exercised by anyone under Natural Right or Arbitrary Divine Right. This was done with the establishment of courts and their jurisdictions: everyone may defend himself against an attack under Natural Right, as Natural Right is simply silent on such matters of competence and the question of who is allowed to use force. However, most countries have established a regular system of criminal prosecution and of punishment under human laws. Where such systems exist, the authority to use force is limited to certain institutions that have received this authority by virtue of Human Right. The use of force is thus

84 Cf. IBP, I.I.x.4.

monopolised with the respective holder of the authority. To anyone else the use of force is prohibited. In that sense Human Right may restrict the existing freedom under Natural Right, as this "freedom" is not legally defined but merely the consequence of the silence of Natural Right on this matter. However, there may be cases where such institutions of authority do not exercise their competence to use force effectively. This may be due either to legal or to factual reasons, i.e. either because legislation of the state is defective and fails to protect the rights of individuals, or because the state refrains from enforcing its laws. Moreover, there may be cases of urgency in which there is insufficient time for the individual to seek recourse to the legal remedies provided for by the state. In such cases the ancient freedom of self-defence is revived, and everyone is entitled to exercise self-defence or render assistance to others by using force.[85] Another example for a field spared out by Natural Right in which Human Right may come into play is that of proprietary rights: as we shall see in the following chapter, Natural Right does not require any system of proprietary rights; such rights are solely introduced by Human Right. Human Right devises the content of such property rights, the objects to which proprietary rights may relate, how they can be acquired, transferred, and relinquished, etc. Yet Natural Right and Arbitrary Divine Right may nevertheless impose certain consequences on the establishment of proprietary rights under Human Right, such as the duty of an owner to assist someone else by granting access to his property, etc.

The interrelation between Human Right and Arbitrary Divine Right is similarly intensive. In his work on the relationship between religion and the state in Holland and Westfrisia, *Ordinum Hollandiae ac Westfrisiae Pietas vindicata*, Grotius claims that jurisprudence cannot be divided into separate jurisdictions on temporal and spiritual matters respectively.[86] Therefore Human Right may regulate what is theologically evident within the limits set by Arbitrary Divine Right. Moreover, it may decide upon issues that are not clearly spelt out by Arbitrary Divine Right, e.g. the performance of ceremonies, the dates of religious holidays, and the like. This we shall examine in more detail in the following.

2. The Scope of Human Rule

As already explained above, Grotius conceives sovereignty as an indivisible, comprehensive highest authority within a state. Though sovereign authority can be exercised not only by individuals or single institutions, but also jointly by several institutions at the same time, it is nevertheless one single power

85 Cf. IBP, I.III.i.; H. Grotius, *De Imperio*, III.

86 Cf. OP, 110 b 41.

that cannot be split up by allocating its functions to different holders without losing its "sovereign" quality. Moreover, we have seen that the power entailed by sovereign authority covers all aspects of government, temporal and spiritual alike.

Given the conventional distinction between divine or spiritual matters and earthly or temporal matters, which had been set out by the traditional doctrine of the spiritual and the temporal swords, Grotius here takes a rather original outlook in employing his understanding of sovereignty to tear down the walls between spiritual and temporal matters of rule. Many contemporary Protestant theologians and ecclesiastical lawyers argued in favour of a separate ecclesiastical government which was to be distinct from the civil government; however, in developing Luther's teachings on the two governments further, the "Episcopal theory" took the view that the temporal ruler of a state could at the same time obtain the position as highest bishop (*summus episcopus*) of the church in his territory.[87]

Grotius, however, took a different path in elaborating upon the administration of spiritual matters. In particular, the aforementioned distinction of the powers of the ruler as temporal head of the Church from his powers as temporal ruler could hardly be reconciled with Grotius' views on sovereignty, unless the temporal was disjointed from the spiritual sovereignty, which was sometimes done by later Roman Catholic canonists in order to argue in favour of a sovereign position of the Roman Catholic Church in international relations.[88] Therefore we are now to ask whether the subjection of the citizens to the sovereign power also covers matters that pertain to religious doctrine: Can the highest civil power, which relies on the human establishment of the state, extend to matters that are not of a merely human nature?

---

87 M. Heckel, *Staat und Kirche nach den Lehren der evangelischen Juristen Deutschlands in der ersten Hälfte des 17. Jahrhunderts*, pp. 237 et seq.; C. Link, *Herrschaftsordnung und bürgerliche Freiheit: Die Grenzen der Staatsgewalt in der älteren deutschen Staatslehre*, pp. 301 et seq.; C. A. Stumpf, *Kirchenrecht als Bekenntnisrecht: Die Verbindung von Erlanger Theologie und geschichtlicher Rechtswissenschaft im Leben und Werk von Adolf von Scheurl*, pp. 289 et seq.

88 On the idea of spiritual sovereignty and the doctrine of the Church as *societas perfecta* in its modern shape cf. H. F. Köck, *Rechtliche und politische Aspekte von Konkordaten*, pp. 38 et seq.; O. Kimminich, "Die internationalen Beziehungen der Kirchen und das Recht auf freien Verkehr", in: E. Friesenhahn, U. Scheuner, J. Listl, D. Pirson (eds.), *Handbuch des Staatskirchenrechts der Bundesrepublik Deutschland*, vol. II, pp. 217 et seq.; in consistent application of this theory M. Baron de Taube and M. Aleksandrovich, "La position international actuelle du Pape et l'idée d'un ‚droit entre pouvoirs' (ius inter potestates)", *Archiv für Rechts- und Wirtschaftsphilosophie*, 1 (1907/08), pp. 307 et seq., advocated a participation of religious powers in international relations; a similar approach is taken by H. Brandweiner, *Die christlichen Kirchen als souveräne Rechtsgemeinschaften*, pp. 245 et seq.

We find hardly any comments on the issue of the powers of "temporal" rulers with respect to "spiritual" matters in Grotius' works *De Iure Praedae Commentarius* and *De Iure Belli ac Pacis libri tres,* except on the general task of the ruler to ensure the common good for his citizens also with respect to the fostering of religion. Yet, a quite detailed account on the relationship between the state and the Church can be found in two treatises Grotius produced in the context of the quarrels between the Arminians and the Counter-Remonstrants in and around 1614: firstly the *Ordinum Hollandiae ac Westfrisiae Pietas Vindicata,* a rather polemic refutation of the attacks of Sibrand Lubbert on the States of Holland published in 1614, and secondly *De Imperio Summarum Potestatum circa sacra,* in which Grotius takes a more abstract as well as more detailed (and more irenic) approach to the powers of magistrates with respect to spiritual matters; this latter treatise was also written in 1614, but revised several times until 1617, and published only posthumously in 1647.[89]

The controversy between the Remonstrants and the Counter-Remonstrants, which reached a peak with the appointment of the Reformed theologian Conrad Vorstius at the Academy of Leiden in 1613, provides the historical background for these two works. Vorstius was thought to be sympathetic to the Arminian cause; therefore the Counter-Remonstrants and in particular Lubbert not only took the opportunity to heavily criticise the appointment of Vorstius, but also challenged the jurisdiction of the state in ecclesiastical matters in general, including the power of the state to appoint theologians of a particular direction to academic and other posts.[90] Lubbert bases his objection mainly on the magistrates of the state lacking the requisite competence for intervening in affairs of the Church. There are two reasons behind this objection: on the one hand Lubbert asserts that the separation between State and Church is ordered by divine law; on the other hand he doubts that magistrates ever can have sufficient theological knowledge to do justice to things peculiarly spiritual.[91]

At the heart of the problem was the perception of the nature of prophecy as an office to expound the Holy Scripture and its relation to the clergy. Were the prophets identical with the clergy? If so, did the gift of prophecy suffice as qualification to join the clergy, or was an additional ordination required? Lubbert claims that prophecy is a *munus,* an office granted as gift by God.[92]

---

89 Cf. on the genesis of *De Imperio Summarum Potestatum circa sacra* H.-J. van Dam, "De Imperio Summarum Potestatum circa Sacra", in H. J. M. Nellen, E. Rabbie (eds.), *Hugo Grotius, theologian: Essays in Honour of G. H. M Posthumus Meyjes,* pp. 19 et seq.

90 This also included a quarrel about the sovereignty of the single provinces of the Netherlands, for which Grotius argued, cf. J. I. Israel, *The Dutch Republic and the Hispanic World, 1606–1661,* p. 446.

91 S. Lubbert, *Responsio ad pietatem Hugonis Grotii,* 108 a 54.

92 D. M. Sprackling, "Divine and Human Law in Hugo Grotius", pp. 77–78.

The holder of this office receives the ability of judgement by virtue of the appointment to the office. Lubbert conceives the prophetic office as residing in synods of theologians, in the ministry, in teachers, and in theological academics[93], thereby displaying a traditional Calvinistic position regarding the holding of ecclesiastical offices.[94] In this sense prophecy here has to be understood as the capability of interpreting the Holy Scripture correctly.[95] This ability was sufficient in itself to establish the authority over spiritual matters, while an additional appointment or ordination by other human beings would have led to an unsound human interference with the divine providence active in granting the gift of prophecy.

This was contrary to Grotius who supported the Arminians' case: as we have already seen, Grotius regards the Gospel as plain and its content as readily accessible to anyone with an average ability to read and understand the written word. This has an impact on Grotius' understanding of prophecy: in his view it is not an office in itself, but merely a gift, like the gift to heal or to speak in tongues.[96] This gift is already evident in anyone who actually reads the Holy Scripture.[97] Accordingly, laity and clergy are not distinct from each other with regard to a specific prophetic disposition. Instead the ability to read the Holy Scripture is granted in principle to laymen as well as to clerics.[98] Hence, there can no be objection to lay magistrates themselves reading and interpreting the Holy Scripture and applying the Law of the Gospel.

This should already suffice to explain the historic background before which Grotius developed his views on the competence of the state with respect to things spiritual. In order to grasp his views on the jurisdiction of the state in religious matters it seems advisable mainly to rely on his *De Imperio* as the more theoretical as well as the more elaborate of the two treatises; yet, wherever appropriate, the analysis of *De Imperio* will be supplemented by Grotius' observations in *Ordinum Pietas*.

---

93 S. Lubbert, *Responsio ad pietatem Hugonis Grotii*, 108 b 28 et seq.

94 Cf. D. M. Sprackling, "Divine and Human Law in Hugo Grotius", p. 78.

95 Cf. J. Calvin, *Institutio Religionis Christianae*, 4.3.4 et seq.; 4.8.9.

96 In this context Grotius takes the same line as Hooker in his refutation of the Puritan understanding of clerical offices, cf. R. Hooker, *On the Law of Ecclesiastical Polity*, V.lxxviii.6.

97 Cf. OP, 110 b 23.

98 Cf. ibid., 103 a 5.

2.1. Unity of Matter

In *De Imperio* Grotius starts his argument by dealing with the nature of spiritual matters, and asks whether there is actually any need for a separation of the respective jurisdictions for them: he does not define what distinguishes a spiritual from a temporal matter; for him this would be futile anyway, since he argues that the nature of spiritual matters does not require any different treatment by a distinct jurisdiction. Moreover, he claims that the supreme sovereign power includes the authority (*imperium*) over spiritual powers due to a unity of matters, spiritual and temporal. In this respect, he exhibits sympathy towards Calvin, who had refuted the adversity between religious and political realms which had been claimed by Luther, even though Grotius' Erastianism is in principle more in line with Lutheran than with Calvinist concepts.[99]

Grotius' views on this subject mainly rely on three different types of arguments. Firstly he states that there is no requirement in the Gospel for the establishment of a separate jurisdiction or administration for spiritual matters.[100] Referring to Romans 13: 1, Grotius claims that St. Paul himself had not drawn a distinction between spiritual and temporal persons; all matters, spiritual as well as temporal, are put under the authority of the one highest power. This reference to Romans 13 appears, however, to rest on rather weak grounds, for the administration of spiritual matters could hardly have been St. Paul's concern. The matter at stake for St. Paul was to remind the early Christians not to disregard the temporal authority in the expectance of Christ's early Second Coming, but to be loyal to it in very temporal matters. Nevertheless, there is certainly some truth in Grotius' challenge of the classic doctrine of the two authorities in that it does not occur in the Holy Scripture itself, save for rather weak allusions.

Grotius furthermore refers to the kingship of Solomon in the Old Testament. The Jewish people had been ordered to be obedient to their rulers in all respects, regardless of whether the ruler's orders concerned spiritual or temporal matters. Grotius' reference to this Old Testament kingship might be surprising, as it was in essence a concept of sacred rule by a king ordained by God, while Grotius himself rejects at least the general necessity of a supernatural foundation of the state or of immediate divine interference in the human establishment of the state. Yet, this should not bewilder us: Grotius' argument is that neither the Law of the Gospel nor Mosaic Law requires a separate administration of sacred matters. For this purpose an exceptional divine origin of royal power is rather irrelevant. In any event, Grotius concludes that there is at least no prohibition in the Holy Scripture

99 Cf. H. Höpfl, *The Christian Polity of John Calvin*, pp. 172–187.
100 Cf. H. Grotius, *De Imperio*, I.2.

for rulers to handle sacred matters under their own general jurisdiction. While Grotius does not claim any explicit divine commandment for the taking charge of spiritual matters by a state's authority, there is at least no opposing rule either. Instead, Arbitrary Divine Right merely allows for the exercise of the state's authority in spiritual matters implicitly by not distinguishing them from temporal matters and by not claiming differences between their respective authorities.

Secondly, Grotius states that the unity of matter between spiritual and temporal concerns is also to be accepted because of natural reason[101]: natural reason requires that the highest civil power includes the authority over spiritual matters, because otherwise it would not be the highest power alone, but only in conjunction with another power that includes this very authority over spiritual concerns. Then, however, the civil power would in this respect be subordinate to the latter, spiritual, power; yet by definition the highest civil power has no power equal to itself. This comment, however, could hardly in itself serve as a satisfactory explanation for the jurisdiction of the state over spiritual matters, as it still remains possible to think of a distinctly spiritual sovereignty independent of the temporal authority, as some Canonists had done.[102] However, such a distinction would be in contradiction to Grotius' idea according to which the one sovereignty can only be shared by several institutions jointly, but cannot be split up into several functions, e.g. spiritual and temporal. This resembles Grotius' statement in *Ordinum Pietas* according to which human and divine jurisprudence cannot be separated from each other[103]; therefore any Human Right that does not take account of Divine Right is crippled and mutilated.[104]

Grotius carries his argument even further: if there were any separation between the highest power over non-spiritual and spiritual matters, any action that falls into the spiritual as well as into the non-spiritual category would either be determined by several authorities at once – which is impossible in Grotius' opinion – or there would have to be established a certain kind of order and hierarchy; in this case, however, there would again be one authority which possesses the highest power, which ultimately would have the supreme jurisdiction over spiritual as well as non-spiritual matters. The only other alternative to this would be chaos, which would present a fierce contradiction to natural reason. That chaos would result from any separation of the power over spiritual from that over temporal affairs is

101 Cf. ibid., I.iii.

102 Cf. H. de Wall, "Protestantische Theorien über die Beziehungen ziwschen Kirche und Staat im Heiligen Römischen Reich Deutscher Nation", pp. 177 et seq., 187 et seq.

103 Cf. ibid., 110 b 41.

104 Cf. D. M. Sprackling, "Divine and Human Law in Hugo Grotius", p. 81.

elaborately illustrated in *Ordinum Pietas*.[105] Here Grotius refers to the Flemish controversies, where he believes the Church had claimed too many powers for itself. In a rather self-congratulatory fashion Grotius here asserts that the province of Holland had set a good example in bringing religious peace by imposing restrictions regarding religious disputes[106], in referring, *inter alia*, to his own measures taken in his official capacity as Attorney General of Holland and later as a member of the Committee of Councillors. During the tenure of these offices he also composed his *Decretum pro pace ecclesiasarum*, which was adopted as regulation by the states of Holland, so as to pacify the religious quarrels within the provincial Church.[107]

The third argument on which Grotius bases his thesis of the unity of matter is the obligation of rulers to foster religion.[108] Grotius here claims that it is the ruler's responsibility to work for the good of the people, in particular of his citizens. Grotius also refers to this in *Ordinum Pietas*, in which he claims the common good to serve as justification for the government holding authority over temporal as well as over spiritual matters.[109] Here he cites Augustine, who had argued in favour of the ruler's duty to command the good and prohibit the bad.[110] This responsibility is in Grotius' opinion not restricted to the ruler's obligation to ensure some sort of earthly happiness; he also has to strive for ensuring that the commonwealth of which he has charge loves God and is loved by God. Remarkably, Grotius does not really distinguish between a Christian type of divine love and a non-Christian one: instead, he claims that even the pagan philosophers who merely had "the light of nature" had acknowledged true happiness to lie in obedience to God.[111] As not only external peace, but also the striving for the piety of the people must be a chief end of any rule, the authority of the ruler must include the Right to pursue these ends, which means that it also includes the power in spiritual matters.

While this is true for any kind of authority, it certainly applies even more to Christian authority.[112] Grotius is keen to stress that religion is a prerequisite for any kind of happiness[113] and even for temporal prosperity[114], because piety secures divine rewards and religious people are likely to have

105 Cf. OP, 125 a 25.

106 Cf. ibid., 125 b 35.

107 Cf. H.-J. v. Dam, *De Imperio Summarum Potestatum Circa Sacra*, pp. 20 et seq.

108 Cf. H. Grotius, *De Imperio*, I.iv.

109 Cf. OP, 99 a 30.

110 Cf. ibid., 115 b 15; this principle also becomes apparent in the Augustine doctrine of *nulla iustitia sine vera religione*.

111 Cf. H. Grotius, *De Imperio*, I.v.

112 Cf. ibid., I.vi

113 Cf. ibid., I.x.; cf. Sprackling, "Divine and Human Law in Hugo Grotius", p. 89.

114 Cf. ibid., I.xi.

a peaceful and harmonious disposition.[115] Moreover, as Grotius emphasises in *Ordinum Pietas*, peace within the Church and within the state are inseparable, wherefore rulers have to take specific care of God's Right.[116] In addition, Grotius sees advantages in the acknowledgement of the ruler's power over spiritual matters: he fears that certain pastors might be disposed to incite public uproar if the state failed to provide discipline amongst them. Moreover Grotius is optimistic that the ruler may help to suppress and overcome superstition.[117]

Yet, the religion fostered by the ruler of a state needs not be true Christianity under the regime of Natural Right; a false religion might suffice to ensure that a commonwealth and a state are relatively well governed.[118] This statement in *De Imperio* resembles the conclusion to *De Iure Belli ac Pacis*, according to which those who do not worship their own gods deserve punishment, even if it is not the Christian religion that is discussed here.[119] As far as human beings establish a state, the respective ruler will take the responsibility to foster religion, just as the ruler has to foster obedience to the applicable law. This obligation to foster religion is therefore a duty of rulers that can be traced back to the obligatory principles of Natural Religion. The ruler has to foster the true religion to the extent that it has been revealed to him, which confirms the moral general principle that there is an individual responsibility of all human beings on an international as well as on the national level. In other words, as far as the true religion has not yet been revealed to him, the ruler is still under an obligation to foster religion in general.

This view regarding the ruler's duty to foster religion is indeed remarkable, as Grotius elsewhere displays quite a negative, though relatively mild, account of the sin of idolatry, which is normally only for God to punish.[120] In taking this rather positive view regarding any religion Grotius, however, differs from the classic position taken by Augustine, who had asserted the necessity of true religion for justice. Grotius' statement that Augustine had claimed that the Roman Empire had been supported by God because the Romans had cherished their religion even though it was a false religion, is certainly a misrepresentation: Augustine, in particular in *De civitate Dei*, had presented an analysis of the Roman imperial idea, which according to Augustine had only been supported by "good disciplines" – *boni mores* – but not by the right religion.[121] As the Romans in fostering these good

115 Cf. ibid., I.xii.
116 Cf. OP, 110 b 41.
117 Cf. H. Grotius, *De Imperio*, I.xiv.
118 Cf. ibid., I.xiii.
119 Cf. IBP, II.XX.li.
120 Cf. ibid., II.XX.xlvii; II.XX.xiv.2.
121 Cf. A. Augustinus, *De Civitate Dei*, IV and V passim.

disciplines had only pursued their own selfish ends, Augustine believed that the pagan Roman Empire was bound to fail in the end. As a contrast to these virtues of self-love, Augustine presents the ideal of Christian religion as the only basis on which true justice could exist. Grotius' general idea of the ruler's comprehensive authority hence contradicts Augustine's outlook on the matter in an extremely important point: Augustine is unwilling to accord any legitimacy whatsoever to any religion which denies the redemption of mankind by Christ. Grotius, however, acknowledges that Natural Religion as such already possesses some legitimacy and therefore is able to provide the grounds on which true natural justice can flourish, even though Natural Religion will never reach the degree of perfection and high moral standard which the Christian religion teaches, as only the latter can show the way to eternal salvation.

While Grotius certainly takes a specific Christian point of view on religion, he ultimately does not base the obligation of rulers to foster the exercise of religion and religious piety on Arbitrary Divine Right: in the course of his argumentation he mainly relies on a duty of piety flowing from Natural Religion, dwelling on Christian sources as well as on pagan philosophers. It thus may be inferred that this obligation to foster religion is in fact an obligation whose origin lies in the obligation of natural piety as part of Natural Right. Grotius' view on this matter thus may be seen as a reference to the Aristotelian claim to ensure a good life within the state, though he would certainly argue that the natural duty to foster religion will be given a particular shape by the Christian truth.

2.2. Unity of Authority

The duty to foster religion, which Grotius established in the introductory sections of *De Imperio*, leads to the question of who has the authority to judge over all matters, spiritual or temporal. So far, Grotius' argumentation had merely exposed a favour to a unity of matter; yet, the fact that the subject is in principle the same does not yet necessarily mean that the authority to be exercised over these matters also has to be the same. Moreover, the question has to be raised to what extent the authority to judge over all matters rests with the ruler of a state, and which matters have to be left to God and divine providence to decide upon.

In *De Imperio* Grotius states that any human act which can be known and is not already morally defined is subject to the temporal ruler's authority. Relevant to the ruler's authority are mainly external human acts, i.e. acts that are externalised[122], whereas internal actions, such as thoughts, etc., are hardly

122 Cf. H. Grotius, *De Imperio*, III.i.

suitable to be subject to this authority, as they cannot normally be discerned by the ruler. There is, however, the possibility that internal acts are linked to external acts; for example, the internal act of intending to deprive someone of his property and to assume that property for oneself is linked to the external act of theft. The same is true for attempted acts which do not yet completely enter the external sphere.

Another distinction Grotius makes in this context is that between defined acts and undefined acts: Defined acts are acts that are either obligatory and therefore "necessary", or unlawful and therefore "impossible".[123] With respect to the moral definition of acts we have to ask who is entitled to define them. Grotius takes the view that human acts can in principle be defined by Human Right as well as by Natural Right or Arbitrary Divine Right.[124] The Divine Right has priority over any Human Right. Therefore only those acts can be defined by human beings that are not already defined by God[125], i.e. either by Natural Right or by Arbitrary Divine Right. Thus, if the state orders something contrary to Divine Right, the citizens have to obey God rather than the ruler, though they may not use force as a means of disobedience to the state.[126]

Though Grotius distinguishes between divine authority and human authority, he shows no interest in a distinction between what is conventionally called "spiritual acts", which include acts of prayer or worship, the administration of sacraments, acts of penitence, and the like, on the one hand, and temporal acts, such as trading, passing sentences, inflicting punishment, and so on. The difference between the two is irrelevant for the distinction between divine authority and human authority: divine authority is universal and therefore also extends to any human authority. Grotius' understanding of metaphysics as Right renders such a distinction futile; for example, in his concept punishment is closely connected with restoring justice. In restoring justice, the judge implements the divine will, and at the same time administers a human office.

Grotius claims that there are indeed some matters that are altogether unsuitable for human authority, as they can only be morally defined by God. Faith and thought may be but two examples. Certainly there is an obligation to have faith, at least in the sense of natural piety. Yet, acts of faith only affect one's internal disposition. The obligation to have faith cannot be effectively enforced by other human beings.[127] Likewise, certain human thoughts may be contrary to Natural Right, but it can only be judged by God himself whether

123 Cf. ibid., III.ii.
124 Cf. ibid., III.iii.
125 Cf. ibid., III.iv.
126 Cf. ibid., III.v; III.xiii.
127 Cf. ibid., III.ix.

or not a human being harbours such thoughts. Though such acts are certainly subject to Divine Right, be it Natural Right or Arbitrary Divine Right, its enforcement has to be left to divine providence. It is thus not so much the borderline between spiritual acts and temporal acts that is in Grotius' view decisive with respect to the scope of human authority, but rather the question of whether an act is susceptible to public observation and enquiry that renders it subject to human authority.[128] It is just more likely that genuinely spiritual matters, such as the necessary inward disposition when accepting sacraments, have already been morally defined by God. Moreover, more care to discern the will of God is to be applied when dealing with matters of spiritual relevance, as errors in religion are more dangerous than any other failings. Yet, apart from the aforementioned qualifications, spiritual matters in this respect have to be treated like temporal matters.

Grotius' radical distinction between acts in the public domain that are susceptible to public observation and enquiry, and acts that remain outside the visible realm becomes even more apparent in *Ordinum Pietas*, in which Grotius claims that there cannot be any distinction between spiritual matters and temporal matters in the public domain[129]: referring to the Puritan Anglican theologian William Whitaker, Grotius asserts that an assembly of bishops is itself by no means any more sacred than any other congregation or assembly. Hence, the authority of the sovereign ruler includes, *inter alia*, the convening and presiding over synods, the election of its members, and the ratification or vetoing of the resolutions by synods, just as it comprises similar powers with respect to any other assembly of public relevance.[130]

Moreover, the moral definition of a divine act does not necessarily mean that it cannot be subject to human authority under any aspect. Though some acts, such as the profession of faith, may be defined morally by God in their substance, their mode of performance normally is not. This is to say that human authority may regulate such modalities, which may include, *inter alia*, the time and place of public worship, the symbols to be applied, the designation of religious holidays, and the like. While it is certainly not for a temporal ruler to abolish or introduce Christian holidays as days for religious celebrations, a temporal ruler may determine on which date a holiday is to be celebrated, by which ceremonies, and the like.

In addition to that, human authority may reinforce God's commandments or prohibitions. Just as certain principles of Natural Right have been reinforced by Arbitrary Divine Right in the Decalogue, Human Right may reinforce Natural Right or Divine Right. In this case it is a matter of human authority to exercise physical coercion or punishment. Yet, while matters of

128 Cf. ibid., III.xv.

129 Cf. OP, 113 a 48.

130 Cf. ibid., 101.

the divine authority may be reinforced through human authority, this does not necessarily have to be the case: hence the divine will does not require human rulers to punish any breach of the divine will under any circumstance and at any price. There may indeed be situations in which the ruler is not under an obligation to punish certain offences against Arbitrary Divine Right, because, say, a punishment would fail its aim – for example, it is rather pointless to wage a penal war because of a breach of Arbitrary Divine Right if it is already clear from the outset that the opponent's forces are too strong to be defeated. Nevertheless, the divine will is still valid, even without such reinforcement.

2.3. Unity of Power

So far Grotius seems to allow for a totalitarian royal and for a totalitarian priestly regime, as well as generally for other forms of regime. He certainly greatly stresses the fact that any sovereign government by definition comprises all authority, and that a sovereign ruler has to be independent from any other human institution. However, Grotius does acknowledge that there is a distinction to be made between spiritual rule and temporal rule. Yet, he fails to elaborate on what the precise difference is and what the particular specifications of spiritual rule as opposed to temporal rule are. Grotius merely states that, though pastors are subordinate to the sovereign ruler, they do not derive their power from him, as they do not act on his behalf, but do something which the ruler could not do.[131] Grotius here appears to take up the claim raised in the course of the Reformation, according to which the legitimacy of the Church's authority is dependent upon the prevention of any conflation between the spiritual and the temporal mandate; what it actually means to him, however, remains unclear.

Under Natural Right, Grotius deems it possible to join together the spiritual power of the priest and the temporal power of the ruler.[132] Yet, standing in the Gelasian tradition dominating in Western Christianity[133], he sees such a combination of the priestly power and the royal power as prohibited under Arbitrary Divine Right: under the Mosaic Law the priestly power had been deprived of any ruling power so as to limit its importance for worldly affairs. The Law of the Gospel also separates the royal from the priestly power, but this Grotius believes merely to serve a practical purpose: the pastors thus should be enabled to take charge of their respective priestly

131 Cf. H. Grotius, *De Imperio*, II.ii.

132 Cf. ibid., II.iii.

133 Cf. Gelasius, "The Bond of Anathema", in O. M. T. O'Donovan, J. Lockwood O'Donovan, *From Irenaeus to Grotius: A Sourcebook in Christian Political Thought*, p. 178–179.

power without having to carry a further burden in administering temporal affairs. Grotius thus rejects the traditional views on this issue, as expressed, for example, in the Convocation Book, which regarded the temporal ruling power as in principle subordinate to the priestly power.

There is, then, also a distinction between the pastoral government and the proper temporal government discernible in Grotius' elaboration on the matter. As pastors are prohibited to exercise coercive power under the Law of the Gospel, they merely fulfil their functions in a suasive and declarative fashion.[134] Hence, Grotius conceives the Church as a stranger on earth, not vested with any power to command.[135] Moreover, the Church is in Grotius' opinion a legal entity established by Divine Right. Its government is bound to act upon the consent of the Church[136]; thus, the Church has a "constitutive government" internally.[137] "Internal" government of the Church is here to be understood in contrast to the "external", outwardly directed government of the Church, i.e. the civil government, which *inter alia* determines the legal appearance of the Church establishment.

Nonetheless, the consequences of Grotius' distinction between the pastoral government and the temporal government still remain unclear. It may be suggested that he likens the structure of the "internal" ecclesiastical government to that of the civil government; the main difference with the internal ecclesiastical government would then be its incapability of resorting to the use of force in order to pursue its functions, as it is bound to act in a suasive and declaratory fashion. This means that the content of what the internal ecclesiastical government teaches in exercise of its suasive power depends on what the members of the Church believe to be the right and necessary doctrine. Still, the source of the power of the Church is to be found in the divine will, and not in any sort of human establishment of the Church. This also supports the suggestion that Grotius regards sovereignty only as a category of the Human Right of Nations, but not of Natural Right or Arbitrary Divine Right.

Thus it is possible for Grotius to uphold his thesis that a state is sovereign although the Church does not derive its power from it: this power of the Church is merely suasive and declarative, without entailing any power to command and to interfere directly with the affairs of the state. It is a wholly different type of power than civil power: though the state has a plenitude of powers, it is a plenitude of earthly powers. The Church on the other hand lacks earthly powers completely, but can only act in the aforementioned

134 Cf. H. Grotius, *De Imperio*, IV.viii.
135 Cf. ibid., IV.x.
136 Cf. ibid., IV.xi.
137 D. M. Sprackling, "Divine and Human Law in Hugo Grotius", p. 95.

declaratory and suasive fashion, as in exercising the power of the keys[138], or in particular in the prescription of penance, which Grotius regards exclusively as giving counsel[139], thus distancing himself from the earlier tendency of the Roman Church, which employed measures of penance in order to exert political influence on an international level.[140]

The power Grotius hereby ascribes to the Church does not at all curtail the completeness and comprehensiveness of the civil powers of the state in relation to the ecclesiastical organisation; in particular, he does not equate the civil powers in spiritual matters with the powers of the Church. Rather, he defines a distinct set of powers of the Church, which are assigned to the Church by divine will. The state still has power in temporal as well as in spiritual matters. Hence, the state may define things that are not already morally defined; it may use force in spiritual matters as far as there are no rules of Natural Right or of Arbitrary Divine Right to the contrary. The state has the power of the sword, and the ruler may enforce spiritual matters that are defined.[141] Grotius states that the king's authority may thus even be called spiritual as it pertains to spiritual as well as temporal matters.[142]

Here Grotius comes close to Luther, who had regarded the enforcement of certain ecclesiastical issues, for example the discipline of the clergy, as falling into the temporal realm and therefore being subject to the earthly government.[143] This may illustrate how both Luther and Grotius are indebted to the Marsilian and Ockhamist tradition. At the same time, Grotius is indebted to Calvin in jettisoning the adversity between the temporal and the spiritual realm, which sometimes had been perceptible in Luther, and which Calvin had already rejected in refuting the Anabaptists.[144]

Though there are, of course, certain personal qualities which Grotius sees as advantageous to rulers in order to help them to govern spiritual matters rightly, it is rather the office of the government that is of primary importance regarding the handling of spiritual affairs.[145] Grotius regards the relevant rules of the Law of the Gospel as easy to identify, for he is very optimistic about the plainness of the Holy Scripture and of religious principles as such.[146] Here Grotius argues as follows: What is necessary in relation to

---

138 Cf. H. Grotius, *De Imperio*, IX.vii.

139 Cf. ibid., IX.viii.

140 Cf. C. A. Stumpf and P. R. Melot de Beauregard, "Die Entwicklung der staatlichen Souveränität im Spiegel der kanonistischen Völkerrechtslehre", *Der Staat*, 42 (2003), pp. 459 et seq.

141 D. M. Sprackling, "Divine and Human Law in Hugo Grotius", p. 96.

142 Cf. H. Grotius, *De Imperio*, II.vii.

143 Cf. M. Luther, *Von weltlicher Obrigkeit*, pp. 25 et seq.

144 J. Calvin, *Institutio Religionis Christianae*, IV.20.2.

145 H. Grotius, *De Imperio*, V.viii.

146 Ibid., V.ix.

doctrinal matters certainly has been revealed and stated very clearly, in particular in the Holy Scripture. If something is uncertain or disputed, one can be confident that it is not important, for otherwise it would have been laid down more explicitly. In particular, principles with respect to salvation only exist in a limited number and can be detected and perceived from the Gospel very easily. Consequently, the ruler's apprehension of the Holy Scripture can be expected to be just as good as that of anyone else. Neither is there a certain theological qualification required in order to qualify the ruler to judge spiritual matters, nor does theological ignorance disqualify the ruler when deciding upon spiritual matters; theological knowledge may enhance the quality of the rule and the exercise of civil power, but it is not an absolute prerequisite for handling spiritual affairs. In *Ordinum Pietas* Grotius further claims that the best solution to the problem of theologically unknowledgeable state officers is to make them knowledgeable, but not to deprive them of the power to make decisions.[147] Yet, the decisive factor remains the office: otherwise, if training or any particular expertise were required, some kings might be regarded as unable to make decisions with respect to the temporal realm as far as they do not have any training in "temporal" law, and even with pastors one could not always be sure whether they are sufficiently skilled in theological matters.[148] Grotius, in so emphasising the relevance of the office, may also have endeavoured to vindicate his own interfering in ecclesiastical affairs as member of the magistrate of Holland, e.g. by advising the magistrate of Goes on deposing ministers or in the prohibition to form a new congregation in Rotterdam.[149]

As to the question of whether the Christian faith is requisite to administer a state office properly, Grotius displays no enthusiasm with respect to pagan or heretic rulers who might then also be in charge of administering the Church; here he may have thought of Byzantine emperors who had been regarded as heretics. Nevertheless, Grotius seems willing to accept their rule on the grounds that God could work through evil men as well as through good men. However, as regards heretical rulers, the acceptance of their rule could only be temporary, as Grotius would probably regard the heresy of rulers as a breach of Arbitrary Divine Right, which can in principle present a justification for their deposition.

Just as the judgement of the ruler is not always right with respect to temporal matters, it will neither always be correct in spiritual matters. In this respect Grotius in *De Imperio* develops an *ultra vires* doctrine regarding the

---

147 OP, 115 a 53.

148 Ibid., 111 a 28-32; cf. D. M. Sprackling, "Divine and Human Law in Hugo Grotius", p. 79.

149 H.-J. v. Dam, "De Imperio Summarum Potestatum Circa Sacra", pp. 20 et seq., fn. 6.

powers of the ruler in religious matters[150]: as far as an act by the ruler contravenes any higher authority and in particular the authority of God, as displayed in the principles of Natural Right and the Law of the Gospel, the ruler acts beyond his powers (*ultra vires*). Thus the act of the ruler is not only contrary to Right and illegal, but also void. Minor mistakes, however, may render an act of the ruler merely illegal; such an act can then still be regarded as valid and effective.[151]

A ruler who administers spiritual matters has to form his own judgement on matters that are to be decided. The ruler is the appointed officer to decide any matter, and his decisions are not dependent upon any factor other than what he sees fit. Grotius is very much in favour of the ruler hearing and also to some extent relying on advice.[152] Yet, it is again the ruler who has to weigh the advice given. Consequently, the ruler has to assess which advice is best and most according to the Holy Scripture.[153] Preference is given to quality over quantity of advice. Moreover, the ruler may act against all and any advice given to him, but should be very careful and have good reasons when doing so.[154] Again Grotius stresses the personal responsibility of the individual to contribute to the common good nationally as well as internationally according to the authority granted to him.

In this respect Grotius displays grave doubts regarding the institutions of synods, which may be motivated by historical examples of general councils of the Church, whose authority had been in dispute. Consequently, Grotius regards synods not as divinely ordained assemblies of the Church, but just as assemblies like any other human assembly.[155] This also becomes apparent from one argument brought forward in *Ordinum Pietas* to support Grotius' statement that rulers should have a right to veto decisions of synods: rulers cannot be expected to propagate what they do not believe, and thus must have a say in the decision-making of a synod.[156] Nevertheless, in *De Imperio* Grotius urges the ruler to pay attention to the synod: he should not act against the advice of the synod without good reason.[157] In this context, we can again see how much Grotius stresses the notion of the constitutive government of the Church: the synod is in his system the one institution in

---

150 H. Grotius, *De Imperio*, V.xi.

151 Ibid., V.xiv.

152 Ibid., VI.ii.

153 Ibid., VI.iii.

154 OP, 117 a.

155 Cf. R. Hooker, *On the Law of Ecclesiastical Polity*, III.ii.1. Hooker thus shifts away from the medieval idea of an ecclesiastical convocation separate from the state's parliament; on this see J. Lockwood O'Donovan, *Theology of Law and Authority in the English Reformation*, p. 151; C. A. Stumpf, "The Christian Society and Its Government", pp. 169 et seq.

156 OP, 115 b 6; cf. D. M. Sprackling, "Divine and Human Law in Hugo Grotius", p. 82.

157 Grotius, *De Imperio*, VII.xiii.

which a consensus within the Church with respect to ecclesiastical affairs is most likely to be reached.

With respect to doctrinal issues Grotius pursues a line of minimalist irenics: the ruler's part in decisions about the right doctrine is not so much to decide upon the adoption of the right doctrine, but rather to resolve the problem of which questions are relevant for salvation – and which are not – and to state what clearly can be deducted from God's Right. The ruler's task does not lie in the fields of theological disputations – he simply has to decide, and where no decisions can be made on the content, he has to resolve that no decisions on this are to be made.[158] Thereby the ruler preserves peace and concord within the state as well as within the Church, which Grotius implicitly regards to be identical with the state in terms of its membership and territorial scope.

Nevertheless, Grotius acknowledges that there are problematic matters of faith which can give rise to doubts about the proper way of dealing with spiritual matters. Here it is not so much for the ruler to decide which opinion to follow, but instead it will be rather his task to suppress disputes on questions unnecessary for living piously, and in particular for salvation.[159] This Grotius also spells out very clearly in the *Ordinum Pietas*[160]: he regards it by far less hazardous to leave some questions open than to effect innovation in controversial issues of a doctrinal nature.[161]

Grotius takes the religious responsibility of the sovereign ruler probably more serious than any other representative of the so-called rationalist state-theory[162]: the sovereign ruler is responsible for fostering religion and administering spiritual matters. In so doing he has to comply with the supreme legal orders provided by God in Natural Right and Arbitrary Divine Right. The responsibility of the ruler is conferred to him together with his sovereign position by virtue of the appointment to his office and the respective submission of the people to his authority. Though this appointment will in most cases rely on a human decision, the office is nevertheless closely connected to duties under Natural Right and Arbitrary Divine Right, some of which will refer to temporal issues only, but some of which – and probably even the more important ones – will also concern particular religious issues.

In arguing in favour of a comprehensive authority of the ruler which covers temporal as well as spiritual matters, Grotius distances himself to a great extent from the traditional Christian perspective of a separation between temporal and spiritual powers. While the notion of such a

---

158 Ibid., VI.ix.

159 Ibid., VIII.vi.

160 Cf. OP, 111 a 510.

161 Grotius, *De Imperio*, I.xiii.

162 D. Wolf, *Die Irenik des Hugo Grotius*, p. 34.

separation is not completely absent from Grotius' elaboration, for he still conceives of a distinct power of the Church which is to be exercised in a declaratory and suasive fashion, he strongly emphasises the responsibility of the ruler to seek the good for the state and its citizens in spiritual as well as in temporal aspects. At the same time, Grotius distinguishes himself from the old Christian understanding according to which legitimate authority requires the acknowledgement of the true Christian religion: he certainly contends that Christianity is more perfect than any other religion. Nevertheless, Grotius also conceives of a legitimate pagan authority which is truly seeking the good for the people entrusted to it – though the pagan authority still lacks the proper understanding of the redemption of mankind through Christ, which Grotius deems necessary for the ultimate maintenance of an order of true justice.

There are certain parallels to the Islamic concept of rule, which like Grotius entrusts one authority with both spiritual and temporal functions.[163] Various Islamic legal scholars have conceded limited legitimacy to the authority exercised by unbelievers.[164] Nevertheless, the Islamic tradition overall adheres to the idea that the Islamic community of the *umma* necessarily comprises all Muslims of all nations, while Grotius – as noted above – conceives of a multitude of sovereign authorities which are independent of each other and meet each other in international relations on an equal level. For Grotius there is no major difference in sovereign authority held by Christians or by non-Christians.

In joining temporal and spiritual functions in the authority of the ruler, Grotius' concept greatly contrasts the modern liberal understanding brought forward in particular by John Rawls in his *Law of Peoples*: while Rawls certainly would agree with Grotius in entrusting the state authorities with the task to seek the common good for their respective societies, he would exclude any religious or moral duties from the state authorities[165]; while Grotius derives his idea of the common good from the divine justice entailed in both Natural Right and Arbitrary Divine Right, Rawls determines the common good along the lines of his concept of justice as fairness. Thus for Rawls the common good ultimately corresponds to the greatest possible freedom of the individuals, which would be incompatible with specific religious functions of the state's authority. This is not to say that Grotius seeks to limit a legitimate degree of freedom of the individual human beings as citizens of a state. Yet, he puts greater emphasis on the individual responsibility of every human being, which then also entails the right use of authority by the ruler as an individual, who has to uphold divine justice,

163 Cf. C. A. Stumpf, "Völkerrecht unter Kreuz und Halbmond", pp. 85, 100.
164 Khadduri, *The Islamic Law of Nations*, pp. 52 et seq.
165 Cf. J. Rawls, *The Law of Peoples*, pp. 166 et seq.

whereas the citizens in this respect have their own responsibility to contribute to the common good in particular through adhering to the principles under which they have submitted themselves to the ruler's authority. This leads us to the question of how the mutual relations between the ruler and the citizens are organised after the establishment of a state's authority.

V. The Organisation of Authority

Dealing with Grotius' political thought, one cannot help but be overwhelmed by the literature that has been written about his adherence to a particular brand of political theory and about his proper interpretation in the context of some school or other. Throughout the history of political ideas there have been manifold attempts to find a particular tradition in which Grotius stands.[166] The aims and results of this scholarly interest in Grotius' approach to the internal organisation of the state could hardly be more diverse. For example, regarding his views on government Grotius has been characterised by some authors as being favourable towards authoritarianism.[167] Others have regarded him as defender of the idea of peoples' sovereignty or of the idea of a well-balanced social contract.[168] Finally, there are also interpreters of Grotius who have simply criticised him as being extremely vague or even as self-contradictory in his views on states and the powers of rulers, so that his approach was deemed irrelevant for the history of political thought.[169]

We will therefore ask in the following how the people of a state relate to sovereign authority in Grotius' concept and what the mutual obligations between rulers and the citizens are. In so doing, we will find out that Grotius is in the end quite prepared to accept any kind of internal organisation of the state – hence, he sees an absolute monarchy as much a legitimate form of government as a parliamentary democracy. However, he thus implicitly rejects an idea that came up with some political authors of his time – the idea that in all states the people are the ultimate sovereign that can appoint rulers and dismiss them as they see fit.

---

166 It should suffice to mention the most frequently used political directions to which Grotius was seen to belong: as supporter of absolute regimes as well as early human rights advocate; on Grotius' relationship to the political doctrines during his time cf. H. Bull, "The Importance of Grotius in the Study of International Relations", p. 71–72.

167 E.g. Y. Onuma, "War", in Y. Onuma (ed.), *A Normative Approach to War*, p. 102; T. Tadashi, "State and Governing Power", ibid., p. 143.

168 E.g. E. Reibstein, *Volkssouveränität und Freiheitsrechte: Texte und Studien zur politischen Theorie des 14.–18. Jahrhunderts*, vol. I, pp. 210 et seq.

169 Cf. on the variety of interpretations K. Nabulsi, *Traditions of War: Occupation, Resistance, and the War*, pp. 146 et seq.; and C. Link, *Hugo Grotius als Staatsdenker*, pp. 22 et seq.

However, Grotius also rejects those authors in medieval Christian jurisprudence, according to whom only the absolute rule of monarchs was a legitimate form of government. As we have seen above, the establishment of states and of the ruler's authority is a mere human act, even though God and his Right endorse this establishment. Grotius nevertheless comes to results similar to that of medieval Christian jurisprudence as he acknowledges that there may be rulers in accordance with God's design for a human order who may not be dismissed by their subjects, unless such right of dismissal has been reserved by the people in the act of appointment.

Likewise, Grotius' position is also quite distant from the views of classic Islamic jurisprudence on the organisation of legitimate rule. Like the medieval Christian tradition, Islamic jurisprudence also regarded the ruler as God's officer whose powers could not be restricted by human constitutional arrangements.[170] While Islamic jurisprudence certainly supposed that a ruler requires advice from theologians and lawyers for discharging his tasks, it was nevertheless the task of the ruler himself to take or reject such advice. Yet, the position of the ruler stemmed from divine will, wherefore this position could not be questioned by human revolutionary acts.

Finally, Grotius is here also at variance with the modern liberal theories on government in refusing to show any distinct sympathy towards democratic forms of government. John Rawls, for example, distinguished between various types of societies in international relations according to their type of government.[171] For Rawls, the only fully legitimate form of government is a liberal democratic one, and thus only such societies can enter into full international relations on the basis of a transnational social contract. Close to such liberal societies are those societies which have at least a decent consultation hierarchy in their internal constitution. Thus, such "decent societies" are also able to join in the aforementioned social contract between "well-ordered" societies, as they also allow for their people to join in the discourse on the common good. Excluded from such international relations are, however, societies which are not well-ordered in Rawls' sense, as they are absolutist monarchies, even if they are "benevolently" absolutist, or because they are simply "outlaw states". Grotius on the other hand rejects such categorisations, as he refuses to pass judgement on the moral quality of internal state constitutions. For him international relations are governed by the categories of Divine Right and Human Right, whereas the question to what extent the people of a state share in its government is quite irrelevant for him.

170 B. Krawietz, *Hierarchie der Rechtsquellen im tradierten sunnitischen Islam*, pp. 353 et seq.
171 Cf. J. Rawls, *The Law of Peoples*, pp. 4 et seq.

1. The People and the Sovereign Power

There has been an extensive discussion by political theorists on whether or not Grotius is to be seen as opponent to the theory of peoples' sovereignty.[172] Given the variety of interpretations of Grotius in scholarly literature it seems preferable to examine what Grotius himself actually has to say about the organisation of authority, rather than to turn to more or less favourable interpretations of what he might or should have said, in order to integrate him more neatly into a coherent system of ideas.

It is certainly possible to use quotations from Grotius to support both views: Grotius argues that a people can transfer all power of government by submitting itself to an appointed ruler irrevocably and absolutely. This may suggest an original sovereignty of the people. Yet, as far as a ruler has been appointed and has been vested with the power to rule as a sovereign, there does not seem to be very much left of the people's sovereignty.

At the heart of the problem is Grotius' statement according to which sovereignty is always held "commonly" by the state, and "properly" by one or more persons.[173] The common sovereignty thus corresponds to what modern concepts call external sovereignty, whereas proper sovereignty corresponds to what is called internal sovereignty. Grotius refutes the claim that all sovereignty is common sovereignty residing with a popular body. Grotius certainly can conceive democratic forms of government[174]; nevertheless, he denies that all states have to be democracies. This still allows for the inference that Grotius holds all states to be organised as democracies originally, before the ruler is appointed and proper sovereignty is conferred upon him. The alternative conclusion would be that in Grotius' views originally only common sovereignty resided in the people, and that proper sovereignty only came into existence when it was conferred in a constitutive act upon some ruler or the people itself; this was the conclusion Vitoria had reached in his own concept.[175]

There are good reasons to follow the latter interpretation of Grotius: Grotius certainly acknowledges the theoretical possibility of a democratic and nevertheless sovereign state[176], though he appears to concede to Vitoria

---

172 In favour of Grotius as representative of this theory is, amongst others, E. Reibstein, *Volkssouveränität und Freiheitsrechte*, vol. I, pp. 210 et seq.; this is refuted by L. Barschak, *Die Staatsauffassung des Hugo Grotius*, p. 13.

173 Cf. IBP, I.III.vii.3.

174 Cf. ibid., I.III.xix.

175 Cf. F. de Vitoria, *De Potestate Civili*, I.III.

176 For examples which suggest that Grotius held democracies to be possible, at least theoretically, cf. IBP, I.III.xix.; ibid., I.III.viii.6.; ibid., I.IV.viii.; III.XV.viii.; moreover, in ibid., I.III.xi.3 Grotius hints to an example of "democratic" monarchy, i.e. a monarchy established on democratic terms.

at least that no sovereign power can exist before a state is established in submission of the people to a certain institution. Such an institution may be for instance a single ruler, a royal family, a ruling class, or even the whole people itself as democratically organised popular sovereign. The democratic outset of the state is merely one of several possibilities of organising a state, and by no means necessary or even the best one.

As to the question of whether all states were democracies originally, Grotius probably would answer that most of them were at least formed in a popular process out of the natural human society: as explained above, the establishment of a state is accomplished by people submitting themselves to a ruler. Grotius describes this in terms of a consensual association and submission of the people to the ruler.[177] Surely, it is not a democracy of our modern design, for the members are represented by the heads of families; however, it is a representational democracy, for individual human beings represented by the heads of their families join together to submit to rule.[178]

Grotius comes close to Vitoria in denying that prior to the consensual association and submission of the people there is sovereignty: sovereign authority pertains to sovereign rule, and before submission there is no object of rule. However, the consensual establishment of the state is not the only legitimate way of conferring or acquiring rule: it is also possible that a ruler obtains his rule by conquest in a just war or through divine appointment without the subjects or their representatives becoming actively involved in such a process – hence, voluntary submission of a people may be replaced legitimately by coercive subjection of a people, as far as the subjection is warranted by Right.

Grotius sternly refutes the idea of a popular sovereignty as the only legitimate form of organising a state: anyone can voluntarily submit to slavery; Roman law as well as Jewish law had explicitly provided for the submission to slavery. Just as much can a whole nation submit itself to a ruler with the effect that it confers to this single ruler all rights of government without retaining any rights for itself.[179] It would be wrong to argue that no people would deprive itself of its sovereign rights; the assertion that such a complete transfer of rights from a people to a single ruler could not be presumed is for Grotius simply incorrect. He believes that there is the possibility of alienating one's personal freedom: the act of adopting a particular constitution, the raising of a proper sovereign rule, is not an act of alienation of powers, but rather an act of creating powers which before the adoption of the constitution did not exist.[180] Just as there are different forms

177 Cf. ibid., II.V.xxiii.
178 Cf. ibid., II.V.xvii.
179 Cf. ibid., I.III.viii.1.
180 Cf. ibid., I.III.viii.10.

of life, of which none is better than another and which one is free to choose as one sees fit, so is a people free to choose any form of government for itself, including the absolute subjection to one sovereign ruler.[181]

Grotius is not denying that rule may be granted revocably as well as irrevocably; nor does he object to the possibility of popular sovereignty or of a democratic form of government. However, such phenotypes of democracies cannot be expected in any situation, and in particular they are required neither under Natural Right nor under Arbitrary Divine Right, nor even under the Human Right of Nations. An undemocratic form of government is in itself by no means less legitimate than a democratic one. Grotius is no advocate for an absolutist form of government; he is, however, certainly an advocate against any form of popular sovereignty by necessity.

We have seen that Grotius presents a remarkable contrast to the liberal concept of John Rawls' Law of Peoples: while Grotius displays relative indifference in relation to the internal organisation of rule and of authority in any state, the constitutional arrangements become extremely relevant for the classification of states in Rawls' international society of peoples. Thus, only "well-ordered" societies which are either liberally organised in a state, or at least are organised "decently" by establishing an internal consultation hierarchy through which the will of the people can be pronounced, are fully eligible to participate in the international social contract which provides the basis for the international Law of Peoples.[182] States with other internal structures than those Rawls conceives – for example, "outlaw states", "societies burdened by unfavourable conditions", and "benevolent absolutisms" – do not qualify for such participation as these states are not "well-ordered". For example, while "benevolent absolutisms" tend to honour human rights, they do not grant their respective peoples a meaningful role in making political decisions. The participation of the people in the making of political decisions is for Rawls relevant as his concept of justice as fairness requires the possibility of discourse in defining legal regulations.[183] For Grotius, such a discourse is not relevant: the overarching framework for international as well as for national affairs is provided by Natural Right and Arbitrary Divine Right, which obligate not only the states but also the individuals, rulers and citizens alike. This is not to say that all citizens except the rulers are deprived from a meaningful role for the preservation of justice. Instead, responsibility is distributed to each individual by human constitutional arrangements. To

181 Thus it seems that Grotius did not at all conflate sovereignty with natural justice as D. Kennedy, "Primitive Legal Scholarship", *Harvard International Law Review*, 27 (1986), pp. 85 et seq., appears to claim, cf. P. P. Remec, *The Position of the Individual in International Law According to Grotius and Vattel*, p. 75.

182 Cf. J. Rawls, *The Law of Peoples*, pp. 4–5, 35 et seq., 71 et seq.

183 Cf. J. Rawls, *A Theory of Justice*, pp. 65 et seq.

grasp this concept better, we shall now analyse Grotius' views on the relationship between rulers and citizens.

2. The Relationship between Rulers and Citizens

As we have seen, Grotius conceives of various alternatives for the establishment of sovereign rule over a people and for the organisation of authority. The most liberally organised republic is for Grotius as legitimate a form of organising the state as an absolute monarchy. However, relatively little has been said so far about the relationship between the ruler and his subjects. Thus, in the following we shall first investigate what competence rulers have to limit the freedom of the citizens, before investigating the legal position of citizens under the authority of their rulers.

2.1. The Competence of the State to Limit the Freedom of the Citizens

The reason why human beings come together under the framework of a state lies in their desire to protect themselves and to enjoy a common benefit.[184] With the establishment of the state the natural freedom of the individual will be limited accordingly. Previously, the natural freedom of the individual was only limited by the framework of Natural Right and Arbitrary Divine Right. In the absence of commandments or prohibitions under Natural Right and Arbitrary Divine Right, human beings are free to act or not to act as they choose. With the establishment of the state, however, a new category of Right emerges within this sphere of freedom – Human Right, and in particular the Human National Right that is put into force by the state.[185]

Grotius regards the establishment of a court system as one of the most important limitations of human freedom by the establishment of the state. Due to the institution of judicial courts the original freedom of self-defence, which was permissible under Natural Right, is severely restricted[186]; self-defence is now only justified insofar as there is no access to the courts.[187] Therefore the ruler assumes a monopoly of exercising force in relation to his subjects. The restriction of the ancient freedom of self-defence relies solely on the human establishment of rule; it is possible to restrict the natural freedom to use force by Human Right, as this natural freedom is not granted to individuals due to a positive commandment by Natural Right or Arbitrary

184 Cf. IBP, I.I.xiv.1.
185 Cf. ibid., I.I.xiv.1.
186 Cf. ibid., I.III.i.2.
187 Cf. ibid., I.III.ii.1.

Divine Right, but merely in a reductive sense due to the absence of any commandments or prohibitions to the contrary.

Another important feature of the establishment of the state is the acknowledgement of the eminent faculty of the ruler over the legal positions of his subjects. When describing this faculty as one aspect of his second definition of Right, Grotius distinguishes between the general faculty, which is normally applied to the relationships amongst private individuals and remains on a coordinative level, and the overriding faculty of the eminent right, which is stronger than the former type of faculty, and also entails a subordination to the holder of the right. This eminent faculty rests with the community against the individual for the sake of common benefit. Thus the paternal power of the father and the power of the master over his servants are subordinate to the more eminent royal power. Consequently, the right of the king in relation to any single property for the common benefit is greater than that of the individual owner of the relevant property for his own benefit. Hence everyone is more obliged to the commonwealth for common concerns than one is obliged to one's own creditor for his concerns.[188]

While the eminent faculty of the state in relation to its citizens can be qualified as part of Human Right, the fact that the human society out of which the state emerges finds its own root in the natural order indicates that it is dominated and governed by Natural Right. This has an impact on the relationship between society and its members, and consequently, any eminent faculty of society to its members must be regarded as part of Natural Right in substance, as a right of the greater part over the smaller part. Consequently, the eminent faculty is an element of attributive justice. The eminent faculty of human society is already existent under Natural Right, whereas that of the state belongs to Human Right as far as it presupposes the voluntary act of association.

2.2. Legal Obligations of the Citizens to Their Ruler

Grotius does not expound his views on the obligations of the individual citizens to their ruler in detail in *De Iure Belli ac Pacis*. Yet there are a few comments which at least help to get a rough idea on such obligations.

There is first of all a general duty of citizens to be obedient to their state and the ruler. Grotius deals with this duty implicitly when commenting on the views of some people according to whom kings are only to be obeyed as far as they govern their people in a good manner.[189] Though Grotius agrees that no one has to follow a manifestly unjust order, he nevertheless dismisses

188 Cf. ibid., I.I.vi.
189 Cf. ibid., I.III.ix.1.

the distinction between good orders and bad orders as unfeasible for determining the limits of the citizens' obedience: as evaluating the quality of state acts is highly complicated, it cannot be left to the individual citizens to judge which order to follow and which not.[190]

However, mere practicality would be a less than satisfactory argument to explain Grotius' conclusion. In particular, it could not sustain the inadmissibility of disobedience where the injustice of a commandment by the state or the ruler is manifest. Though Grotius clearly accepts that there can be such cases, he holds that the duty of obedience persists nevertheless. Grotius implicitly argues in favour of a general duty of citizens to obey their superiors because of their respective political authority; as soon as political authority comes into play, it may not be exchanged by an external moral authority. This is a consequence of the submission to rule[191]: though there is not necessarily a duty for a free man to submit to any rule, it is nevertheless possible to do so, even to the effect that one does not retain any freedom at all. Grotius' aim is to allow for political authority to be the overriding instance within the political realm, even if this means overriding any other kind of moral authority.

This is in clear contrast to Rawls' idea of the Law of Peoples. Rawls, for example, advocates a right of individual human beings to refuse military service for unjust wars, which according to Rawls would be a most effective means to prevent any unjust wars.[192] However, the assumption that any individual will be able to discern the justice or injustice of military force seems rather naïve. While Grotius certainly acknowledges a personal and individual responsibility of all human beings under Natural Right and Arbitrary Divine Right, still the respective responsibility of a private individual and that of a ruler vested with sovereign authority are fairly different in scope: for Grotius, it is an aspect of the individual's responsibility to submit to the responsibility of the ruler, and thus the individual has to accept the consequences which follow from this submission.

The obligation of the citizen to be obedient hence not only derives from the Human Right of the state, but also exists under Natural Right and Arbitrary Divine Right, respectively. The principles of expletive justice command to render to others what is due to them. If one submits to the rule of state, then obedience is due to the state as a consequence of expletive justice. Furthermore, a similar duty of obedience is entailed by Arbitrary Divine Right as, according to God's will, we have to render obedience to our superiors.[193] In addition to that, in the New Testament Christ has com-

190 Cf. ibid., I.III.ix.2.
191 Cf. ibid., I.III.viii.1.
192 Cf. J. Rawls, *A Theory of Justice*, pp. 331 et seq.
193 Cf. IBP, I.II.vii.3.

manded us to give to the emperor what is due to him.[194] Therefore, Christians are in Grotius' views even more obliged to render obedience to the state than any other people.

2.3. Rights of the Citizens in Relation to the State

Nowhere in *De Iure Belli ac Pacis* does Grotius explicitly elaborate upon the obligations of states to their citizens. Though it may be suggested that in certain cases there might be a right of a citizen to be protected by his state, or rather an obligation of the state to protect its citizens, Grotius actually does not say so explicitly. However, it is worthwhile to enquire to what extent citizens may have rights in relation to the state.

2.3.1. Basic Rights of Citizens?

Grotius does not comment on the existence of any basic rights or human rights of human beings against states in the modern sense. As has already been demonstrated above, the notion of subjective rights in the modern sense of basic subjective rights is absent in Grotius' definition of Right in general as well as in his concept of Natural Right and Arbitrary Divine Right in particular. Human Right, as envisioned by Grotius, certainly allows for the creation of mutual rights and obligations which result in subjective rights.[195] It is therefore a question to be decided in each individual case whether there are basic rights, such as for the protection of property, the freedom of movement, and the like, granted by a state. However, it seems that this is not normally to be expected.

Moreover, it appears to be rather doubtful whether such a notion of subjective basic rights of citizens against their states could really be reconciled with Grotius' idea according to which a state has to foster the common good, including the fostering of religion: in case the ruler's opinion on what is good and what is bad for society diverges from that of an individual citizen, Grotius would certainly allow for the state's views to prevail. If there really is some sort of concept of basic rights to be enjoyed by individual citizens in Grotius' system, it would indeed be very limited and very relative, and in any case only derivative in character.

---

194 Cf. ibid., I.IV.iv.1.

195 Cf. C. Link, *Herrschaftsordnung und bürgerliche Freiheit*, pp. 144 et seq.

2.3.2. Right of Resistance

Now the obligation of citizens to render obedience to their superiors is not an absolute and not an unconditional one; as far as orders of the ruler prove to be overtly unjust, they do not have to be complied with according to Grotius. It remains to be examined what position Grotius takes with respect to civil disobedience, or active or passive resistance of citizens against the authority of the state. We have already seen that with the establishment of the state, Grotius deems most of the right to self-defence to be taken away from individuals. As far as there is recourse to the courts of a state against any violation of rights, there is no longer any need for self-defence.[196]

The same applies to self-defence of individuals against their rulers. Therefore, in principle, no citizen may exercise any self-defence against acts of his ruler. Grotius sees this principle confirmed by the fact that the respect for the sovereign is protected by special laws in many states, wherefore it is a very grave offence to disrespect the state by resisting its acts.[197] The same is confirmed by Arbitrary Divine Right: according to Grotius, Jewish law had ruled out disobedience against the High Priest or other persons that have been called to rule the state, and had even provided that such disobedience be punished by death.[198] In the New Testament Christ had commanded to render to the emperor what is due to him. Grotius interprets this statement from the Gospel to mean that Christ had even required more obedience from his followers towards the state than Jewish law or any other law had. Moreover, Christ ruled that obedience should be combined with patience where necessary.[199] This Grotius regards to be confirmed by St. Paul, who had stated that anyone who resists the government's commandments resists the commandments of God. Moreover, according to Grotius, St. Paul had demanded Christians to submit to the orders of the government and not to exercise any resistance. Refraining from resistance against superiors is not only an obligation vis-à-vis other human beings, but also vis-à-vis God. From this Grotius concludes that we have to accept the ruler and the authorities of the state, as God has approved of their appointment. God has endorsed the government's institution of commanding and obeying in the Old Testament as well as in the Gospel for our own benefit.[200] Though there may be time and again rulers that do not govern well, these instances must be regarded as exceptions. Grotius therefore asserts that the institutions of instruction and corresponding obedience are the most eminent prerequisites for a well-ordered public life.

---

196 Cf. IBP, I.IV.ii.2.
197 Cf. ibid., I.IV.ii.3.
198 Cf. ibid., I.IV.iii.
199 Cf. ibid., I.IV.iv.1.
200 Cf. ibid., I.IV.iv.

According to Grotius, not even minor state authorities are allowed to resist injustice that is inflicted upon them by their superiors.[201] Here Grotius implicitly dismisses the idea of an ephorate by necessity, i.e. institutions designed to act as warden of the government in counselling it, correcting it, and in the extreme even removing it from office.[202] Among those who had proposed this idea was Beza, who identified the ephorus with the parliamentary estates[203], as well as Althusius, who regarded the ephors as the people's representatives.[204] Though Grotius refrains from giving any opinion on the possibility to introduce an ephorate explicitly, it may be assumed that for him it would rather be a matter of the constitution to provide for such wardens. In any case, Grotius holds such an office not to be necessary; in particular, as far as a parliament is provided for by the constitution, such a parliament does not necessarily have the competence of counselling or criticising the ruler, let alone the power to remove him.

After having asserted the principle that obedience should be paid to the ruler of the state, Grotius asks whether this principle is always valid and binding, or whether there are at least some exceptions, in particular in the case of the gravest and most obvious danger. Here Grotius firstly states that though God's laws are usually phrased rather generally, they still allow for exceptions in cases of emergency[205]: though God has the power to send human beings to death, his laws do not always presuppose such a strict interpretation. Grotius realises that God's laws could command human beings to be virtuous even in the case of danger to their life, which, for example, is particularly true in the case of soldiers who must not leave their duty in the case of very grave and unavoidable perils. Yet such explicit commandments are in Grotius' views very thoroughly considered and normally only imposed in cases of need.[206] Any application of laws has to take account of human weakness. Furthermore, the establishment of the state is solely dependent on the will of those men that lay its foundation; by this they confer the civil power of the state to the respective ruler. If these founders of the state were asked whether they preferred to let all citizens rather perish than engage in violent resistance against the power of their superiors, Grotius assumes the founders would allow for the right of resistance, since this could avoid a coup against the state or the killing of many innocent people.[207]

201 Cf. ibid., I.IV.vi.1.

202 Cf. O. M. T. O'Donovan, *The Desire of the Nations: Rediscovering the Roots of Political Theology*, p. 240.

203 Cf. T. Beza, *Du droit des magistrats*, III.8.

204 Cf. J. Althusius, *Politica methodice digesta*, XVIII.48.

205 Cf. IBP, I.IV.vii.1.

206 Cf. ibid., I.IV.vii.2.

207 Cf. ibid., I.IV.vii.2.

Then it needs to be enquired whether Grotius believes that God commands man to suffer death rather than to defend himself against injustices committed by his superiors. In this respect it has to be remembered that Grotius takes the establishment of the state primarily as a human act, without Arbitrary Divine Right coming into play so far.[208] It was an exclusively human decision to join together under the roof of state, based on the weakness of each individual, in order to commonly protect each other against external violence. By this human foundation of the state the power to govern the state is conferred to the rulers, as is claimed in 1 Peter 2: 13. Surely God has approved of the establishment of the state and the entrusting of rulers with civil power, which explains why this has been called a divine institution as well. Yet, though God approves of the human establishment of the state and of human laws, he does not confer upon them a specific divine quality.

We have already seen above that Grotius thinks that a higher degree of patience is required from Christians by Christ. Nevertheless, Grotius still holds that it is permitted to Christians to resort to escape in cases where their life is threatened by their superiors.[209] This, of course, seems to allude to Grotius' own experience after his incrimination in the course of the Synod of Dort in 1617/18, even though, strictly speaking, he then did not have to fear for his life, but had only been given a life sentence. Yet, Grotius is not willing to admit anything beyond such passive resistance. He even asserts that the Christian religion has been strengthened by the willingness of the martyrs to suffer injustice. Therefore, according to Grotius, it is right to surrender to the state in any circumstance; in general, active resistance is not a legitimate remedy for Christians.[210] Regarding other people, who are not bound by the Law of the Gospel or who have so far refused to accept it, however, there seems to be a broader right of self-defence against unjust rulers, whereas the law of Christ demands a greater degree of patience in this respect than had been required before, even under the old Arbitrary Divine Right.

Yet Grotius regards some active resistance to be legitimate, for Christians and non-Christians alike. Nevertheless, in the examples given by Grotius in this context, it is not a fully legitimate power of the ruler against which resistance is exercised; in all these examples the power exercised is illegitimate, either because the ruler is subordinate to the people, or because he is no longer the ruler, or because an exception has been agreed upon. Thus, the conventional prohibitions of active resistance do not apply.

For example, it may be that the original power of a state has already been overturned and replaced by a new ruler who cannot claim the same

---

208 Cf. ibid., I.IV.vii.3.
209 Cf. ibid., I.IV.vii.8.
210 Cf. ibid., I.IV.vii.15.

legitimacy as the old one. Is there then nevertheless the same duty of obedience on the part of the population? Grotius' answer is no: if a new power has been established wrongfully it does not have the same legal status as a conventional legitimate power. Yet, Grotius still argues in favour of a provisional obedience. Thus, the orders of the new power should be acknowledged and obeyed in the meantime. Remarkably, this is not because of a new legitimacy of this power, but rather can be explained as compliance with what Grotius imagines to be the wish of the rightful government as government-in-exile: the rightful government would or at least should wish to preserve peace and order amongst the people.[211] Thus, the orders of the newly established power are only legitimate because of what Grotius thinks would be the presumptive will of the old power. The provisional character of any of the commandments of the new power is moreover underscored by Grotius' additional remark that such obedience would not have to be rendered to any commands by which the new power could stabilise its position.[212] Nevertheless, customary complaisance can legitimise a usurping power.

It remains to be asked if and when such new rulers may be deposed from their power or even be killed. Here Grotius firstly points out that where the new ruler has assumed his power due to an unjust war, the Right of War remains applicable.[213] Therefore the new ruler may be treated like any other enemy to the extent that he may even be killed. Furthermore, there is a right of self-defence if this is supported by the authority of the true holder of the civil power within a state.[214]

Apart from these exceptions, Grotius regards it as inadmissible to depose the usurper or to engage in active resistance against him.[215] In any case Grotius believes it possible that the true holder of power prefers the maintenance of peace to dangerous and bloody uproar. At least it is uncertain whether the legitimate holder of power wishes any extreme measures to be taken; the decisive criterion is then what a true government, were it in place, would require. In such cases a decision has to be taken either in favour of peace or in favour of freedom, the latter being the riskier choice. Such decisions must not be left to individuals; the choice is for the entire people to make.[216] Only if there is a high probability that the usurper can be removed, may respective actions be taken; otherwise, where it is doubtful what the chances of any active resistance against the illegitimate holder of

211 Cf. ibid., I.IV.xv.1.
212 Cf. ibid., I.IV.xv.2.
213 Cf. ibid., I.IV.xvi.
214 Cf. ibid., I.IV.xviii.
215 Cf. ibid., I.IV.xix.1.
216 Cf. ibid., I.IV.xix.2.

power are, the preference of doubt should be given in favour of peace and of a provisional acceptance of the illegitimate rule.[217] According to Grotius, it is still possible that God himself mandates individuals to enforce his judgement upon rulers.[218]

VI. Conclusion

Grotius' views on Human Right and on the nature of the state, his opinions on the character of sovereignty, and his ideas regarding the relationship between the state and its citizens lead us to conclude that there are two main features that are relevant for our further examination of his theology of international law.

States are a merely human establishment, although they rest on the basis of human society as part of the natural order. Consequently, they lack a divine quality in substance. It is for human beings to decide whether they want to establish a state, while there is in principle no divine commandment or any natural necessity for a people to organise itself within the framework of a state. The establishment of states is undertaken for the benefit of human beings. However, God approves of the human establishment of states: though God does not provide for states in the creational order, he presupposes states in the Law of the Gospel. The social appetite of human beings is the main incentive to establish a state; the main purpose of human beings in establishing a state is the common good of the citizens, including the protection of the citizens against external dangers, the maintenance of internal peace and order, and other benefits; yet, again, such benefits are benefits for human beings.

There is no divine appointment or commissioning of the temporal ruler; the state is not a sacred institution. However, God approves of the establishment of the state, but leaves the human quality of its establishment unchanged. Nevertheless, Natural Right and Arbitrary Divine Right do take account of the established state. Both categories of Right affect the political life within the state by governing the conduct of any political agent, rulers and ruled alike.

The second important feature of Grotius' theory of the state and of sovereignty is the general idea that all citizens, as well as all individuals engaging in ruling, governing, and administering the state, are in principle bound by the same categories of superior Right. Any human being, be it in

217 Cf. ibid., I.IV.xix.3. on the consequences see Tadashi, "State and Governing Power", p. 143.

218 Cf. IBP, I.IV.xix.4.

his capacity as ruler, lawmaker, civil servant, citizen, or mere member of mankind, is bound by Natural Right and Arbitrary Divine Right before and after the establishment of a state. Though the establishment of a state leaves the principles of Divine Right untouched, there are yet additional consequences from Natural Right and Arbitrary Divine Right due to the establishment of a state. These additional consequences mainly affect the application of Natural Right and Arbitrary Divine Right within a state, and differ in accordance with the individual position of human beings as rulers or citizens: due to Natural Right as well as Arbitrary Divine Right there is an additional duty of the ruler to foster the common good in his capacity to rule, which is a consequence of the establishment of the state and the conferment of the right to govern the state upon him. Likewise, Natural Right and Arbitrary Divine Right both impose an additional duty of obedience on the ruler's subjects. This duty depends on the respective positions of human beings, not only as human beings in the universal human society, but also as citizens and rulers of the state.

Still, one has to ask whether Christianity makes any difference in relation to Human Right in general and the establishment of political authority within Christian states in particular. If the state really is a human foundation, it needs to be asked where Arbitrary Divine Right comes into play. It seems that Grotius' system here entails a distinction between two different levels, firstly the individual level of the single human being acting within the framework of a state, and secondly the more general level of the commonwealth of a state as a whole.

On the individual level, every Christian is bound by the Law of the Gospel. Grotius explicitly conceives the prescriptions of the Gospel as law; it is in his opinion undoubtedly binding for any Christian in any and all of his doings, as well as in what he leaves undone. Therefore, we cannot distinguish between a Christian as a mere human being on the one hand and a Christian as citizen of a state on the other: in any of his acts as citizen, a Christian will have to take the Law of the Gospel into account. In relation to his position as subject, the Christian citizen's faith will have an impact mainly upon his duty of obedience towards the ruler. As we have seen, Grotius does not regard a Christian citizen only to be bound by the same degree of obedience to superiors as anyone else, but by an even greater degree. Thus, the Christian subject will, for example, abstain from active resistance against the government even in those cases in which resistance would be permissible for citizens under Natural Right. A Christian citizen hence will only exercise the limited passive resistance that has been allowed by Christ or perhaps even refrain from exercising any resistance at all and instead resort to patient suffering. Likewise, a Christian ruler will feel bound by the Law of the Gospel only to impose such human laws which are not contrary to the Gospel. Thus Christianity will make a difference regarding states, first and foremost on the individual level, by forming a specific Christian bond amongst the citizens as well as amongst those Christians who engage in the business of government.

On the more general level we find the distinctive feature of a Christian state primarily in the pursuit of the common good. This opens up the way for additional questions: Firstly, what is the common good to be pursued by a Christian state in contrast to another state? And secondly, what is a "Christian state" in contrast to a "non-Christian state"?

In order to answer the first question it is helpful to recall that Grotius includes within the common good to be pursued by a state the requirement to strive for compliance with God's wishes in order to please God. How can God be pleased by citizens? From what we have learned about Grotius' views on the relationship between Natural Religion and Christianity we can conclude that a Christian would not give an answer that is entirely different from the answer that a non-Christian person would give; yet, Grotius would expect the Christian's answer to be more detailed: a Christian has a particular understanding of what is necessary in order to gain eternal salvation, while a non-Christian lacks this perspective. The Christian citizen is assisted by Gospel Law in his assessment of alternative ways of conduct; he has the benefit of a rather specific and detailed code of behaviour in the Law of the Gospel, whereas a non-Christian would solely have to rely on the more difficult method of rational reasoning, producing rather vague directives for right conduct. Therefore, what is regarded as common good by a Christian will correspondingly deviate from what is conceived as common good by a non-Christian, certainly in terms of precision, but probably in terms of content as well.

This still leaves open the second question of what can be called a Christian state in the Grotian sense. Obviously, a certain amount of Christians may live in states which cannot be called Christian at all. This already becomes clear from Grotius' favourite references to the early stage of Christianity[219], when – as he thinks – the memory of the teaching of Christ was still fresh, but the state in which Christians lived – the Roman Empire – could not in earnest be called Christian yet. It will therefore be insufficient just to count the numbers of Christians in order to determine the religious determination of the state. The decisive factor will be the religious conviction of the ruler: according to the Grotian concept it is for the holder of the sovereign power to ensure that the state is striving for the common good; therefore it is also for him to determine what is necessary in order to reach the common good. Consequently, it is the ruler's responsibility to rule which religion is to be exercised publicly within the state. The ruler will be obliged

219 On Grotius' fondness for ancient sources cf. G. H. M. Posthumus Meyjes, "Hugo Grotius as an Irenicist", in: The Grotius Committee of the Royal Netherlands Academy of Arts and Sciences (eds.), *The World of Hugo Grotius (1683-1645)*pp. 48 et seq.

to adopt the Christian religion as official religion if he is personally bound by the Law of the Gospel, i.e. his choice may in that case be narrowed down to one religion that may be adopted legally. Accordingly, the adjective "Christian" is only to be used with respect to a state whose holder of the sovereign power is Christian. A state is a Christian state if the Law of the Gospel takes a supreme position. Once a state has become a Christian state, the ruler may not de-Christianise it by legislating idolatry. *Vice versa,* a state is a non-Christian state if the holder of the sovereign power has either accepted a non-Christian religion or accepts no religion at all.

The Grotian concept thus mediates between the traditional Christian concept of an individually binding system of Divine and Human Right applying to rulers and subjects as individuals on the one hand and the modern view of states as geographically defined entities as exclusive legal subjects of the modern system of public international law on the other. However, Grotius puts a stronger emphasis on the autonomous role of human beings in the establishment of states and of the ruler's authority, as well as in devising constitutional arrangements which meet the needs of the situation of any particular people.

Similar parallels and differences can be found in comparing Grotius' concept of Human Right and human rule with that of classic Islamic jurisprudence. Like the medieval Christian jurisprudence and also like Grotius, the Islamic tradition distinguished between the state and the rule of the Islamic community and those of unbelievers according to the separation between the realm of Islam and the realm of war[220]: like the Christian tradition Islamic jurisprudence ties human acts of the ruler directly to divine will, whereas Grotius' concept allows for a wider discretion of the ruler as individual in how to implement the divine will in the world and how the common good of a people is to be sought.

A main difference between Grotius' views on Human Right and human rule and modern liberal theories is Grotius' indifference to the internal organisation of states. While liberal theorists such as John Rawls define circles of states in accordance with their internal constitutional arrangements, e.g. their consultation procedures in their internal legislation, Grotius considers, in principle, all alternatives of constitutional arrangements as equal in their moral value. Grotius distinguishes between different circles of states only according to the sets of Divine Right that apply to rulers and subjects, so that a distinction can be drawn between Christian and non-Christian states, but not according to their respective internal organisation.

In its consequences Grotius' perception of a state as Christian or non-Christian will have implications not only for the laws that a state adopts, but also for its conduct in its international relations. This we shall see in the

220 Cf. C. A. Stumpf, "Völkerrecht unter Kreuz und Halbmond", pp. 85, 100.

following chapters, which are devoted to two different aspects of Grotius' views on international relations, the territorial dimension of International Right and the function of war as a judicial process between states.

Chapter 4

Proprietary Rights

I. Introduction

Following the general thesis that Grotius presents a theology of international law which centres around the individual as morally responsible agent in the international arena, it is now time to analyse the relation between the individual and things by examining Grotius' perception of proprietary rights. Under this rubric we will turn to the institution of property in Grotius' legal system, as well as to territorial matters.

Before we embark on our examination we need to recall the traditional Christian view of proprietary rights. Proprietary rights and territorial matters only played a rather marginal role in early Christian ethics. This may be explained by the lack of wealth of the members of the early Christian communities on the one hand, and by the fact of their relative quantitative irrelevance in their political environment on the other. When these conditions changed, and Christian ethics dealt with the matter of proprietary rights more thoroughly, the institution of proprietary rights was more or less accepted as a necessary evil in the post-lapsarian world.[1] Thus, even if private ownership is legitimate it still should be used for the common benefit. As to the legal principles governing proprietary rights, the early Christian rulers had no reason to deviate from the traditional Roman legal concepts of ownership with their focus on a balance of strength between the legal agents and on an equitable shape of respective rights and obligations.

As to matters of territory and the territorial dimension of rule, there had been no reason for the Christian tradition to treat them differently from conventional "private" property rights.[2] Yet even when territorial matters became increasingly relevant following the settlement of European peoples after the great migration of Germanic tribes, the territorial right of rule was initially developed along the line of the existing principles of proprietary

1 Cf. O. M. T. O'Donovan, "Christianity and Territorial Right". in: A. Buchanan, M. Moore (eds.), *States, Nations, and Borders: The Ethics of Making Boundaries*, pp. 127 et seq.

2 Cf. J. A. Brundage, *Medieval Canon Law*, pp. 80, 105 et seq.

rights. Even when a distinct right of territorial domination emerged in the first centuries after the beginning of the second millennium, this right still was defined in analogy to the categories of proprietary rights.[3] Up to the end of the Middle Ages, in particular in the 14th century, authority over land was mainly viewed in analogy to property rights in the strict sense of the term, i.e. as title to a certain piece of land, rather than as an authority over the place a nation dwells in. However, from the end of the Middle Ages onwards there emerged the idea that rule could also have a territorial dimension reaching beyond the mere ownership of the land on which the people to which authority pertained settled.[4] However, specific legal categories to characterise this territorial dimension of authority as something different than property rights in the strict sense only developed subsequently. In any case, a new terminology had not yet been fully developed by the time Grotius wrote his treatises on International Right.

Hence, while territorial matters had no great significance for the "homeless" Christians dispersed in the early communities around the Mediterranean Sea, who took greater interest in reflecting on the transcendent home of eternal salvation than in defining an earthly territory of their own, this attitude changed when Christianity assumed the status of an official religion of the Roman Empire. However, this resulted in an identification of the "Christian" territory with the reaches of the Roman Empire itself. Then a shift occurred with the European movement of expansion to lands overseas. The Old Testament concept of a land promised by God to his people was refined by medieval theologians: just as God had promised in the Old Testament his Jewish people the land of Israel, he had promised the Christians as his new people the world in its entirety with the advent of Christ on earth. Consequently, infidels could not rightfully hold dominion over any land. This theory was, however, sternly refuted by the moral theologians of the School of Salamanca, who argued that belief itself was no pre-requisite for any rightful exercise of dominion or authority.[5]

If we compare the Christian perception of proprietary rights with its Islamic counterpart, we may note various parallels. According to early Islamic

---

3 Cf. O. M. T. O'Donovan, "Christianity and Territorial Right", in: A. Buchanan, M. Moore (eds.), *States, Nations, and Borders: The Ethics of Making Boundaries*, pp. 136 et seq.

4 Cf. H. G. Walther, *Imperiales Königtum, Konziliarismus und Volkssouveränität: Studien zu den Grenzen des mittelalterlichen Souveränitätsgedankens*, pp. 261 et seq.; F. A. von der Heydte, *Die Geburtsstunde des souveränen Staates: Ein Beitrag zur Geschichte des Völkerrechts, der allgemeinen Staatslehre und des politischen Denkens*, pp. 20 et seq.

5 Cf. H. F. Köck, *Der Beitrag der Schule von Salamanca zur Entwicklung der Lehre von den Grundrechten*, pp. 112 et seq.

jurisprudence, all things belong to God as creator of everything.[6] Thus, every property belongs to God. Yet, God grants man a right of possession. In classic Islamic legal theory there arose, however, a controversy over whether God had granted mankind this right collectively, or whether he had left the mode of distribution to man.[7] The latter view finally prevailed, and thus Islamic law soon acknowledged the transfer of individual property rights and the right of inheritance between individuals with certain qualifications. However, we may note here that a great extent of the Islamic legal theory's attention to proprietary rights concentrates on the rightful use of spoils gained through wars against unbelievers.[8]

The traditional position of the Islamic law of nations in relation to matters of territory equals the respective approach by early Christianity. In this respect we have to consider that the environment in which Islam and its jurisprudence emerged was characterised by the huge wastelands of the Arabian deserts, which was thinly populated by Nomads, whereas virtually the entire population resided in a few oases. Thus, it took centuries before a geographical delimitation of territories became necessary. This is, however, not to say that Islamic jurisprudence was completely indifferent to territorial matters: the important distinction between the realm of Islam and the realm of war gained territorial implications quite early, even though the religious character of effective rule by believers or unbelievers remained the decisive criterion for defining the borderline between the two realms.[9] The territorial notion of property rights increased immensely in the interest of Islamic jurisprudence in the course of the 20th century, when matters of natural resources such as oil, gas, and water became relevant for the Arab countries' economies.

If we compare these religious traditions of proprietary rights with the contemporary outlook taken on these issues by the "Western" perception of public international law, we are bound to note that the respective proprietary institutions are now firmly established beyond doubt. The shift from religious traditions of public international law to secular traditions goes hand in hand with the substitution of personal structures of rule by geographically

---

6 Cf. K. A El Fadl, "The Unbounded Law of God and Territorial Boundaries", in A. Buchanan, M. Moore (eds.), *States, Nations, and Borders: The Ethics of Making Boundaries*, pp. 214 et seq.

7 Khadduri, *The Islamic Conception of Justice*, pp. 138, 217 et seq.

8 Khadduri, *The Islamic Law of Nations: Shaybani's Siyar*, pp. 53 et seq.

9 Cf. C. A. Stumpf, "Völkerrecht unter Kreuz und Halbmond: Muhammad al-Shaybani und Hugo Grotius als Exponenten religiöser Völkerrechtstradition", *Archiv des Völkerrechts*, 41 (2003/1), pp. 86 et seq.

defined territorial states in the course of the 17th and 18th centuries.[10] This increasing significance of geographical borders finally resulted in an inclusion of a territorial dimension in the definition of statehood. Most significantly, the German legal scholar Georg Jellinek developed in the beginning of the 20th century the doctrine of the three elements of statehood: a state thus requires a people of its own, a government structure of its own, and a territory of its own.[11]

While it is today widely acknowledged that many state borders have been drawn quite arbitrarily, the territorial integrity of states is now a generally accepted principle of public international law. At the same time, matters of proprietary rights are still controversially discussed in legal practice; the problem of private property as fundamental human right and the related problem of the admissibility of an expropriation of private owners, as well as the demand for a new economic world order, may suffice here as examples for the contemporary debate.[12] For the modern theoretical concepts underlying proprietary rights in modern public international law we may once more refer to the concept brought forward by John Rawls in his theory of international law[13]: According to John Rawls, the point of the institution of property is that, unless a definite agent is given responsibility for maintaining an asset and bears the loss if he fails to do so, that asset tends to deteriorate, and the same is true for a people's territory. Furthermore, Rawls argues that it does not follow from the fact that boundaries are historically arbitrary that their role in his concept of the Law of Peoples cannot be justified: there must be borders of some kind, and any inequalities of power and wealth have to be remedied by a duty of assistance of the powerful and wealthy for the benefit of the weak and poor.

Grotius approaches the issue of proprietary rights in the context of his treatment of the just reasons for war in *De Iure Belli ac Pacis*, as well as in *De Iure Praedae Commentarius* and in his textbook on the jurisprudence of Holland, *Inleiding tot de Hollandsche Rechts-geleertheyd*. In the following we will see that his understanding of proprietary rights presents a turning point from the Christian tradition to the modern concept of property and territories. While Grotius is certainly firmly rooted in the Christian tradition, he is nonetheless already paving the way for a modern understanding of the institution of property and state territories. We will endeavour to show this

---

10 Cf. C. A. Stumpf, P. R. Melot de Beauregard, "Die Entwicklung der staatlichen Souveränität im Spiegel der kanonistischen Völkerrechtslehre", *Der Staat*, 42 (2003), pp. 459 et seq.

11 Cf. G. Jellinek, *Allgemeine Staatslehre*, p. 396 et seq.; see also Article 1 of the Montevideo Convention on Rights and Duties of States dated 26 December 1933.

12 Cf. R. Dolzer, "Wirtschaft und Kultur im Völkerrecht", in W. Graf Vitzthum (ed.), *Völkerrecht*, pp. 493 et seq.

13 J. Rawls, *The Law of Peoples*, pp. 38–39.

through an examination of the terminology, the origin and function of proprietary rights, the acquisition and termination of proprietary rights, and finally the limitations of proprietary rights.

II. Categories of Proprietary Rights

The two distinct rights that Grotius is concerned with when dealing with the institution of proprietary rights in general and rights relating to territories in particular are authority (*imperium*) and dominion (*dominium*). It should be noted, however, that the English terms "proprietary right" and "property right" may be misleading in this context and hence require some explanation as regards Grotius' concept of territorial authority: though Grotius quite often deals with both the *imperium* as well as the *dominium* at the same time when discussing proprietary rights, only the latter is to be conceived as a property right in the strict sense as a right of private ownership, while the former pertains to those rights that derive from the power of the ruler in relation to land which is inhabited by the people under his rule. Notwithstanding this, Grotius frequently applies a terminology which is peculiar to property rights to authority, and with respect to this it should be justified to refer to the territorial authority as property right in the wider sense. Hence, in the following the term "property right" will be used for rights *in rem*, denoting in particular the dominion, while the term "proprietary right" is used as the more general term, which is roughly equivalent to what Grotius calls *suum* or *nostrum*, and contains property rights as rights *in rem* as well as rights *in actus aliquos*, including, *inter alia*, authority.

According to Grotius, there are two kinds of rights which can be obtained by way of occupation, which he regards as the most natural and original way of assuming proprietary rights: authority on the one hand and dominion on the other, as far as the latter can be distinguished from the former.[14] If this statement is taken at face value, authority appears to be the proprietary right which a ruler has over the territory of his rule, while dominion seems to be a proprietary right in a stricter and narrower sense as the property right of the individual private owner. It might then seem that in Grotius' opinion the difference between authority and dominion is rather one of quantity than of quality. Additional support for this assumption can be derived from the fact that Grotius claims that dominion may be included in authority. Authority and dominion may, according to Grotius, be combined; the latter is obviously sometimes included in – or, perhaps better, attached to – the former. This

14 Cf. IBP, II.III.iv.1.

would indicate that Grotius altogether follows the conventional method of addressing territorial rights to rule in terms of the right of ownership.

Yet, such an interpretation is not entirely satisfactory as an explanation for the relationship between authority and dominion in Grotius' exposition. By introducing the distinction between authority and dominion Grotius rather seems to acknowledge a conventional understanding of authority and dominion as major and minor proprietary rights, without, however, showing much of an inclination towards aligning himself to this tradition. Moreover, from the fact that authority and dominion sometimes go together, we may also conclude that at other times they do not. From this we may infer that there is also a difference between these two terms which cannot sufficiently be expressed by employing the language of quantity.

Authority then has a twofold dimension in Grotius' concept: Primarily, authority relates to human beings as authority to rule over a people; human beings can even be its exclusive object, as is the case with migrating peoples that are moving to a new habitation. Only secondarily does authority also relate to land as the territory of a state.

This becomes clear when Grotius points out the difference between authority and dominion as regards their respective acquisition: although it is possible to obtain authority as well as dominion by one action, dominion can be transferred to citizens and foreigners alike, while authority always remains with the one person or institution that holds the right to rule. From this it is clear that authority is not simply a greater right in a quantitative sense than dominion, but also of a qualitative difference: authority is primarily a right of the ruler in relation to his subjects, and in a secondary sense it is also a right of the ruler in relation to the state and to the citizens. This is confirmed by Grotius' claim that the ruler's authority includes an eminent faculty (*ius eminens*) with respect to the dominion held by his subjects.[15] As the sovereign ruler holds absolute power over his subjects, he also holds absolute power over their property rights. This absolute power over property rights derives from the ruler's eminent faculty. Though there can be original acquisition of dominion by way of occupation, the possibility of original acquisition of dominion can be excluded by the state that has authority over things, for example in order to control the settlement of newly acquired land: a settlement by private individuals on wasteland may be followed by a grant of the respective property right to such land by the ruler. Consequently a settler will not obtain a property right to land by an act of original acquisition through occupation, but only by way of transfer from the ruler. This may become relevant for the state's right to assert its sovereignty over such land, because otherwise the state would not be in the position to

15 Cf. ibid., I.I.vi

control settlement of the land, and would be kept from intervening if settlers decided to direct their allegiance to another ruler.

Yet, even though authority then is the "greater" right than dominion, dominion still can exist without there being a state. In this case the holder of dominion may, under principles yet to be outlined, exclude other parties from using the thing to which this dominion relates. However, as soon as there is an established ruler with territorial authority over the land in question, this authority has precedence over the dominion, as it is the greater right that includes the eminent faculty.

Authority in its territorial aspect can thus be defined as a right of the ruler over a certain territory which in principle excludes other sovereign states to exercise any rights of their own over the territory in question. This resembles very much the modern understanding of the territorial integrity of sovereign states, as a generally accepted principle of public international law, without however implying that other states or potentially even individuals are excluded from enforcing the overarching principles of Natural Right or of Arbitrary Divine Right even in the territory of other states. At the same time Grotius still comes close to the classic understanding of territorial authority in terms of property rights in presenting the territorial aspect of authority as a right of the ruler over a territory in the public domain in the sense of an equivalent to the dominion as property right in the private domain.[16]

III. Origin and Function of Proprietary Rights

We will now turn to an analysis of the nature of proprietary rights in his system of Right. For this we first have to ask for the origin of proprietary rights as conceived by Grotius, before we examine the function he accords to them.

1. Origin of Proprietary Rights

As regards the origin of proprietary rights, Grotius follows the traditional stance of the Christian understanding of ownership, which also corresponds to the respective Islamic position in many ways. According to Grotius, God granted the right to everything to all human beings twice in the course of history: first, immediately after creation, and second, after the Great Flood.[17]

16 This can be illustrated very aptly by reference to Grotius' treatment of the institution of feudal tenure in his work on the laws of Holland. Cf. H. Grotius, *Inleiding tot de Hollandsche Rechts-geleertheyd*, II.xli. et seq.

17 Cf. IBP, II.II.ii.1

Initially, all things were held as common property, from which anyone could take what was required for maintaining oneself. This common property was not a proprietary right as right in a strictly subjective sense; rather it was a universal use that was permissible then.

Significantly, Grotius does not claim that a renewed donation of all property had been effected with the redemption of mankind in Christ. By this he obviously sets himself in a tacit contrast to some of his predecessors, in particular canonists and Roman Catholic theologians, such as Giles of Rome and his work *De ecclesiastica potestate* and James of Viterbo, whose *De regimine christiano* had prepared the soil on which Boniface VIII could plant his bull *Unam Sanctam*.[18] According to this doctrine, the coming of Christ had resulted in a complete reordering of proprietary rights, and the Church had assumed authority over all territories, to be exercised by her on behalf of Christ. Hence, the Church had been vested with the capacity to donate, transfer, and withdraw any authority over any territory in any part of the world in its absolute free discretion; this goes hand in hand with the idea that the rebirth of mankind through the redemption by Christ resulted in a re-allocation of all earthly property, and that Christ as king of kings and as lord of lords had assumed the right to all temporal property.[19] The argument was that the Church, acting through the Pope, had been entrusted with the task to act as intermediary between God and human beings in every sense, including *inter alia* the attribution of proprietary rights. In conferring the rightful dominion to temporal lords, it was therefore for the Church to determine who was worthy or unworthy of obtaining or holding dominion, the implication being, of course, that heretics and pagans were perfectly unworthy of property.

Grotius had elaborated upon such claims in *De Iurae Praedae Commentarius* and refuted them with the argument that Christ's rule was not of this world and therefore could not apply to, and in particular did not abandon, the existing order of earthly governance over territories.[20] Thus the claim of Spain and Portugal to overseas territories, which rested on a grant by the Pope, was invalid. While God had donated everything to everyone twice, the coming of Christ had had no effect on proprietary rights.

There are two important features of Grotius' theory of proprietary rights to be noted, which will return time and again as an underlying theme in his entire treatment of territories as the proprietary right of the states pertaining to their territory. The first is the idea that God's will itself does not provide or indeed support individual property rights or the appropriation of things as private property in the sense of excluding other people from the substance or

---

18 Cf. "Extravagantes communes" I. 8.1., in *Corpus Juris Canonici*.

19 Cf. Giles of Rome, *De ecclesiastica potestate*, 6 et seq.; J. Viterbo, *De regimene christiana*, 1.8.

20 Cf. H. Grotius, *De Iure Praedae Commentarius*, I., XII.

uses of the thing owned. Hence, Natural Right, under which God's donation of all things to mankind after creation had been effected, and Arbitrary Divine Right, as expressed in the subsequent donation of all things from God to all mankind after the Great Flood, only accomplish the common property of human beings to all things. Neither is the institution of single private property rights devised by Natural Right, nor are such private property rights entailed in Arbitrary Divine Right.

It remains to be asked whether the afore-described communal property right to any good granted by God to mankind is part of Natural Right or of Arbitrary Divine Right. Very likely it is both, as the communal property right had been introduced by God in creation as well as in acts of will subsequent to creation. Of course, Natural Right and in particular the principle of expletive justice is tied to these newly created proprietary rights, wherefore they are also subject to the protection of the legal order of justice under Natural Right. Moreover, though Arbitrary Divine Right cannot be applied to all of mankind, but only to those who have received notice of it, the communal property right is a right of the entire mankind as this donation was addressed to all, regardless of the personal applicability of Arbitrary Divine Right.

The original introduction of single property rights and their allocation to individuals had then taken place under what Grotius regards to be a tacit agreement.[21] Consequently, proprietary rights are part of Arbitrary Human Right, in particular the Human Right of Nations. However, Natural Right and Arbitrary Divine Right both acknowledge the invention of single property rights, as well as the introduction of territorial authority, to the effect that any violation of such proprietary rights results in injustice.[22] Moreover, as we shall see in due course, the holding and acquisition, and the exercise of proprietary rights are also affected and governed by certain principles of Natural Right or Arbitrary Divine Right.[23] Furthermore, even after the introduction of single property rights – and of the territorial authority of rulers to whom the same principles apply – still the ancient communal property right devised by Natural Right and Arbitrary Divine Right applies: though the introduction of single property rights under Human Right has not been excluded by the factual existence of communal property rights under Natural Right and Arbitrary Divine Right, such single property rights cannot grant the owner a position that excludes all former notions of the common property rights. We will return to this in the further course of our examination.

According to Grotius, the single property rights were introduced when human beings started to pursue various arts, for which Grotius sees the "tree

21 Cf. IBP, II.II.ii.5.

22 Cf. ibid., I.I.x.1.

23 Cf. ibid., II.III.iii., vi.

of knowledge" of the Garden of Eden as a symbol. Grotius points out two vices which had resulted in the division and distribution of the original communal property right: ambition and vanity; moreover, overall conditions had become increasingly sophisticated, so that property had to be allocated firstly to tribes, and subsequently to families; movable goods had become subject to single property rights prior to immovable goods.[24] Thus Grotius follows here the traditional negative account of the origin of single property rights: his reference to the symbol of the Garden of Eden already indicates a post-lapsarian character of proprietary rights. The introduction of single property rights thus is not only forged by the vices of ambition and vanity, but also designed as a stronghold against these vices. Arbitrary Divine Right has to take account of the fallen nature of human beings. It is designed to help preserve the human existence against the vices which may arise in the absence of property rights. Yet, the introduction of proprietary rights by the Human Right of Nations has not resulted in a complete distribution of all things and subsequent conversion of all common property in single property, but there still are some things that remain common property, some of which are not even subject to subsequent acquisition by way of occupation. These shall be dealt with later in greater detail.

It is interesting to note the different outlook Grotius takes in relation to the origin of private property rights in comparison in particular to Thomas Aquinas: while Grotius aligns the development of private property rights to the fallibility of human nature, but nevertheless regards this development as legitimate in the light of a preservation of order in a post-lapsarian society, Thomas Aquinas had held the establishment of proprietary rights to be legitimate because of the authority conferred on mankind in creation to take care of and distribute all goods on earth.[25] Thus, in establishing property rights, man reinforces and specifies his natural dominion over earthly goods. Compared to this positive account of property rights, Grotius' explanation of the origin of proprietary rights rather presents an excuse than a justification. The fact that human beings do not necessarily have to regulate their possessions by the invention of single property rights is illustrated by Grotius' reference to the example of the native people of America, who had not felt the necessity of introducing proprietary rights because of the simplicity of their living conditions. Likewise, certain Christian communities have abstained from allocating proprietary rights because they share everything amongst their members in strict penitence and because they are motivated by a strong mutual love.

Overall, in his views on the origin of proprietary rights Grotius follows a traditional Christian approach, which at the same time finds a parallel in

---

24 Cf. ibid., II.II.ii.2 et seq.

25 Thomas Aquinas, *Summa Theologica*, 2a2ae 66 et seq.

classic Islamic legal theory: proprietary rights are rather a necessary evil than a blessing for mankind. Nevertheless, Grotius acknowledges the positive effects of the introduction of proprietary rights as an order which at least in principle is designed to ensure peace within human society in relation to the use of assets. Furthermore, Grotius probably would also subscribe to the idea brought forward by John Rawls, who argues that the institution of property is to prevent assets from deteriorating due to a lack of individual responsibility.[26] However, in the following we shall see that Grotius still endorses a communal responsibility of the holder of single proprietary rights under both Natural Right and Arbitrary Divine Right.

2. Function of Proprietary Rights

From Grotius' theory of the origin of proprietary rights as well as from his general concepts of Natural Right and Arbitrary Divine Right we may infer that proprietary rights, whether dominion or territorial authority, are not ends in themselves. In order to establish rightful ownership or territorial authority, and in order to transform something from the prior state of common property to the subsequent state of individual property a legitimate purpose is needed. Such a rightful purpose must be something beyond the mere will of holding or acquiring any object. This bears relevance, of course, for colonial enterprises, as traditionally the supposed lack of sustainable use of land had served as justification for the European expansion to territories overseas.

As we shall see later in greater detail, it is impossible for Grotius to appropriate land – in particular dominion over land – without any legitimate intention to use it for some rightful purpose. Nevertheless, the scope of rightful purposes in Grotius' concept may be relatively broad: he does not appear to question any extension of trade enterprises just for the purpose of making individual gains. Consequently, Grotius does not display any concern in relation to the European settlement activities in North America, as he believes the land to have been waste or at least not to have been used sustainably by the indigenous peoples for themselves.

There are yet further observations to be made in this context. Certainly, Grotius claims that foreigners who wish to settle in wastelands must be granted permission to do so, although he does not explicitly state that authority has to be granted to them.[27] Moreover, we may take it that it is more an obligation of the state to grant this permission than a right of the settlers to have this permission granted to them, as Grotius does not contend

26 Cf. J. Rawls, *The Law of Peoples*, pp. 8, 39 et seq.
27 Cf. IBP, II.II.xii.

a positive subjective right under the Human Right of Nations to this effect. Yet, in any case there is no claim for settlers to obtain authority over any wasteland over which authority has already been acquired by someone else. Moreover, it may be suggested that in the granting of dominion the principles of attributive justice have to be observed, which leaves the holder of authority granting such dominion relatively far-reaching discretion as to the question to whom it is to be granted. Of course, this discretion may be narrowed down in the case of existential needs, but that qualification was hardly ever relevant in the case of colonial conquests.

From this account it may be questioned if Richard Tuck is correct in interpreting Grotius' reference to Seneca's quotation according to which it is no "Favour, properly so called, to permit a Man to light a Fire by ours" in the sense that "[t]here is no ownership in things which are of no use to their owners, and therefore other people have a *perfect* right to occupy them".[28] For his thesis Tuck offers the following explanation: "Drawing in Gentili, though characteristically without acknowledgment, Grotius argued (II. 2. 17) that it followed from this that 'if there be any waste or barren Land within our Dominions, that also is to be given to Strangers, at their Request, or may be lawfully possessed by them, because whatever remains uncultivated, is not to be esteemed a Property, only so far as concerns Jurisdiction [*imperium*], which always continues the Right of the ancient People'".[29]

What Tuck is establishing here, yet possibly without considering the particular context in which Grotius develops his arguments, is an idealist relationship between Grotius on the one hand and Boniface VIII on the other, stating that both had endeavoured to justify the European colonial powers' conquest of those wastelands which had not been used by the native population. However, this is not what Grotius said, nor is it probably what he actually had in mind when explaining his thoughts on the occupation of proprietary rights.

Firstly, the quotation of Seneca to which Tuck refers is used by Grotius in the context of his elaboration upon the limitation of proprietary rights. Surely, fire is not a "thing" that can be appropriated according to Grotius anyway. Thus, Seneca's remark is more important here for Tuck than for Grotius. Secondly, contrary to what Tuck reads in Grotius, Grotius' treatment merely allows for the harmless use of private property – dominion – by anyone, without it automatically becoming a suitable object for the appropriation by others. That the discretion of the state holding authority regarding the decision to grant dominion may be narrowed down because of the principles of attributive justice is to be acknowledged; however, from this

---

28 Cf. ibid., II.II.xi.

29 Cf. R. Tuck, *The Rights of War and Peace: Political Thought and the International Order from Grotius to Kant*, p. 105.

we can only infer an obligation of the state to adequately consider a request for granting dominion, but not a right of the foreign settlers to automatically occupy wasteland as it pleases them. That unused property may turn into relinquished property and therefore become no one's property which is again susceptible of appropriation by others, is again a different matter and not relevant in this context, as no one had claimed that the wastelands on which the colonial settlements were undertaken had been relinquished by former owners. Yet, such a relinquishment of proprietary rights occurs according to its own principles, and Grotius would probably not argue, as Tuck seems to imply with his reference to the native American Indians, that territorial authority over any land which is presently not used by the current holder of the territorial authority may automatically be assumed by anyone else.

Furthermore, Tuck's assertion that Grotius' opinion on this subject was specifically designed to provide the legal grounds for the European colonial activities, probably goes a bit too far: After having described the Northern American activities of the Dutch at Grotius' time, Tuck claims: "These recent activities focused Grotius's attention on the implications of his general theory of property for the occupation and ownership of uncultivated land"[30]. Yet, Tuck does not produce vindicable evidence for his thesis. In particular, he does not prove that Grotius here thought more of contemporary colonial endeavours than of Mongolian nomads moving through Central Asian deserts. The only hint remarked by Tuck in this respect is Grotius' use of the word "America" when stating that some native people were still able to do without private property rights. What Tuck appears to miss in his compilation of quotations from Grotius' works is the distinction between the dominion as private property right and the territorial authority as proprietary right in a broader sense, the latter of which Tuck mistakenly believes Grotius to have ruled out altogether. While Grotius certainly supports the legitimacy of Europeans occupying former wasteland overseas for the purpose of cultivating and acquiring dominion over it, he is not going so far as to allow for an acquisition of territorial authority over unused territories. Hence, Europeans could have claimed dominion through their occupation of wastelands in North America; however, they could not have obtained territorial authority over it.

Thus, the dominion as well as the authority of relinquished things may be acquired by anyone. Proprietary rights are designed to fulfil a certain purpose, they are not ends in themselves. However, the purpose of dominion has to be distinguished from the purpose of authority. There may be land which is unused and not subject to dominion; such land may be occupied, by which dominion over it may be acquired. However, this is not to say that authority over such land may be acquired as well. Authority to a certain piece

30 Cf. ibid., p. 104 et seq.

of land may be held on legitimate grounds, even if there is no dominion over it or at least if dominion over it is not supported by any specific purpose.

IV. Acquisition and Termination of Proprietary Rights

Grotius' comments on the acquisition and termination of proprietary rights may be viewed primarily as a discussion of rather technical aspects of property law. Nevertheless, we shall see that these comments also reveal his perception of proprietary rights in their function as determining individual moral responsibility. As such they are not only of relevance from a moral-theological perspective, but still have an additional impact on the modern system of public international right.

1. Acquisition of Proprietary Rights

Grotius deals with two different ways of acquiring proprietary rights, along the lines of classical Roman property law[31]: proprietary rights can either be acquired originally, by which the respective proprietary right comes into existence, or derivatively, by way of transfer of an already existing proprietary right.

1.1. Original Acquisition of Proprietary Rights

In relation to Grotius' remarks on the original acquisition of proprietary rights, we must note that his idea of proprietary right focuses on the substance of the property concerned, and less on its precise definition, e.g. by drawing exact borderlines to the proprietary rights of others. Consequently, Grotius was probably not as keen on positive documentation of the content of the proprietary rights as some of his successors had been.[32] This is perhaps also significant of Grotius' age, where borders were not regarded as fixed as they had been later, and where the delimitation of countries was less undertaken by defining geographical borderlines, but still on the basis of personal allegiance of the individual to his people.

There are two different ways of original acquisition: first, original acquisition had taken place by way of division, when human society was

---

31 M. Kaser, *Römisches Privatrecht*, pp. 113 et seq.

32 Cf. Nabulsi, *Tradition of War: Occupation, Resistance, and the Law*, pp. 167 et seq.

established – this is the tacit agreement already mentioned earlier.[33] With this tacit agreement, resolved sometime in the early ages of mankind when human society was formed, proprietary rights were introduced, and though not everything had yet been appropriated, most things at least became susceptible of appropriation.

Now that this division has taken place, original acquisition of territorial authority as well as of dominion can only be effected by way of occupation. New rights of ownership can still be created, but not new property.[34] Thus, by the creation of limited new rights, certain rights which are already entailed in the older rights are identified and specified in the subject as well as in the object to which they relate. Hence, all pieces of land had already been in existence since the moment of creation and were from the moment of God's donation to mankind subject to the ancient communal property right. By the occupation of a limited piece of land, it becomes specified as an object of a single proprietary right, dominion or territorial authority. The nation occupying such piece of land becomes the subject of this proprietary right. Nonetheless, certain aspects of the ancient communal property right still persist.[35]

1.1.1. Prerequisites of Occupation

Grotius conceives of a number of prerequisites that are necessary in order to accomplish the acquisition of proprietary rights through occupation. There are personal prerequisites with respect to the person for acquiring proprietary rights, as well as material prerequisites as regards the object to be appropriated.

According to Natural Right, one cannot seize things unless one is capable of rational thinking. Yet, the Right of Nations also allows minors and mentally disabled persons to acquire and hold proprietary rights. As Natural Right is the Right of reason, it seems only logical to presume that primarily only those human beings who are actually rational creatures participate in legal discourse. Yet, Natural Right does not vest human beings with rights in the classical subjective sense, but only explicitly commands or prohibits, and grants licences by being silent about certain matters. Thus, Natural Right does not prevent human beings incapable of rational reasoning from holding proprietary rights; it is simply not concerned with their legal position as regards proprietary rights, but leaves such issues open for regulation under Arbitrary Divine Right and Human Right. The Right of Nations as part of Human Right can support such minors and mentally disabled people as

33 Cf. IBP, II.III.i.

34 Cf. ibid., II.III.ii.

35 Cf. ibid., II.III.i.; removal of false opinions and clarifications in II.III.ii, iii.

members of the human race, meaning that their fellow human beings may act on their behalf. Therefore, the Human Right of Nations in this context merely devises something in addition to Natural Right, but not against it. However, while human beings incapable of rational reasoning are able to hold proprietary rights under the Right of Nations, they are not in the position to exercise them: in contrast to the mere holding of proprietary rights, the exercise of proprietary rights in the sense of acquiring, transferring, and relinquishing them again requires the use of rational reasoning, of which such people are incapable. Such acts could not be performed against Natural Right and therefore Grotius is not willing to allow the Right of Nations to accord such exercise of proprietary rights to minors and mentally disabled people.[36]

1.1.2. Material Prerequisites

There are also a number of material prerequisites that impose limitations upon what can be appropriated in a factual way. The most important principle in this regard appears to be the possibility to effectively exercise such proprietary rights over the thing to be appropriated. This is relevant in particular in relation to the appropriation of territories. In modern public international law the ideas brought forward by Grotius are still influential in relation to the determination of maritime zones.[37]

Parts of the land surface will certainly qualify for appropriation. However, there are many things susceptible of appropriation without having been appropriated so far: Such things are, for example, waste and unused land, islands in the sea, wild animals, fish, and birds.[38] There are two different ways of subjecting things to single property rights: Firstly, things can be made subject to a proprietary right through occupation by society, by a single nation, or by its rulers. Typically this also results in the gaining of authority over the respective thing. Secondly, single property rights can be created by individuals, which is done through assignation rather than through occupation.[39] By such assignation the dominion may be gained derivatively. In this context, Grotius acknowledges that it is possible to occupy land in a very general manner, without parcelling and distributing it to individuals.[40] Such

36 Cf. ibid., II.III.vi.

37 Cf. G. Hafner, "Räumliche Regime und Nutzungen über die und jenseites der Staatsgrenzen", in H. Neuhold, Hummer, Schrummer (eds.), *Österreichisches Handbuch des Völkerrechts*, pp. 328 et seq.; W. Graf Vitzthum, "Raum und Umwelt im Völkerrecht", in W. Graf Vitzthum (ed.), *Völkerrecht*, pp. 410 et seq.

38 Cf. IBP, II.II.iv.

39 Cf. ibid., II.III.iv.

40 Cf. ibid., II.II.iv.

land is then already singled out of the common property of all of mankind, without there yet being any particular owner who holds dominion over it.

Proprietary rights to the sea and parts thereof are to be treated differently: Grotius thinks that the sea had not been covered by the afore-mentioned tacit agreement. This idea still survives in the modern law of the seas, for example, in the contemporary concept of the deep seabed as common heritage of mankind.[41] Yet, according to Grotius, the sea is not susceptible of appropriation due to a natural reason: it cannot be limited.[42] Though this cannot prevent the appropriation of coastlines or even of coastal waters, as far as these can be occupied effectively, the high seas will have to remain common property. Intending to align himself with the Roman-Christian legal tradition, Grotius here points out that an appropriation of the sea or parts thereof had not been admitted under the Right of Nations from early ages until the time of Justinian; there had not even been a claim to appropriate partial rights with respect to single uses of the sea, such as fishing.[43] Roman law also had claimed that the sea is common to all and not the sole property of the Roman citizens. Moreover, Roman lawyers, according to Grotius, had distinguished clearly between the public property of the Roman people and property that was common to all, probably including non-Romans. In denying the susceptibility of the sea of appropriation Grotius certainly pursues an aim which has not lost any of its relevance until today: the sea is considered by Grotius as well as by lawyers today as the most important medium for communication between nations as well as a source for a variety of natural resources: in claiming the "freedom of the sea" and in conferring to it the status of common heritage of mankind, modern public international law thus still seeks to preserve open access to the sea.[44]

Nonetheless, Grotius explicitly accepts that certain parts of the sea may be susceptible of appropriation. In such a case, the effective occupation of the sea is undertaken by the state's fleet, which then exercises control over this part of the sea; moreover, coastal water may be controlled effectively from the coast.[45] This observation regarding the effective occupation of the sea by naval means appears to be a concession of his position to the view taken by John Selden[46], who claimed that an occupation of the sea is possible by way

41 Cf. I. Brownlie, *Principles of Public International Law*, pp. 20 et seq.

42 Cf. IBP, II.II.iii.2

43 Cf. ibid., II.III.ix.

44 Cf. W. Graf Vitzthum, "Raum und Umwelt im Völkerrecht", pp. 410 et seq.

45 Cf. IBP, II.III.xiii.2.

46 J. Selden, *Mare Clausum seu De dominio maris libri duo*; cf. M. C. W. Pinto, "The New Law of the Sea and the Grotian Heritage, International Law and its Sources", in W. P. Heero (ed.), *Liber Amicorum Maarten Bos* (1989), pp. 54 et seq.; C. G. Roloefsen, "The Sources of Mare Liberum: The Contested Origins of the Doctrine of the Freedom of the

of using a fleet. Selden thus refuted Grotius' assertion brought forward in *De Mare Liberum* according to which an effective control of seas could not be possible at all. Thus, according to Selden and contrary to Grotius' opinion as expressed in *Mare Liberum,* the waters around the British Isles could be controlled effectively by the British fleet and consequently were susceptible of appropriation. The second observation regarding the effective control of the coastal waters from the coast strongly resembles the idea of subsequent maritime lawyers according to which coastal waters belong to the coastal state up to the distance which could be reached by a cannon ball fired from the shore. This 'cannon-shot'-doctrine was later to become the measure by which coastal states in many parts of the world defined their territorial sea.[47]

Therefore, one could have private property as well as public property with respect to parts of the seas in line with the principles described above under Natural Right; however, the Right of Nations could even limit the mere appropriation of parts of the sea; where such a rule of the Human Right of Nations exists, no appropriation by human beings is permissible.[48] However, such a rule of the Human Right of Nations which prohibits the appropriation of dominion does not necessarily prevent the assumption of authority over the seas or parts of the seas.[49]

The issue of proprietary rights to the sea is an extremely prominent topic of Grotius' thought on International Right; his famous treatise on the freedom of the seas, *Mare Liberum,* was devoted to issues connected herewith. While many of his other ideas have been forgotten or were re- or misinterpreted, this original idea remained influential even up to the present day. However, from a modern point of view and in particular taking into account the developments of modern maritime technology, it can be doubted whether Grotius' arguments against the non-appropriability of the sea are still convincing: as we know, at least now, the sea is not inexhaustible, for which the traffic jam on various oceans and many over-exploited fish stocks are but two examples. The fluidity of the water does not lead Grotius to deny the appropriability of more limited waters, such as ponds or rivers; therefore, using it as reason against the appropriability of the seas seems inconsistent. Moreover, the sea also has land at its bottom and thus the seabed could in any case be appropriated. Here it probably would have been more consistent for Grotius to argue with a non-appropriability of certain communal

---

Seas, International Law and its Sources", in W. P. Heero (ed.), *Liber Amicorum Maarten Bos*, pp. 143 et seq.

47 Cf. R. R. Churchill and A. V. Lowe, *The Law of the Sea*, pp. 71 et seq.

48 Cf. IBP, II.III.x.3.

49 Cf. ibid., II.III.xiii.1.

property rights. Such a concept is, for example, used in the establishment of the legal status of the sea as common heritage of mankind.

1.2. Derivative Acquisition of Proprietary Rights

Next to the original acquisition of proprietary rights there is the possibility of acquiring such rights by way of transfer from the current holder of the existing right. Such a derivative acquisition of proprietary rights is either done by way of voluntary action of transfer, by way of a law ordering the transfer, or by acts performed in the course of a just war. We may here restrict our attention to certain aspects of Grotius' exposition of this subject which still remain relevant for contemporary public international law.

According to Grotius, the transferability of a complete proprietary right is provided for by Natural Right.[50] Just as proprietary rights may be created, they may also pass to another person. The details of Grotius' comments on this subject need not interest us; they follow the lines devised by Roman law.[51] For our purposes it will suffice to focus here on the implications of Grotius' remarks on the transfer of proprietary rights for the self-determination of certain parts of a country.

In this respect it first has to be pointed out that traditionally most concepts of public international law deny single parts of a country any right to disaffiliate themselves from the rest of the country. This is true for Christian authors on the subject as well as for Islamic legal tradition: both traditions are only willing to accept the right of any community to disaffiliate itself from their previous connections in order to turn to the "right" creed, and thus, for example, become part of the *respublica Christiana* or the *dār al-Islām,* respectively. Any other disaffiliation is impermissible. The same is true for modern public international law, which displays no great sympathy for any separatist activities.[52]

In this respect Grotius overall follows the general inclination in the religious as well as the modern traditions of public international law only to accept transfers of proprietary rights which are based on the consensus of all parties involved. Thus, for example, any transfer of territorial authority has to be effected by the true holder, which can either be the ruler or the people.[53] It is then also possible to transfer parts of proprietary rights.[54] Moreover,

---

50 Cf. ibid., II.VI.i.1.

51 Cf. M. Kaser, *Römisches Privatrecht* (1992), pp. 113 et seq.

52 Cf. K. Hailbronner, "Der Staat und der Einzelne als Völkerrchtssubjekte", in W. Graf Vitzthum ed.), *Völkerrecht,* pp. 206 et seq.

53 Cf. IBP, II.VI.iii.

54 Cf. ibid., II.VI.iv–viii.

such a transfer can be effected with respect to single parts of a country, in which case consent of the relevant part is required. According to Grotius, this is because the individual parts can maintain themselves independently from the main body of the country and are connected with the rest of the country only due to their will.[55] Consequently, the entire country will not normally have the right to give away parts of the country without the consent of such parts. Likewise, the single part has not normally the right to separate itself from the rest of the country.[56] An exception is only to be made in extreme cases of need, when the single part could not preserve itself without disaffiliating itself from the rest of the country.[57] Grotius does not assert any obligation for the parts to sacrifice themselves unconditionally for the sake of the whole. Grotius' concept of established territorial sovereignty could not be reconciled with any retention of rights implying territorial self-determination of individual parts of a state, except in extreme situations. Likewise, this concept of established territorial sovereignty is irreconcilable with unilateral acts of abandoning single parts of the territory. The requirement of the people's consent is also helpful in shedding fresh light upon Grotius' views regarding territorial authority: though he does not believe that the citizens always retain the right to govern themselves or always have the right to decide upon the form of their government, where they do have that right, they share the holding of authority. Hence, where the people elect a ruler, this ruler remains bound to the terms under which he (and his family) were elected. Thus, the ruler does not have the right to transfer his rule if he has not been clearly vested with this right. The question of how much of this authority he could transfer to others is consequently dependent on the way he has been vested with this authority by his people. Though he has the right to enjoy the fruits of his authority, he does not have the power to make dispositions on the proprietary right of authority itself without the consent of the people, as the people in this sense retains common sovereignty. However, it is possible that a ruler is granted full authority, including the power to make dispositions on such authority, in which case his subjects do not retain any rights or do not impose any conditions upon the granting of this power. The ruler will then be free to transfer his authority over people and territory as he pleases.

55 Cf. ibid., II.VI.iv.
56 Cf. ibid., II.VI.v.
57 Cf. ibid., II.VI.vi.

2. Termination of Proprietary Rights

Proprietary rights in general and the right of authority in particular are terminated as soon as the holder of the respective proprietary right – the family or the respective people – dies without leaving the right to a successor, or if the main parts of the respective property perish.[58] While in the former case it is the holder of the respective right, i.e. the legal subject of the right, that comes to an end, in the latter case the legal object to which the right refers ceases to exist. Proprietary rights also come to an end if they are abandoned by the holders; in this case the object to which the right relates becomes susceptible of the occupation by a new holder.

2.1. Termination of the Holder of the Proprietary Right

Grotius' remarks on the termination of proprietary rights due to the death or the dissolution of the holder deserve some attention in light of his concept of a perpetuation of legal subjects.[59] According to Isocrates and Emperor Julian, states cannot die, as they belong to corporal things that consist of several subjects under one name. Plutarch claimed that peoples have one sense; the lawyer Paulus held that peoples have one soul; this sense and this soul cannot die. Nevertheless, a people can indeed perish, either if the relevant parts without which the whole body could not survive cease to exist[60], or if the relations amongst the individual members of the body are abandoned[61]; the latter is the case if the community of the people is dissolved because of public uproar, pestilence, or violence in the course of war. Moreover, the body of a people can be deprived of its legal shape if the perfect community is terminated[62]; such termination can happen, according to Grotius, if all of its members are subjected to slavery. Here Grotius is at variance with Thomas Hobbes, who held the citizens necessarily to be dependent upon the state in a slave-like fashion, whereas Grotius, despite allowing for the submission of a people into complete slavery, conceives a general dependency of the state upon the community of its citizens and their personal freedom.

Noteworthy are also Grotius' observations on what cannot be regarded as a termination of the perfect community: If a people leaves its home in order to move to another location it retains its identity as far as the shape as perfect

58 Cf. ibid., II.IX.iv.
59 Cf. ibid., II.IX.iii.
60 Cf. ibid., II.IX.iv.
61 Cf. ibid., II.IX.v.
62 Cf. ibid., II.IX.vi.

community is preserved.[63] This underlines the mere secondary importance of territorial dimension of the state: a people could in principle present a perfect community without effectively occupying a territory of its own. The territorial requisites of modern public international law are absent from Grotius' concept of international relations. Though Grotius certainly believes a state normally to have a territory of its own, this is not necessarily so. Nomads have as much of a capacity to establish a state as any settled people. In any case, the territory is irrelevant for the identity of a state; thus, a state as a perfect community will remain in existence if its people decide to leave their settlements and jointly migrate to another place.

Irrelevant for Grotius is also the internal constitution of a state: Grotius stresses that the Roman people had remained the same, whether they had been governed by kings, consuls, or emperors.[64] Likewise, a change of the constitution does not affect the identity of the state. The identity of a state relies exclusively on the bond between the citizens and the common desire to live together in an order of established rule, wherever this living-together may be undertaken and however this established rule is organised. This has relevance for mergers and demergers of nations: if two nations merge to become one nation, their respective rights held prior to this merger are not lost, but will be held communally by the newly merged people.[65] In the case of a nation that demerges into separate nations, the new separate nations will be independent from each other, but still hold in common what had been common to the former common nation. The same is true for parts of a people that emigrate in order to settle in a colony.[66]

These principles can also be applied to determine the legal status of the former Roman Empire, an issue in which many older and contemporary lawyers have taken an interest.[67] Here Grotius displays himself as a stern opponent of the traditional doctrine of the Middle European constitutional lawyers, according to whom the rights and authority of the Roman Empire had been assumed by the German kings.[68] Grotius' objection to such a legal continuity can perhaps be explained by the efforts of the Dutch people to escape the authority of the Holy Roman Empire of German Nation undertaken at that time. Moreover, Grotius certainly was aware that the effort to deny the legitimacy of German claims to the inheritance of the Roman

63 Cf. ibid., II.IX.vii.

64 Cf. ibid., II.IX.viii.

65 Cf. ibid., II.IX.ix.

66 Cf. ibid., II.IX.x.

67 Cf. H. Dreier, "Kanonistik und Konfessionalisierung: Marksteine auf dem Weg zum Staat", *Juristenzeitung*, 57 (2002), pp. 3 et seq.

68 Cf. C. A. Stumpf, P. R. Melot de Beauregard, "Die Entwicklung der staatlichen Souveränität im Spiegel der kanonistischen Völkerrechtslehre", *Der Staat*, 42 (2003), pp. 459 et seq.

Empire may have pleased his French hosts who had always looked rather askantly at the universal Roman claims of their "Roman-German" neighbours.[69]

Consequently, Grotius does not acknowledge any transfer of the authority of the Roman people to the German people.[70] Instead he argues that the Roman people have retained their original identity up to the present day. This is even though other people have mixed with the Romans, despite the extension of Roman citizenship to people living in other parts of the Roman Empire, and despite the transfer of the imperial residence from Rome to Constantinople. By neither of these acts or incidents could the Romans have been deprived of their original authority. Nor could the election of Charlemagne and his successors as Roman emperors have altered this legal situation as they were only elected as Roman Emperors in person and had always distinguished their imperial Roman authority from their respective authority as Frankish and Lombard kings. When the Franconians divided up into the West Franconians with hereditary kings and the East Franconians with elected kings, the Romans decided to accept the East Franconian Kings as Roman Emperors. However, the Romans, according to Grotius, still retained a right of approval to the rule exercised by the Emperor as far as their affairs were concerned.

Interestingly, Grotius claims that in exercising their right of approval, the Roman people are represented by the Roman bishop, who expresses approval on their behalf and in so doing performs the coronation of the Emperor. This is hardly an accurate account of the constitutional history, at least as far as the time from the 9th century onwards is concerned, though it certainly was a popular view held by numerous lawyers.[71] Nevertheless, Grotius thus manages to explain that the German King receives his authority over Germany merely by virtue of his election by the German electors in accordance with the German constitutional tradition. The German King, however, only obtains his position as Roman Emperor and as King of Italy by the approval of the Roman people. By this he holds full authority over the entire Roman Empire – though Grotius unfortunately does not explain what he believes this empire precisely to consist of. It thus seems that Grotius indeed thinks the Pope may exercise certain rights pertaining to the office of the Roman Emperor during the vacancy of this office, such as the appointment to offices and the granting of fiefs. Overall Grotius' account is

---

69 Cf. on this "separatism" propagated by medieval canonists in France H. G. Walther, *Imperiales Königtum, Konziliarismus und Volkssouveränität*, pp. 78 et seq.

70 Cf. IBP, II.IX.xi.

71 Cf. C. A. Stumpf and P. R. Melot de Beauregard, "Die Entwicklung der staatlichen Souveränität im Spiegel der kanonistischen Völkerrechtslehre", pp. 459 et seq.

strikingly liberal in relation to the Pope's position, considering him being a representative of a Protestant legal tradition.

2.2. Abandonment of Proprietary Rights

Just as one can appropriate things that belong to no one, one can relinquish the proprietary rights one holds. Relinquishing proprietary rights means to leave one's own proprietary rights for others to appropriate. By relinquishing proprietary rights, the respective property is returned to its original state, which, as we may take from Grotius' previous observations, is not the state of something that is owned by no one, but that of full common property of everyone.[72]

Grotius' comments on the relinquishing of proprietary rights may be particularly helpful to illustrate his views on the inter-relation between Human Right, Arbitrary Divine Right, and Natural Right. Firstly, Grotius acknowledges that the principle according to which the legal effects of an acquisition of relinquished proprietary rights by way of an acquisition through lapse of time (*usucapio*) solely belongs to Arbitrary Human Right, as time does not have any legal effect under Natural Right. Grotius expresses his discomfort with this principle though[73]: it would seem that there can then be no acquisition through lapse of time in relation to rights between sovereign nations. As they are not subject to Arbitrary Human Right, the principle of acquisition through lapse of time does not apply to them. Apparently, Grotius not even holds that there may be an acquisition through lapse of time under the Human Right of Nations, as this would presuppose that all or at least many nations acknowledge such a legal principle. Such acknowledgement would indeed be hard to establish. However, Grotius realises that a complete denial of any form of acquisition through lapse of time under Natural Right runs the danger that causes for war could be multiplied, because the peace-making impact of acquisition through lapse of time cannot take effect between nations.

Grotius' remark that "nothing happens because of time, although everything happens within time" (*nihil enim fit a tempore, quamquam nihil non fit in tempore*) provides the solution for this dilemma. It signifies that time is relatively irrelevant with respect to the shaping of rules of Right or of law. Though the application of Right might change because of or along with the progress of time, the content of Right remains the same. Yet on the whole Grotius is rather sceptical about progress in time. This already becomes apparent in his rarely hidden affection for Patristic authors and his orientation

72 Cf. IBP, II.III.xix.1.
73 Cf. ibid., II.IV.i.

towards the views expressed by ancient philosophers and lawyers, whereas his contemporaries are rarely considered whenever he is looking for a confirmation of his theses. For him the progress of time helps to obscure the genuine sources and true understanding of them. It is therefore not surprising that Grotius does not accord any legal relevance to it. Progress of time could neither itself alter the legal status of things, nor could it amend proprietary rights attached to things. Nonetheless, time may serve to establish a presumption of a certain attitude concerning an omission of acts. Alternatively, the absence of any specific expression of will during a certain period of time may result in the alteration of the legal status of a proprietary right. This is, however, not to say that time itself effects alteration.

Grotius states that legal consequences which are dependent on will cannot be effected merely by will alone as long as it is not externalised.[74] However, human beings can externalise their will not only by explicit expression, but also by acts[75] or even the omission of acts.[76] The nature of human society does not allow for a will to be denied its effect, as far as this will has been made sufficiently discernible.[77] Therefore, no one can deny the clear meaning of his own words or actions. Legally, someone seems to approve if he is silent although he is present and could actually verbalise his disapproval explicitly; similar principles apply to the coming into existence of customary law.[78] Consequently, the relinquishing of property can only be concluded from any omission to act if the omitting person knows the effect of this omission and is free to act.[79] Though the use of force in the deprivation of property normally excludes the freedom of will, if time has passed since that force has ceased to be effective it may be concluded that the former owner has meanwhile voluntarily omitted to recover the lost property. Moreover, as time passes the previous owner has the possibility to learn about the legal effect of his omission to recover the property.[80] Therefore, the passing of time indicates that the former owner has voluntarily and knowingly abandoned his proprietary rights.

If a proprietary right has not been exercised during a long period of time, it can be assumed that there is no longer any owner or holder of this proprietary right.[81] Interestingly, Grotius also dismisses the complementary position according to which a will to relinquish proprietary rights could not be presumed solely because of the progress of time, by claiming that the

74 Cf. ibid., II.IV.ii–iii.
75 Cf. ibid., II.IV.iv.
76 Cf. ibid., II.IV.v.
77 Cf. ibid., II.IV.iii.
78 Cf. ibid., II.IV.v.2.
79 Cf. ibid., II.IV.v.3.
80 Cf. ibid., II.IV.vi.
81 Cf. ibid., II.IV.vi–vii.

good of human beings could be presumed: no one would like to leave someone in an unjust situation, e.g. by possessing something without having rightful ownership for a long time.[82] It is then not only the presumption to relinquish proprietary rights that becomes apparent in the progress of time, but also the presumption that any former holder of the relevant proprietary right is willing rather to concede the acquisition of a proprietary right by another person than to claim his property after a long time from the new possessor and to bring distress upon him.

The sources quoted by Grotius in this context even confirm that for this presumption the actual intentions of the former owners are irrelevant. Thus, land that was left waste for a long time and has subsequently been inhabited by others cannot be claimed back rightfully by its former owners.[83] Therefore, the progress of time entails a healing effect for the lack of title, as it helps to base a presumption of the will of the former owner upon it, which cannot be proved to the contrary.

It may sound somewhat peculiar that Grotius on the one hand claims that single property rights have been introduced *inter alia* because of the human vices of vanity and ambitiousness, while, on the other hand, he asserts that human beings could be presumed rather to abandon property than to leave someone else unjustly holding what belongs to them. Yet, the explanation for this can be found in Grotius' ambivalent image of human beings: on the one hand, they have a post-lapsarian tendency towards moral failure; on the other hand they are not entirely evil, so that they are still capable of good intentions, at least for the purpose of establishing legal presumptions.

As regards the abandoning of authority as proprietary right, Grotius claims that the same principles apply. While authority is of great value, it can also turn into nuisance. Therefore it cannot be presumed that human beings would wish to uphold their proprietary rights under any circumstance.[84] Yet, the chief consideration for Grotius in this respect is the desire to remove all doubts from the legitimacy of the rule. It is thus justified to apply the principles of the acquisition of relinquished property also to authority. Consequently, a long-existing rule may not be overturned by those who doubt the legitimacy of its original acquisition.[85]

More difficult is the question of how much time there has to pass before the afore-mentioned presumption of will of the former holder of the proprietary right to abandon it can be supported. Grotius hesitates to give a definite time frame, though one hundred years in his opinion can sometimes

82 Cf. ibid., II.IV.viii.
83 Cf. ibid., II.IV.ii.
84 Cf. ibid., II.IV.viii.
85 Cf. ibid., II.IV.viii.3.

be regarded as sufficient as this entails a normal lifetime as well as the passing of three generations.[86]

As far as sovereign authority has been acquired by force, it may not be removed forcefully by the subjects. Any forcefully acquired sovereign authority may after some time transform into a sovereign authority that is held with the tacit consent of the subjects.[87] Thus usurped rule can become legitimate rule, not because of the original unjust act of usurpation, but either because of a subsequent tacit transfer of authority by the people governed, as far as they had had the right to govern themselves, or by prescription and acquisition of the right to rule from the former ruler, if this former ruler has not exercised his rule effectively or can otherwise be presumed to have abandoned it.

There remains the question of whether future generations could lose their proprietary rights by the presumption of a tacit renunciation.[88] The dilemma is that both alternative possibilities for answering this question give rise to doubts: if unborn human beings, i.e. future generations, cannot lose their rights before being born, the idea of a presumption in favour of a legitimate acquisition of property in absence of an externalised will to the contrary is bound to fail. This is because most rights can be inherited; even if the owner refrains from exercising his proprietary right and thus appears to have abandoned it, his unborn heir still retains his right of inheritance. Thus a prescription of proprietary rights would only apply in very rare cases. However, if one were to claim that future generations could be deprived of their rights before being born, one would have to overcome the general legal principle according to which the keeping of silence cannot harm those who are not capable of speaking.

Grotius solves this dilemma by asserting that future generations cannot hold any rights. Thus, if a people holding authority itself decides to alter its will, no injustice is committed against future generations, because these future generations could not yet have acquired any right to participate in the decision-making. A prescription of proprietary rights thus is possible. However, Human Right may stipulate otherwise and therefore may provide for rights of future human beings. This could be done by way of regarding those future generations as being born for the purpose of holding certain rights. Thence, any acquisition of proprietary rights fictionally held by unborn human beings is impermissible. However, these rules of Human Right cannot be presumed, but have to be spelt out very clearly.

86 Cf. ibid., II.IV.vii.

87 Cf. ibid., II.IV.xiv.

88 Cf. ibid., II.IV.x.

V. Limitations of Proprietary Rights

As the Christian legal tradition holds that the institution of proprietary rights is a necessary evil in a post-lapsarian situation, there have been various attempts of Christian authors to limit the effect of proprietary rights so as to direct the use of assets for the benefit of the common good.[89] Similar approaches can be found in Islamic legal theory, which acknowledges the institution of subjective proprietary rights, but still qualifies such rights in various respects by attaching certain duties of the owner to the respective property.[90] Likewise, there is a strong tendency even in liberal concepts of public international law, such as the one brought forward by John Rawls in his *Law of Peoples,* which aim at emphasising obligations relating to ownership, e.g. the duty of wealthy and powerful states to render assistance to states which are burdened by unfavourable conditions.[91]

As already mentioned earlier, Grotius believes that some aspects of the ancient communal property persist even after the introduction of the single proprietary rights under Human Right. From this Grotius infers that a number of limitations to proprietary rights which narrow their effective scope or limit their exercise may apply in extraordinary cases where the normal status defined by proprietary rights cannot be upheld. A special type of limitation of proprietary rights are obligations that are attached to the holding of proprietary rights. Thus, proprietary rights do not only entail certain powers, but may also impose obligations upon their respective holders.

Limitations of single property rights are in Grotius' view not merely qualifications of the proprietary rights to which they are attached, but are rather to be considered as remaining elements of the older common property which are not altogether superseded by the introduction of single property rights.[92] Hence, single property rights never grant absolute legal positions in the sense that the rights of others are excluded or waived completely. It is not a revival of the former common property that takes place, for example in cases of emergency, but rather an actualisation of the persisting rights of common property: Grotius believes that human beings, when introducing proprietary rights, did not seek to abolish the former institution of common property completely. Here Grotius appears to be close to certain strands of the old Germanic law, which had upheld the communal nature of all

---

89 Cf. J. A. Brundage, *Medieval Canon Law*, pp. 105 et seq.

90 Cf. K. A El Fadl, "The Unbounded Law of God and Territorial Boundaries", in A. Buchanan, M. Moore (eds.), *States, Nations, and Borders: The Ethics of Making Boundaries*, pp. 214 et seq.

91 J. Rawls, *The Law of Peoples*, pp. 105 et seq.

92 Cf. IBP, II.II.vi.1.

property whether owned privately or communally.[93] However, the same view was also common amongst the Scholastics and Thomas Aquinas, who had drawn on the respective principles of Roman law.[94]

One thing that seems rather odd when looking at Grotius' elaboration on the limitation of proprietary rights is the fact that he has surprisingly little to say about additional aspects of Arbitrary Divine Right in general or the Law of the Gospel in particular with respect to this matter. As we shall see, Grotius regards these limitations mostly as elements of Human Right, whereas Divine Right is hardly mentioned by him in this respect. As an explanation it may be suggested that for Grotius it makes more sense to define the limitation of private property rights by human legal categories as private property is in his view of human making. Arbitrary Divine Right is applied in matters such as the purpose for which property is to be used, but is for Grotius less apt to constitute claims to the property of others.

1. Limitations of Proprietary Rights in Cases of Emergency

In a case of emergency Grotius believes that the ancient right of common usage as entailed by the original status as common property and not excluded by the introduction of private property rights becomes relevant again[95]: for example, if food becomes scarce on a ship, everyone has to submit his belongings to common usage. In the case of a fire, one may tear down the house of one's neighbour in order to protect one's own house.

Here Grotius specifically refers to the view of theologians, in particular of Thomas Aquinas, who had not regarded a thief someone who takes from others in order to sustain himself.[96] However, Grotius makes it clear that this is not because the owner has to give to the needy anyway due to his obligations of charity under the Law of the Gospel, but because private property had only been introduced under this mild qualification. By this,

93 Cf. F. Wieacker, *Privatrechtsgeschichte der Neuzeit, unter besonderer Berücksichtigung der deutschen Entwicklung*, pp. 408 et seq.; O. Gierke, *Das deutsche Genossenschaftsrecht*, vol. 1: *Rechtsgeschichte der deutschen Genossenschaft*, pp. 24 et seq.; vol. 2: *Geschichte des deutschen Körperschaftsbegriffs*, pp. 87 et seq.; C. A. Schmidt, *Der prinzipielle Unterschied zwischen dem römischen und dem germanischen Rechte*, pp. 45 et seq.

94 Cf. Thomas Aquinas, *In Ethicorum*, I.1–4; VIII.1–1541; I, 9–27 et seq.; in *In decem libros Ethicorium Aristotelis ad Nicomachum expositio / Sancti Thomae Aquinatis*, ed. Raimondo Spiazzi. On Thomas' concept of man as *animus sociale* see E. Schockenhoff, "Dient die Politik dem Glück des Menschen? Zum Verhältnis von geistlicher und weltlicher Gewalt bei Thomas von Aquin", in C. A. Stumpf, H. Zaborowski (eds.), *Church as Politeia: The Political Self-Understanding of Christianity*, pp. 69, 78 et seq.

95 Cf. IBP, II.II.vi.2.

96 Cf. Thomas Aquinas, *Summa Theologica*, II.67.4.

Grotius obviously does not deny the existence of a commandment of charity entailed by Gospel law which results in an obligation of the owner to give; rather he says that the right of the needy person to take is entailed in the original communal property right which survives the introduction of individual property rights and cannot be excluded by any private owner unilaterally.

However, Grotius acknowledges the necessity of certain restrictions on this right of emergency in order to prevent abuses. First of all, the right of emergency by which the individual property of others is infringed upon is only granted under the principles of subsidiarity. Thus, one can only resort to it if other means to provide remedy fail. Before the right of emergency is contended, one first has to ask the owner or the government for help.[97] The right of emergency is in Grotius' concept only the last resort; only if others do not help voluntarily may one help oneself by seizing the property of others.

Second, the right of emergency does not grant any right against those who are in need themselves.[98] Under equal conditions the right of the rightful owner or possessor prevails. Grotius here primarily appeals to Natural Right. However, the situation is not different under Arbitrary Divine Right: Gospel law only commands us to love our neighbour as much as ourselves, but not more than ourselves.[99] Grotius certainly regards it as praiseworthy if a needy owner shares his goods with other persons in need, though there is no strict obligation to do so.

Third, Grotius claims that compensation has to be rendered to the owner for the expenses incurred in the case of an exercise of a right of emergency. In his view, the right of emergency is not a full right, but one to which a duty of compensation is attached.[100] The same principle applies in the case of war, when property of a neutral party is used.[101]

2. Harmless Use

Next to the use of alien property in cases of emergency there is the possibility to use the property of others harmlessly, provided that such use does not present any illegitimate infringement of the proprietary right.[102] In such cases of harmless use the proprietary right of the owners is not affected, as this use does not diminish the substance of the property. For example, anyone may

97 Cf. IBP, II.II.vii.
98 Cf. ibid., II.II.viii.
99 Cf. ibid., I.III.iii.3.
100 Cf. ibid., II.II.ix.
101 Cf. ibid., II.II.x.
102 Cf. ibid., II.II.xi.

light one's torch at someone else's fire. Such harmless use includes the right to use the water of rivers to which a particular proprietary right relates.[103] Thus the owner of a river may use the river, may erect buildings, and anything that comes into existence within the river or emerges from the river belongs to him. However, the river as flowing water remains common property, so that anyone may drink from it.

2.1. Freedom of Transit

Grotius extends the permissibility of harmless use to all lands and those parts of the sea that are susceptible of becoming public property: these have to remain open for anyone to pass through for rightful purposes, to move to other countries, or to conduct trade with other nations, or to pass through in the course of a just war.[104] For Grotius this is supported by the Old Testament as well as by the history of ancient Greece.

The right of transit as part of the right of harmless use may not be restricted because of the fear of the owners: Rights could never be limited by fear, as there are safeguards against dangers: For example, the right of transit can be restricted in the sense that only limited parts of an army are allowed to pass through the territory at one time, or only without weapons, or other measures may be taken which ensure that the legitimate interests of the holder of authority over the respective territory can be upheld.

From this Grotius infers a general prohibition to exclude others from transit over land, rivers, or secluded parts of the sea under Natural Right. This right of transit has to be acknowledged by the owner of the respective land, regardless of the purpose for which it is used. It also includes the use of the right of transit for military purposes.

The right of transit covers in Grotius' opinion also the traffic of goods. Hence, no one has the right to impede the trade of one nation with another nation, as the permission of trade is for the benefit of the whole human society and harms no one. Overall, Grotius accords great importance to trade as means for human communication: he refers to ancient authorities who had claimed that God had distributed the wealth of the world over the countries in order to make everyone dependent on others and to ensure that human beings become sociable.[105] This may seem like a typical view for a son of the Dutch merchant nation, but it was also shared by Vitoria.[106]

---

103 Cf. ibid., II.II.xii.
104 Cf. ibid., II.II.xiii.
105 Cf. ibid., II.II.xiii.5.
106 Cf. F. Vitoria, *De Indis recenter*, 3.1.

In the context of the traffic of goods, Grotius asks whether customs could legitimately be raised by states. He replies with a qualified yes: customs or similar levies or duties can be charged to foreign traders legitimately as far as such levies present an adequate compensation for services rendered by the state to foreign traders. This may be regarded as an application of expletive justice to international trade: duties can only be claimed rightfully if they are due to the state, and they can obviously be only due to the state if the state in exchange renders services; otherwise duties would constitute unjust gains.[107] Grotius, however, acknowledges that in practice this principle is ignored more often than not. As an example, he refers to Arab leaders, though he certainly could have also pointed to many Middle European states of his time.

With respect to the freedom of transit, it is to be noted that Grotius is here in agreement with most Christian authors on the subject, as well as with the general outlook on this matter of Islamic legal authors with the qualification that a letter of protection is required for any travels of unbelievers through the realm of Iṣlam.[108] However, at the same time this position is not in conformity with the present situation in public international law, which still finds it difficult to accept the principle of a freedom of transit overland, even though there are numerous attempts to overcome the respective restrictions.[109]

2.2. Freedom of Settlement

The right of transit, according to Grotius, also entails the right to rest for a while in the territory of transit and even to erect temporary buildings there.[110] But not even the taking up of a permanent residence may be denied to foreigners as asylum-seekers if they are expelled from their home countries, ask for permission to settle in the country, and undertake to promise allegiance to the existing authorities and institutions for the maintenance of public peace.[111] It would be hard not to take this statement as an allusion to Grotius' own experience as political outcast in the Netherlands and expatriate in France.

Grotius claims that foreign migrants should be allowed to immigrate into other countries. To these migrants a permission to settle and to obtain wastelands has to be granted.[112] Grotius again sees this to be supported by his concept of harmless use of property which always has to be permitted: as

107 Cf. IBP, II.II.xiv.

108 On the *aman* as letter of protection see Khadduri, *The Islamic Law of Nations*, pp. 54 et seq.

109 Cf. R. Dolzer, "Wirtschaft und Kultur im Völkerrecht", pp. 502 et seq.

110 Cf. IBP, II.II.xv.

111 Cf. ibid., II.II.xvi.

112 Cf. ibid., II.II.xvii.

the dominion to wastelands is not claimed by anyone else, there is no reason why foreigners may not obtain it, provided, however, that the existing overlordship remains intact. This bears practical relevance for the colonial enterprises undertaken by various European states at that time, though as we have noted, not in the far-reaching sense which Tuck appears to accord to Grotius' words.

Again we find Grotius in conformity with the approach taken in the religious traditions of public international law to this subject, which generally approves of such right of settlement by foreigners, whereas, again, we find him in this respect at variance with the situation under contemporary public international law.

2.3. Freedom of Commerce

In Grotius' concept, the right to actions follows the right to things. It is obvious for him that everyone has the right to perform such acts as are necessary to sustain one's own life.[113] Thus everyone must have the right to acquire necessary goods at an adequate price, except when the owner needs the relevant goods for himself. The sale of wheat may be prohibited in the event of famine. But even in such a case, foreigners already admitted to one's own territory may not be expelled again; rather the common lack of fortune has to be borne commonly.[114] When dealing with the legal aspects of his economic ethics Grotius certainly goes further than many of his contemporaries and further than the practice of the states that had regularly expelled foreigners in times of need, but had also more often than not prohibited the sale of certain goods to foreigners. This is in particular true for the upcoming mercantilism which already started to emerge in France at Grotius' time.

However, the right to purchase goods or the obligation to sell does not correspond to any right to sell or an obligation to purchase: Grotius confirms that everyone is free to purchase or not to purchase as one likes.[115] To this end, Grotius refers to the example of the ancient Belgians – ancestors of the Dutch – who had refused to allow wine or foreign goods into their countries, as well as to the Arabs, who had sometimes imposed similar restrictions on imports.

Once more Grotius here agrees with the respective Christian tradition of public international law and also with the view of Islamic jurisprudence on this matter. The respective situation under modern public international law is, again, different: while the World Trade Organisation is, generally

---

113 Cf. ibid., II.II.xviii.
114 Cf. ibid., II.II.xix.
115 Cf. ibid., II.II.xx.

speaking, certainly trying to liberalise international commerce, the factual situation is still less favourable to it.[116] Nevertheless, the demand for a liberalisation of commerce is certainly in line with the approach of the liberal perspective of the Law of Peoples as presented by John Rawls.

2.4. Principle of Equal Treatment

Furthermore, the right to acts that are normally conceded to foreigners has to be conceded to all foreigners.[117] This implies a prohibition to discriminate certain foreign nations in relation to other foreign nations. Hence, if most foreigners are allowed anywhere to hunt, fish, catch birds, search for pearls, inherit, sell, and marry local women, then this may not be prohibited to one particular group of foreigners by way of exception, unless this people has committed an act of injustice against the domestic people. Thus there is also a concept of equal treatment in Grotius' theory of Natural Right.

However, this only covers those actions which spring from natural freedom. Only actions which are entailed in natural freedom have to be conceded to everyone in a country, including foreigners.[118] Therefore, it does not present any injustice to refuse to foreigners any action that is not already entailed by natural freedom, but is either only granted as a special favour or as an exception from the law. To refuse a favour, Grotius says, can never be an injustice.

This principle of equal treatment is hard to reconcile with exclusive trade agreements between states. Nevertheless, Grotius holds such agreements to be admissible if the traded goods are made available to third parties at a reasonable price.[119] Grotius here cunningly refers to the contracts that Dutch merchants had concluded with local rulers in East India, very much to the displeasure of English merchants; these trade agreements had been one of the most important subjects of the Anglo–Dutch colonial consultations in 1613, in which Grotius participated as Dutch representative.[120] Even though having been expelled by his home country, Grotius nevertheless continues to defend the Dutch colonial policy. However, it should be fair to suggest that this repetition of the Dutch arguments against the English is rooted in something

116 Cf. W. Benedek, *Die Rechtsordnung des GATT aus völkerrechtlicher Sicht*, pp. 51 et seq.; R. Dolzer, "Wirtschaft und Kultur im Völkerrecht", pp. 502 et seq.

117 Cf. IBP, II.II.xxii.

118 Cf. ibid., II.II.xxiii.

119 Cf. ibid., II.II.xxiv.

120 G. N. Clark and W. van Eysinga, "The Colonial Conferences between England and the Netherlands in 1613 and 1615", *Bibliotheca Visseriana*, 34 (1951), pp. 79 et seq.; G. N. Clark, "Grotius's East India Mission to England," *Transactions of the Grotius Society*, 20 (1935), pp. 45–84.

different than an ongoing allegiance to his home country. Grotius probably wanted to defend himself here against the accusation of contradicting himself in relation to his doctrine of the freedom of navigation, which he had put forward earlier in *Mare Liberum*. While Grotius had claimed – on behalf of the Dutch East India Company – that the right of navigation could not be denied legitimately by the Spanish and Portuguese in East India, the Dutch themselves did limit this very freedom of navigation of other nations in East India merely a few years later. In particular, the Dutch denied the English access to the native rulers in Indonesia in order to secure the rather profitable trade with spices and other natural resources for themselves. When the English confronted Grotius with his anonymously published *Mare Liberum* at the Anglo–Dutch colonial consultations in London in 1613, apparently knowing about Grotius' authorship, Grotius was in need to find a suitable explanation for the apparent contradictions between the claims of the Dutch against the Spanish and against the English. Grotius manages to find a plausible defence of the Dutch practice in applying the principle of attributive justice: if one state undertakes to provide protection for another state, these two states may conclude an exclusive trade agreement by which the protecting state is exclusively entitled to purchase goods from the protected state. However, Grotius adds the qualification that the state so favoured by such exclusive right of trade will be under an obligation to sell the goods thus acquired to other states at an adequate price, though not at cost. Still the making of a gain is permissible, in particular if the state thus favoured renders services to the state with which the agreement has been concluded. This had been the case with the Dutch agreements with East Indian rulers, as these agreements had entailed protection of the East Indian rulers by the Dutch and the building of fortresses in the respective East Indian territories. However, that such protection was hardly an altruistic measure employed by the Dutch is another matter: certainly the protection by the Dutch East India Company for East Indian rulers was designed foremostly for the protection of the Dutch trade interests against interference by other European nations. Grotius then finally admits rather cryptically that civil laws sometimes prohibit such exclusive trade agreements because of common use.

In this respect Grotius also aligns himself with the general tendency displayed in the respective religious traditions of public international law in Christianity and in Islam.[121] The situation under modern public international law is again less favourable to the principle of equal treatment. However, we

---

121 Cf. C. A. Stumpf, "Völkerrecht unter Kreuz und Halbmond", pp. 87 et seq.

may here note that there are various moves on the regional level to remove discriminatory measures.[122]

VI. Conclusion

Overall, in relation to his concepts of proprietary Right and the territorial dimension of rule, Grotius stands in the respective Christian tradition. The modern understanding of territorial states which emerged already in Grotius' lifetime thus cannot draw on Grotius' concept of statehood. However, even in the modern view on territorial rule a tendency towards a rethinking of the traditional concept represented by Grotius can be noted; the contemporary law of the seas, the concept of the high seas and the deep seabed as common heritage of mankind is but one example of a return of modern public international law back to ideas represented by Grotius.[123]

From the analysis of Grotius' views on proprietary Right we may draw two general inferences regarding Grotius' views on proprietary rights and on territorial authority:

Firstly, both dominion as property right in the strict sense of private ownership and territorial authority as proprietary right in a wider sense have a purely human origin. While Natural Right and Arbitrary Divine Right have merely provided for communal proprietary rights, the introduction of individual subjective proprietary rights, dominion and territorial authority, under Human Right is in Grotius' opinion perfectly legitimate. Nonetheless, dominion and territorial authority are by no means necessary institutions. At least in theory, man could do without such individual proprietary rights.

Secondly, the institution of individual proprietary rights reflects the fallibility of human nature. The institution of individual proprietary rights provides a man-made order of the allocation of things to man in the post-lapsarian world. This function at the same time restricts the scope of proprietary rights, as proprietary rights entail a responsibility of the individual holder to make them available also for the common good. This becomes particularly relevant for those aspects of the ancient communal proprietary rights which persist despite the introduction of individual subjective proprietary rights.

In presenting his theory of proprietary rights, Grotius thus is to a great extent indebted to the traditional perception of Christian moral theology vis-à-vis the institution of property: he accepts proprietary rights as a necessary

---

122 Cf. Cullet, "Differential Treatment in International Law: Towards a New Paradigm of Inter-State Relations", *The European Journal of International Law*, 10 (1999), pp. 549 et seq.; R. Dolzer, "Wirtschaft und Kultur im Völkerrecht", pp. 479 et seq.

123 Cf. W. Graf Vitzthum, "Raum und Umwelt im Völkerrecht", pp. 410 et seq.

evil in a fallen world. At the same time Grotius adheres to the traditional tendency of Christian economic ethics in emphasising the individual responsibility of holders of proprietary rights to employ these rights also for the common good, so as to compensate human society for the subjection of formerly common assets to subjective rights. As we have seen, this perception of proprietary rights in the Christian tradition also has various parallels in its Islamic counterpart, which is also in favour of subjective proprietary rights that entail limitations by virtue of the individual's membership in a greater society.

With this approach to proprietary rights as subjective rights entailing a moral responsibility for the common good Grotius may also contribute to the contemporary debate on the establishment of a new economic world order which can combine the existent proprietary order with an enhanced degree of responsibility of the individual for the common good of the international society. John Rawls seeks to reconcile an unequal distribution of assets with a duty of assistance by the more powerful and wealthier members of the international society to those other members that are burdened by unfavourable conditions.[124] Both Grotius and Rawls thus endeavour to reason for an enhanced responsibility of the holders of proprietary rights for the common good of all members of society. However, while Rawls' concept with its liberal outlook on moral theory relies on a respective consensus which he believes to be motivated by a long-term gain for all members of the international society, Grotius argues in favour of respective obligations under Natural Right, Arbitrary Divine Right, and Human Right. The moral responsibility of the individual holder of proprietary rights is in Grotius' concept not dependent upon the religious allegiance of the individual. Instead, it is a moral responsibility which is rooted in every individual's membership in the universal society of human beings, even though Grotius certainly would expect a higher degree of awareness of this responsibility from Christians, who have received explicit orders to render assistance to their fellowmen through divine revelation.

124 Cf. J. Rawls, *The Law of Peoples*, pp. 106 et seq.

Chapter 5

Right to War and Right in War

I. Introduction

Grotius' project pursued in *De Iure Belli ac Pacis* is an exposition of the Right of War and of Peace. Most of what has been said in the foregoing pertains to Grotius' views on Right in the state of peace. It is now time to analyse Grotius' positions in relation to war as the exception to the state of peace. First, however, we will briefly sketch the alternative perceptions of war and their relation to Grotius' own perspective on the Right of War.

The history of man is a history also of war. Virtually everything that may cause a conflict between individuals is also apt to cause a greater conflict between communities of human beings. Consequently, war as a collective form of dispute naturally is of greatest interest to any science concerned with the moral standards of human conduct. In principle, there are various ways of perceiving war, which are, of course, not mutually exclusive in relation to each other.[1]

One rather extreme perspective, which may be labelled as "martial tradition" of war, is that of seeing war simply as a chance to display certain human virtues and qualities, such as fortitude, bravery, courage, ambition, etc., regardless of the incident that gave rise to the occasion of the conflict. This martial attitude to war is not so much concerned with the achievement of any extrinsic aim of the war, but just relishes in certain human qualities which come to the surface in the course of the exercise of military strength. A continuing state of hostility is then also seen as conducive to keeping human beings alert, so as to prevent them from relishing in decadency. The roots of the martial tradition reach back to antiquity; it is, for example, typically ascribed to the historic Sparta, but is in some respect also visible in Cato the Elder, who for example had advocated military training against the moral decay of the population.[2] However, it is also a view regularly endorsed by fascist regimes, which blend it frequently with racial ideologies.[3]

---

1 Cf. H. Münkler, *Gewalt und Ordnung*, pp. 1 et seq.

2 Cf. M. P. Cato, *Originum libri septem*, III.68.

3 On this phenomenon see K. Nabulsi, *Tradition of War: Occupation, Resistance, and the Law*, pp. 103 et seq.

On the other hand, there is also an idealist tradition of war which endorses war as struggle for the achieving of a certain idealised end. To this belong the so-called holy wars, which are undertaken for a religious purpose. The idea of holy wars can be encountered at least in all of the most important monotheistic religions, e.g. the holy wars waged by the people of Israel in occupying the land promised to them by God in the Old Testament[4]; in Islam, the understanding of Jihad by many legal scholars as the holy war against the unbelievers wherever Muslims find them[5]; in Christianity, the crusades against Muslim rule in the Holy Land[6] as well as the missionary wars against pagans in territories overseas.[7] Another, equally relevant subcategory of the idealist tradition of war is the republican tradition of war as a fight against foreign rule or an authoritarian regime for the national self-determination of a people.[8] Wars of colonised people against their foreign colonial powers as well as forceful revolutions within a state are but two examples of this republican tradition of war as a subspecies of the idealist tradition. Characteristic of this idealist approach to war is the subordination of the means to the aims which are pursued through the war. Very illustrative for this is Lenin's statement: If I wish to make an omelette, I have to damage eggs. In this latter respect, the idealist tradition is closely related to the practically orientated understanding of war as pursuit of political aims through different means, which finds famous representatives in Clausewitz[9] and also in Machiavelli.[10] This view of war was prevalent amongst Western lawyers and politicians in the course of the 18th and 19th centuries.

Furthermore, there is also a pacifist tradition, which condemns war absolutely and without any qualifications.[11] This tradition is particularly strong in certain Christian circles, such as the Mennonites as well as in other contemporary Christian groups; according to their interpretation, one should rather suffer evil than inflict evil on other human beings.[12] Therefore, even

4 Cf. C. A. Stumpf, "Vom Heiligen Krieg zum gerechten Krieg", *Zeitschrift der Savigny-Stiftung für Rechtsgeschichte. Kanonistische Abteilung*, 87 (2001), pp. 1–30.

5 Cf. Shafi'i, *Kitab a-Umm*, IV, 84–85.

6 Cf. F. H. Russell, *The Just War in the Middle Ages*, pp. 119 et seq.

7 Cf. C. A. Stumpf, "Völkerrecht unter Kreuz und Halbmond: Muhammad al-Shaybani und Hugo Grotius als Exponenten religiöser Völkerrechtstradition", *Archiv des Völkerrechts*, 41 (2003/1), pp. 91 et seq.

8 On this "republican tradition" see cf. K. Nabulsi, *Traditions of War*, pp. 177 et seq.

9 Cf. C. von Clausewitz, *Vom Kriege*, I.I.24: "So sehen wir also, daß der Krieg nicht bloß ein politischer Akt, sondern ein wahres politisches Instrument ist, eine Fortsetzung des politischen Verkehrs, ein Durchführen desselben mit anderen Mitteln. . . ."

10 Cf. N. Machiavelli, *Discorsi sopra la prima deca di Tito Livio*, II.xi.3.

11 On the Christian pacifist tradition and its relation to the Christian just war tradition see O. M. T. O'Donovan, *The Just War Revisited*, pp. 7 et seq.

12 For examples of the pacifist traditions see J. H. Yoder, *Nevertheless, the Varieties and Shortcomings of Religious Pacifism*, pp. 12 et seq.

defensive wars are to be avoided, for military actions can only achieve earthly aims, while true happiness lies only with God's eternity.

Finally, there is the just war tradition, which is based on early Roman law[13] and from there found its way into Christian moral thought through Isidor of Seville[14], the canonist lawyers of the 11th and 12th centuries[15], and finally the Salamancan school of moral theology.[16] In this tradition war is perceived as necessary evil for the restoration of a just legal order and the enforcement of Right in the international arena, where no state jurisdiction is effective. For the restoration of Right in the case of an ongoing attack it sees defensive wars as justified. However, classic just war tradition also regards penal wars as legitimate if they are undertaken to remedy a violation of Right. A notion of the just war doctrine can also be found in early Islamic legal theory, in which some of the legal scholars held that Jihad was a religiously motivated defensive war against attacks by unbelievers.[17] Thus, while there was continuing hostility inherent in the relationship between the realm of Islam and the realm of war of the unbelievers, there was primarily a personal obligation of the individual Muslim to contribute to the defence of the realm of Islam against attacks by unbelievers, whereas there was no legal necessity to attack the realm of war out of one's own religious or legal initiative.[18]

Under modern public international law wars are generally to be led only within the system of such international organisations as the United Nations.[19] However, the question of whether the use of military force by one state against another has to be authorised by the international society of states is still subject to legal controversy.[20] The position according to which the use of force has been monopolised by the United Nations, which had probably been the prevalent opinion among Western jurists, has recently come under pressure, as military actions, such as the measures employed by NATO in Kosovo and the Operation "Enduring Freedom" performed by the USA, the United Kingdom, and others in Iraq have been undertaken without recourse to the United Nations.

---

13 E. Seckel, *Über Krieg und Recht in Rom: Rede zur Feier des Geburtstages Seiner Majestät des Kaisers und Königs, gehalten am 27. Januar 1915*, pp. 32 et seq.

14 Cf. C. A. Stumpf, "Vom Heiligen Krieg zum gerechten Krieg", pp. 12 et seq.

15 Cf. F. H. Russell, *The Just War in the Middle Ages*, pp. 35 et seq.

16 H. F. Köck, *Der Beitrag der Schule von Salamanca zur Entwicklung der Lehre von den Grundrechten*, pp. 56 et seq.

17 Cf. Ibn Taymiya, *Qua'ida fi Qital al-Kuffar*, pp. 115 et seq.

18 Khadduri, *The Islamic Conception of Justice*, pp. 168 et seq.

19 Cf. M. Bothe, "Friedenssicherung und Kriegsrecht", in W. Graf Vitzthum (ed.), *Völkerrecht*, pp. 626 et seq.

20 Cf. ibid., pp. 621 et seq.

In any case, there is a shift from the classic just war theory to modern public international law in the sense that nowadays only defensive wars tend to be accepted by most contemporary jurists as part of a *Ius contra bellum*.[21] This view is also taken by modern liberal moral philosophy as represented by John Rawls. According to Rawls, in a society of liberal or at least "decent" organised peoples all possible motives for an aggressive war are absent by necessity.[22] Modern public international law and the political theory underlying it thus endorse a combination of the classic just war theory and certain aspects of the pacifist tradition: in theory only defensive wars which are waged after an attack by another state are admissible. Other violations of public international law may only be remedied by peaceful means, but not by penal wars.[23]

Nonetheless, it may be questioned whether the aforementioned theoretical approach to wars is mirrored by contemporary reality. Here the other traditions of war still remain in practice. In this respect the military operation "Enduring Freedom" presents a rather interesting example of study for the alternative perspectives of war, even though it is still too early to determine the tradition in which it stands: as far as the non-compliance of Iraq with the United Nations resolutions on disarmament is taken as cause for the war, it would seem to be a penal war in the sense of the traditional just war theory. If access of certain states to the natural resources of Iraq was the true cause, the attack was based on the political tradition of war represented by Machiavelli and Clausewitz. If the liberation of the Iraqi people from their oppression by a dictator was the true reason for the war, it might be taken as an altruistic republican war.

Amongst the aforementioned theoretical approaches to war, it is certainly a Christian tradition of just war within which Grotius is firmly rooted, and it is indeed this perspective from which Grotius ventures to refute the legitimacy of any other approach to war, be it the martial tradition, the idealist tradition, or the pacifist tradition.

Though there is an inherently positive account in Grotius' exposition of peace, this is, of course, not to say that Grotius conceives war altogether as an abhorrent deviation from what the life of human beings should be. As we shall see, Grotius overall adheres to the idea of the Christian just war tradition in viewing just wars as necessary evils. He thus holds that war may be a suitable remedy for a disturbance of peace. A just war, waged by the right authority and because of a just reason, may achieve a restoration of justice. At the same time Grotius claims that just as Right governs all human acts during peace, there is also Right governing the acts to be performed in

21 Cf. ibid., pp. 606 et seq.

22 Cf. J. Rawls, *The Law of Peoples*, pp. 8, 16 et seq.

23 Cf. ibid., pp. 91 et seq.

the course of war. For him there is indeed a distinct set of Right claiming obedience in war, even though some authors claimed that the rule of law ends where the rule of war starts.

We shall approach Grotius' outlook upon war firstly by clarifying his terminology. In his view a just war is not merely a situation in which random acts of violence are performed by someone against someone else, but it is at least accompanied by some formal requirements; if such formalities are ignored, this will normally indicate that the use of force is illegitimate.[24] Then we will proceed to discuss Grotius' position on the legitimacy of war under Natural Right, Arbitrary Divine Right, and Human Right, through which he distances himself from the pacifist tradition. In the further course we will turn to Grotius' position on the Right to War, which provides certain requirements regarding the justification of wars; here we will see how his position is distinct from any idealist tradition of war. From the Right of War we will then move on to the Right in War in order to see Grotius' criticism of the warfare undertaken by his contemporaries, through which he implicitly rejects the martial tradition of war. By this we shall finally endeavour to fit Grotius' concept of the Right of War into his system of a theology of international law which rests on the personal responsibility of the individual moral agent.

II. Categories of War

Grotius defines war as a condition in which human beings fight with each other forcefully.[25] War is therefore not merely a violent act or violent fight itself, as was suggested by Cicero, but the state of those engaged in combat by armed force. Moreover, according to Grotius, the scope of the term "war" is not restricted to public wars only, as the ordinary use of the word might suggest, but also covers private wars and mixed wars. Simply to be in such a state of combat does not imply anything about one's moral or legal authority, though the question whether someone possesses sufficient authority may bear relevance for the question if a war is legitimately waged by the right party. Grotius is keen to point out that private wars possess manifold similarities with public wars. Wars can therefore be fought amongst public parties or private parties, by the superior against the inferior, or vice versa. Whether or not a war is just, whether or not there is a just reason, a just authority, or a just intention, is irrelevant for the definition of war as such.

---

24 Cf. P. Haggenmacher, *Grotius et la doctrine de la guerre juste*, pp. 250 et seq., pp. 68 et seq.

25 Cf. IBP, I.I.ii.1.

From Grotius' willingness to discuss both public and private forceful conflicts under the rubric of war we can infer that the use of force is at the centre of Grotius' interest: while he certainly accords a distinct quality to the use of force by or against an established authority, it is the responsibility of the individual agent in which he primarily takes interest. This will become clearer as we proceed.

According to Grotius, there are altogether three types of war. In addition to public wars and private wars, there are also mixed wars. A public war is a war waged by someone who holds superior power. A private war is a war waged by someone else, i.e. by someone who holds no superior power. A mixed war is a war which is for one party a public war and for another party a private war.[26] Though in *De iure belli ac pacis* Grotius appears to be more interested in public wars, he nevertheless gives at least some attention to private wars as well. As already explained above, the use of the term "war" for public wars as well as for private wars and for mixed wars enables Grotius to present a rather general theory on the admissibility of the use of force in human interrelations.

1. Private Wars

Grotius regards any condition of a violent fight between parties which do not exercise any particular right of authority as private war.[27] Thus the recovery of a stolen good by violent means, and also any act of punishment inflicted upon the thief by the owner, falls under this rubric.

It is obvious that in the case of an establishment of states, which is undertaken for the protection of the peace of the citizens against any external harm as well as for the preservation of concord and peace amongst the citizens, there is not much space left for private wars. In the case of an established state, which presupposes *inter alia* the appointment of magistrates and the setting up of courts, it will normally be only for the state to settle disputes amongst the citizens, while the resorting of the citizens to violence in order to assert their own private rights would obviously be detrimental to the very purpose of the establishment of the state's authority. Thus, even if someone's right is violated by someone else, he may not try to remedy this violation himself, as this will present an illegal use of force. A dispute has to be referred to the established courts of the state and it is for these courts or for the state authority to provide a remedy for the violation, to effect the return of what is due to someone, and to inflict suitable punishment upon those who have violated rights of citizens.

26 Cf. ibid., I.III.i.
27 Cf. ibid., I.III.ii.

Nonetheless, Grotius argues that there remain private wars that still may be undertaken legitimately even under the established legal framework of a state's authority. While the establishment of a state authority certainly limits the possibility of waging private wars in general, it nevertheless allows for certain exceptions. Even though the original freedom has been limited with the establishment of courts, this freedom remains where there is no effective jurisdiction exercised: a law which prohibits to resort to self-help can claim adherence only as far as disputes can effectively be referred to a judge.[28] Yet, courts may be absent temporarily or permanently. For example, courts are absent temporarily when it is not possible to wait for the judgement because of imminent dangers. Courts may be absent permanently, either in a legal or in a factual sense. The former is the case if the dispute occurs in a place which does not belong to a state and therefore is not under any court's jurisdiction, for example on the high seas, in wastelands, or on uninhabited islands; obviously then there cannot be any rule of Human Right of whatsoever nature that commands the referral of disputes to courts, whereas Natural Right and Arbitrary Divine Right do not prohibit private wars in such cases anyway. The case of a factual absence of judges will become relevant when the subjects do not obey the judges, or when the competent judge refuses to administer his office. In this case the original freedom which existed prior to the establishment of the state's authority will be revived; it will then be for the individual to uphold the rule of Right himself.

Natural Right allows private wars by being silent on this issue. It is Human Right that limits the possibility of waging private wars. Natural Right complies with this decision of Human Right by disallowing private wars after the courts were established and as far as effective recourse to these courts can be sought.

However, the situation might be somewhat different under Arbitrary Divine Right, in particular under the Law of the Gospel as "perfect" Arbitrary Divine Right.[29] Grotius certainly acknowledges that God has obliged Christians to be more patient than anyone else is required under Natural Right or under non-Christian Human Right. God has more right to our lives than we have ourselves, and therefore God could have obligated us that we should rather be killed than kill when we are endangered by others. However, Grotius doubts whether God really has thus obliged us to this extent. There are quotations from the Holy Scripture that could be used to assert this: "Do not avert those who insult you" and "Do not defend yourselves, beloved".[30] Moreover, there are the words that Christ addressed to St. Peter: "Put back your sword in the sheath; for he who reaches for the

---

28 Cf. ibid., I.III.ii.

29 Cf. ibid., I.III.ii.

30 Cf. Matthew 5: 39.

sword, shall die through the sword".[31] Furthermore, there is the image of Christ who has died for his enemies as well. Likewise, there are various authorities amongst the ancient Christians who had been critical of private self-defence, even though they sometimes had at the same time asserted the legitimacy of public wars. Remarkably, Grotius here parts with the Patristic authorities, with whom he otherwise tends to sympathise, and joins the Scholastics, whom he elsewhere tends to despise. He asserts that the patience to be exercised in relation to one's enemies does not present an obligation: the Gospel commands us to love our neighbours as much as ourselves, but not more than ourselves. Thus, in the case of imminent harm it is not prohibited to take care of oneself rather than to take care of others. Even the conventional argument that the victim should not send the attacker to eternal damnation, and thus should not kill the attacker in the course of committing a crime, does not convince Grotius in this respect: the victim might also require some more time for penitence; moreover, the attacker might also have some time left for penitence before he dies.

2. Public Wars

Public wars in the sense applied by Grotius are wars amongst states that do not stand in any relation of subordination to each other, or in other words, wars amongst sovereign states.[32] Public wars can either be formal wars or "less formal" wars. Grotius notes that a formal war has often been referred to as a *bellum iustum*, whereby *iustum* is to be understood in the sense of "legally correct". This is however not to say that only formal wars are admissible.[33]

For a formal public war there are two requirements under the Human Right of Nations: First, the war must be initiated by those who hold sovereign authority in the state. Second, a formal war requires a formal declaration of war.[34]

Informal wars lack these characteristics. They can be waged by a state against private persons and may be initiated from any institution of a state, without necessarily requiring the initiative of the holder of the sovereign authority. Any government authority has the right to wage a war in defence of the inhabitants entrusted to it and in exercise of its power as far as it faces violent resistance. However, Grotius remarks that in light of the dangers which accompany warfare the laws of nearly every state stipulate that only

---

31 Cf. Matthew 26: 52.

32 Cf. IBP, I.III.iv.

33 On the position of the just war literature in relation to informal wars see F. H. Russell, *The Just War in the Middle Ages*, pp. 159 et seq., 307 et seq.

34 Cf. IBP, III.III.

the holder of sovereign authority may initiate the war. The authority to wage war is then subject to the internal regulations of the state. Yet the interpretation of such regulations still has to take account of practical needs; therefore, in certain cases minor authorities may be entitled to use force even without any particular mandate by their superiors. Furthermore, minor authorities can be specifically authorised by the holder of the sovereign power to wage wars; nevertheless, Grotius thinks a merely presumed mandate is normally insufficient except in urgent cases.[35]

The aforementioned definitions of war, of formal and informal wars presented here are for Grotius a sole matter of the Human Right of Nations. They do not possess much relevance for the question of whether any violent action taken is legitimate or whether a war is justified. Nevertheless, this classification of wars is decisive for Grotius' further treatment of the Right to War and the Right in War, for Grotius is mainly interested in the formal war in the sense described above. Nevertheless, certain features of the Right to War and the Right in War may also become relevant for private wars, for mixed wars, or for "less formal" public wars.

III. Legitimacy of War

As we have seen above, the definition of war offered by Grotius does not contain any judgement upon the legitimacy of war, or, more generally speaking, whether it is morally acceptable to exercise violence at all. Yet, Grotius believes that wars can indeed be legitimate under Natural Right and Arbitrary Divine Right, and thus firmly rejects the Christian pacifist tradition of war.

1. Legitimacy of War under Natural Right

In his perception of the status of war under Natural Right, Grotius claims to follow Cicero, who had developed his theory on war in parallel to a Stoic concept[36]: There are certain primary impulses of nature and secondary principles which are to be applied to the primary impulses. The striving of an animal to preserve itself and its conditions, the striving for self-preservation, and the abhorrence of death and those things which appear to contribute to

35 Cf. ibid., I.III.v.

36 Cf. M. T. Cicero, *De Officiis*, I.XI.36; on the Ciceronian doctrine of just war and its impact on the Roman foreign policy see E. Seckel, *Über Krieg und Recht in Rom*, pp. 12 et seq.; A. Heuss, *Die völkerrechtlichen Grundlagen der römischen Außenpolitik in republikanischer Zeit*, pp. 237 et seq.

that animal's perishing, are impulses. No one would choose rather to damage one's own body than to maintain it healthy and appropriate. From there a primary obligation is to be derived to maintain oneself in the natural state, and to hold on to what complies with one's nature, as well as to avoid what is against it.[37]

Furthermore, all human actions have to comply with reason, for reason is more important than the body. This compliance of actions with reason, which Grotius regards as morality, is to be deemed worthier than the aforementioned primary impulses. Though the impulses of nature lead us to reason, reason has to be dearer to us than those primary impulses. As all this is acknowledged by any reasonable human being without the necessity of any further evidence, the examination of the position of Natural Right in relation to war has to start with asking what complies with the primary impulses of nature. Only after having done so may one proceed to those principles which were established subsequently, but are of higher value, and which are not only to be accepted if commanded explicitly but have to be adhered to in every way.

Morality can either prescribe specific rules: in this case the morality of a certain act can be determined precisely; then even the slightest deviation from the rule of morality already constitutes a moral failure. Alternatively there may be rules of morality which allow for moral discretion; in this case the observation of certain moral rules is praiseworthy, but any deviation from such rules is then still permissible without resulting in a moral transgression. In these latter cases divine laws and human laws often transform something which is praiseworthy into something which presents an obligation. Yet, in relation to Natural Right it is (only) necessary to find out whether something can be done without committing an injustice in the sense of acting contrary to rational nature and to human community. The question of whether a certain alternative is more praiseworthy than another alternative is irrelevant in this respect.

In applying the aforementioned principles on war, Grotius asserts that firstly there are no primary impulses which are contrary to war. On the contrary, all natural impulses are favourable to it. This is because the ultimate end of war is the preservation of life and limbs, and the defence or acquisition of those goods that are necessary to sustain life. Grotius' account of the interrelation between nature and war so far strongly resembles the martial tradition of war with its willingness to justify the use of force with the natural disposition of human beings.[38] However, he draws different conclusions from his observations regarding the relationship between nature and war: reason and the nature of the human society are to be considered of higher moral value than the natural inclination of human beings to use force.

37 Cf. IBP, I.II.i.

38 Cf. F. Meinecke, *Die Idee der Staatsräson in der neueren Geschichte*, pp. 189 et seq.

Reason and the nature of human society do not prohibit the application of force absolutely and under any circumstance, but only such use of force which contradicts the principles of human society, i.e. which violates the right of someone else, for the end of human society lies in the preservation of everyone's rights and possessions by joint forces and the co-operation of everyone. This is regardless of whether proprietary rights have yet been introduced, because even if they had not, still everyone would own his life, limbs, and freedom for himself, so that these could not be attacked by someone else without injustice. Likewise, it is permissible to use things which are the common property of human society and even consume them completely. Anyone who prevents someone else from making legitimate use of this access to common property acts contrary to justice. It is therefore not contrary to the nature of human society to care for oneself and to pursue one's own ends, as long as this does not violate the rights of others. Even the use of force is not unjust, as long as the rights of others are not violated. Grotius thus implicitly rejects the martial tradition, which endorses the use of force as an end in itself. Yet by holding the use of force to be legitimate in certain cases, Grotius at the same time disagrees with the absolute rejection of force in the pacifist tradition.

2. Legitimacy of War under Arbitrary Divine Right

From the fact that something is permissible under Natural Right one cannot draw the inference that God could not have devised otherwise under Arbitrary Divine Right, because Natural Right does not prohibit war, but only permits it implicitly. Indeed Grotius acknowledges that the question of whether war is legitimate under the Law of the Gospel is not easy to answer.[39] Nevertheless, he endeavours to prove that God has not prohibited war, and thus refutes the Christian pacifist tradition of war: while he concedes that *prima facie* various arguments could be gained from the Gospel against the legitimacy of war, in the end both the pre-Christian Arbitrary Divine Right as well as the Law of the Gospel permit the waging of wars, even though these sets of Right impose certain limitations on warfare in addition to those derived from Natural Right.

In the greater part of his treatment of the legitimacy of war under the Law of the Gospel Grotius follows the medieval canonists' position as famously displayed in Gratian's Causa 23.[40] The details of Grotius' discussion of arguments for the legitimacy of war and the refutation of counter-

39 Cf. IBP, I.II.v.

40 Gratian, *Decretum*, C. 23; on the canonist tradition of just war cf. F. H. Russell, *The Just War in the Middle Ages*, pp. 56 et seq.

arguments need not interest us; we may here limit our attention to certain illustrative examples from Grotius' exposition. In his analysis of the justification of war under Arbitrary Divine Right in *De Iure Belli ac Pacis* Grotius first analyses the position of the Law of the Gospel in relation to Natural Right and the pre-Christian Arbitrary Divine Right.[41] Grotius believes that the Gospel does not prohibit war. The arguments brought forward by Grotius are, however, not primarily concerned with the justification of war itself, but instead focus on the legitimate use of force by Christians in exercising authority, e.g. by punishing offenders, by resorting to self-defence, and by enforcing rightful claims against others. Thus war is for Grotius simply a problem of upholding the order of Right through the employment of force, which is closely related to the exercise of jurisdiction in human affairs.

Grotius perceives the first and most important evidence for the legitimacy of war under the Law of the Gospel and for the thesis that Christ has not abolished the Right of War altogether in St. Paul's exhortation in his letter to Timothy to make petitions, prayers, callings, and actions of grace for all human beings, in order to strive for a fruitful and peaceful life, in piety and holiness, because this is pleasing to God, who wants that all human beings are saved.[42] From this Grotius draws the following three inferences[43]: Firstly, it pleases God if Christians become kings. Secondly, even as kings they remain Christians. Thirdly, it is pleasing to God if Christian kings secure a peaceful life for other Christians. Grotius believes that the question of how this is to be achieved is explained by St. Paul in his letter to the Romans[44], where he states that the superiors have been appointed by God to do us good; we should have fear if we have done evil, as the superiors have the sword not in vain. By this image of the sword Grotius sees encompassed the power to punish, including in particular, but not limited to, the use of the real sword. Grotius sees the same statement in the second Psalm, which admonishes all kings to receive the son of God with reverence, i.e. to make themselves his servants in their respective positions as kings. Grotius finds additional support for this in Augustine's interpretation of these texts, according to which kings serve God by commanding the good and preventing evil, not only in relation to human society, but also in relation to the divine religion. This also includes the punishment of such acts that are contrary to God's commandments. For Grotius there is then not only a licence for warfare because of the absence of any explicit prohibition to the contrary under the Law of the Gospel, but even an obligation to use force for

41 Cf. IBP, I.II.vi.

42 2 Timothy 1 et seq.

43 Cf. IBP, I.II.viii.

44 Romans 13:4.

the maintenance of Right. The Law of the Gospel then even provides a positive directive to the ruler to ensure a good life in the state by all means, including the waging of war if necessary to defend this good and peaceful order. Due to the task entrusted to the ruler under Arbitrary Divine Right, the ruler cannot even choose to submit to the threat of unrest or of other evil, but is bound to defend his people and to endeavour to restore a peaceful order. On the other hand, under Arbitrary Divine Right the ruler has at least some discretion as to how to achieve this aim; there are no detailed prescriptions apparent for when and how to wage a war, other than the rather general obligation to use force if this becomes necessary.

A further reason given by Grotius for the legitimacy of warfare is one of practicality: If the right of the state to resort to force, by way of both inflicting the death penalty and by waging war, was denied or abolished, a flood of offences would have to be expected as a consequence. If such dramatic a consequence had really been intended by Christ, he would have made this explicit; he would have clearly expressed that no one should be subjected to the death penalty and that no one should bear arms. However, he had not done this, and the counter-arguments usually derived from the Gospel are in Grotius' opinion either quite general or quite dubious in this respect. Reason commands to limit the meaning of such general expressions.

Finally, we shall briefly consider Grotius' refutation of counter-arguments against the admissibility of war under the Law of the Gospel.[45] There is firstly the prophecy of Isaiah, according to which the peoples will turn their swords into ploughs and their spears into scythes.[46] Grotius understands this prophecy as referring to the time when all peoples have accepted the law of Christ and will fulfil it. As soon as this stage has been reached, there will no longer be wars at all as then there will only be Christians who live in a Christian way. Thus, one cannot draw any inference from this prophecy to the situation before this end is reached.

Secondly, there are various arguments against the permissibility of war taken from the Sermon on the Mount.[47] This is in particular the reference to the quotation according to which there should no longer be the principle "eye for eye, and tooth for tooth", but if one receives a blow at one's right cheek, one should also offer the left cheek. From this some authors had concluded that one must not hinder or prosecute injustice, neither in public life, nor in private life, but rather suffer injuries than repay them. Grotius replies to this with a twofold counter-argument: First this exhortation to submit to violence as set out in the Sermon on the Mount is not addressed to superiors, but to individuals as private victims of an injustice committed

45 Cf. IBP, I.II.viii.

46 Isaiah 2:4.

47 Matthew 5.

against them individually. Consequently, the Sermon on the Mount would seem to set out a private ethic designed to coin the conduct of individuals in their social intercourse, without necessarily giving any guidelines in the domain of political ethics within the framework of human society. The order rather to accept injuries than to injure by way of retribution only entails the acceptance of minor injuries such as blows on the cheek, but not major ones, which are conventionally taken as justification of a war. Similar replies are being made by Grotius to the reference to the commandment also to leave the cloak to those who resort to the court in order to win the frock. According to Grotius, this exhortation is simply designed to admonish Christians not to quarrel with each other in pagan court rooms; likewise the Jews had regarded it as an insult of God's name to refer a case pending amongst Jews to alien judges. Instead Christ requires patience from us, so that we shall not quarrel in front of a pagan court about minor things which can be replaced very easily, even if we are fully justified to do so under human laws. In a similar way Grotius counters various other arguments from the Sermon on the Mount, by limiting the scope of its commandments to minor issues and excluding any inference from them to major matters. Thus, the commandment to give as we are requested is qualified by Grotius to mean that we are requested to share our surplus with those in need, whereas a literal interpretation of this commandment might open the way for the conclusion that we have to give anything and under any circumstance if we are requested by someone else to do so. The commandment to suffer minor injuries is to be derived from Christ's more general commandment of patience. However, this does not apply to the suffering of unbearable injuries.

The third counter-argument against the admissibility of war is taken from the commandment to love our neighbours, including our enemies, by which the old Jewish commandment to love one's neighbours and to hate one's enemies had been replaced.[48] However, Grotius holds that the love for one's neighbour can be reconciled very well with the death penalty and with the waging of war: the Jewish commandment to love one's neighbour had already not been interpreted in a way so as to render the death penalty impermissible; Jewish judges could sentence Jewish convicts to death, and there are also various examples in which certain Jewish tribes waged war against other Jewish tribes. Likewise, even if we are ordered to love everyone in light of the coming of Christ, even our enemies, we still may do as the Jews were allowed to do in relation to our neighbours: we may punish them if necessary, and we may wage wars against them. This is true even though the Law of the Gospel prescribes us to pay a higher degree of love to our neighbours than the Jews had to pay according to their laws: we do not have to love everyone in equal measure, but we may still love our father more

48 Matthew 5:43 et seq.

than we love a foreigner. Thence the law of love also orders us to prefer the well-being of the innocent before the well-being of the guilty and to prefer the general well-being of everyone to that of any individual, or in other words: we are to employ attributive justice as justice of judgement in relation to the use of force. We should love in pursuit of the example given by God himself; but God himself has also time and again given preference to wrath over clemency, and has therefore punished those who resisted his will.

Interestingly, Grotius in this context does not follow the example of Augustine, who had demanded that punishment should be guided and directed by the love of the punisher for the one who is punished, and even that punishment was due because of the love ordered to us, just as the loving father punishes his beloved children not despite, but because of his love.[49] Furthermore, Grotius not only rejects the pacifist preference for patience in relation to the suffering of injustice, but even argues in favour of an obligation to uphold justice by all means necessary under the Law of the Gospel.

IV. Right to War

In treating all the different types of war as means to uphold the overall system of Right, Grotius implicitly denies that there is any legitimate reason to wage war beyond the preservation and restoration of justice. In this sense there are only just wars or unjust wars – yet he thus indirectly excludes any idealist wars, such as a holy war or a republican war which is undertaken with the aim to implement any particular idea, such as the conversion of mankind to a certain creed or to reach a new, utopian stage of history.

The traditional just war doctrine had required the following features of any war to qualify it as just war: First, a just war has to be initiated or waged by the right authority. Second, only such wars could be just which were waged because of a just reason. Third, any actions of war had to be accompanied by the right intention, namely the knowledge of the existence of a just reason and the willingness to pursue a war because of this right reason. Further elements had been added to these traditional elements from time to time, the most important of which is probably the appropriateness of measures taken in a war.[50]

The elements of the right authority, the just reason, and the appropriateness of the measures taken can be detected quite easily in Grotius' elaboration on the requisites of a just war. The requirement of the

---

49 For this Augustine tradition see C. A. Stumpf, "Vom Heiligen Krieg zum gerechten Krieg", pp. 23 et seq.

50 Cf. F. H. Russell, *The Just War in the Middle Ages*, pp. 155 et seq.

right intention, however, is less easy to identify; though we may suggest that it is also existent in Grotius' theological system of international relations, which relies on a personal responsibility of the individual moral agent, we are yet to see how Grotius accounts for this requirement.

Yet, before we turn to analyse Grotius' views on just war, we may first note that similar requirements had also applied in the case of other religious traditions of war, such as in the case of holy wars of ancient Israel and in the concept of the Jihad as just war according to the concept of a number of Islamic legal scholars. However, it may be contended that the holy war of ancient Israel was less connected to the idea of the maintenance or restoration of an all-encompassing system of justice, but rather waged according to an explicit divine order on a case-to-case basis which provided the respective just cause. Consequently, the right authority necessary for waging war was granted by an explicit divine mandate.[51] Likewise, the concept of the Islamic Jihad as a just war was founded on the idea of defending the realm of Islam against attacks launched by unbelievers and thus was foremostly a concept of self-defence.[52] Furthermore, Jihad could only be undertaken on an order of the Caliphate or Imamate as the exclusive authority to decide on war.[53] The Grotian understanding of the just war certainly has various parallels with these two religious traditions of war; however, in contrast to these traditions Grotius places a stronger emphasis on the individual responsibility of the agents, in particular of the holders of sovereign authority, while the notion of divine providence exists to a much weaker degree in his concept.

1. Just Authority

According to Grotius, the type of authority required to wage war legitimately depends upon the type of war that is to be waged. While for a private war no special authority is necessary at all – save for the absence of an effective jurisdiction to which recourse could be sought – in the case of a public informal or less formal war in principle any kind of public authority suffices. Yet, the use of force amongst private individuals or minor state authorities presents an exception from the ordinary means of jurisdiction provided within any established state. In his treatment on the Right to War Grotius primarily focuses on the public formal war: a public formal war can only be initiated by the holder of the highest sovereign power of a state, as such a war is the only means to enforce rules of Right in relation to sovereigns, and such rules can normally only be enforced legitimately by other sovereigns as

51 Cf. C. A. Stumpf, "Vom Heiligen Krieg zum gerechten Krieg", pp. 3 et seq.

52 Khadduri, *The Islamic Conception of Justice*, pp. 168 et seq.

53 Khadduri, *The Islamic Law of Nations*, pp. 15 et seq.

their peers. Hence, a public formal war is a war between holders of sovereign authority.

As a general rule, a war is normally waged for one's own ends, though one can also assist others in waging war or wage war on someone else's behalf.[54] For example, if a state has been violated by another state it is primarily for the attacked state to defend itself. If someone's proprietary rights have been violated by someone else, it is for the victim of this violation to recover such proprietary rights for himself. Public formal wars can therefore be regarded as the ordinary self-defence amongst sovereigns as there is no other institution to which recourse could be sought by sovereigns if their rights are violated by others.

Nevertheless, Grotius recognises that it is also possible for a sovereign ruler to assist another party in self-defence. There is no legal restriction that could prevent us from helping others under foreign attack.[55] There are various types of bonds amongst human beings, such as the bond between a state and its citizens[56], alliances[57], friendship[58], or family relations; if no other special bond can be drawn upon, there is yet the common nature of human beings which entitles any human being to render help to others.[59] Thus, interference of a third party on behalf of someone else does not need to be vindicated by a prior alliance; common human nature is enough to license such interventions.[60] Here Grotius follows Vitoria's thesis that sovereign rulers exercise the power to wage war against other sovereign rulers on behalf of human society.[61] It is not a particular right that is enforced in war; rather any public war presents an act of asserting justice in the natural community of human beings. The entitlement to enforce justice in relation to sovereign rulers is, however, limited to sovereign rulers themselves. It should be noted that a similar stance had been taken by Calvin, who thought it necessary for kings to execute public vengeance.[62] This also corresponds to the Islamic doctrine of the Jihad as just war: while every individual Muslim is obliged to participate in a Jihad, any Jihad requires a respective declaration by the Caliphate or Imamate; a war not approved by or on behalf of the Caliphate or Imamate is strictly prohibited.[63]

---

54 Cf. IBP, I.V.i.
55 Cf. ibid., I.V.ii.
56 Cf. ibid., II.XXV.i.
57 Cf. ibid., II.XXV.iv.
58 Cf. ibid., II.XXV.v.
59 Cf. ibid., II.XXV.vi.
60 Cf. P. Haggenmacher, *Grotius et la doctrine de la guerre juste*, pp. 139 et seq.
61 Cf. F. Vitoria, *De Iure Belli*.
62 Cf. J. Calvin, *Institutio Religionis Christianae*, IV.xx.13.
63 Cf. C. A. Stumpf, "Völkerrecht unter Kreuz und Halbmond", pp. 85 et seq.

The general admissibility to render assistance to others in warfare corresponds in Grotius' concept to a respective qualified obligation: the well-being of others does not have to be as close to our heart as our own.[64] The same applies to foreign citizens, who do not have to pursue the interests of a country other than their own.[65] This is again consistent with Grotius' more general notion of self-defence: though he seems to be in favour of a duty of the state to assist citizens who suffer violations of their individual rights – as the protection of individuals is the very purpose for which a state is normally established – Grotius would hardly go as far as to assert any obligation of individuals to assist other human beings that are attacked. Individuals are not under the same general obligation to protect their fellow-individuals as the ruler is in relation to his subjects.

The question of who has to initiate a just war is to be distinguished from the question of who may participate in a just war. Grotius here claims that according to Natural Right all subjects may be employed in a war.[66] Nevertheless, special laws as part of the national Human Right frequently exclude certain groups of individuals; for example, slaves were excluded from warfare under Roman law; moreover, the clergy is usually exempt from warfare as the acts required from combatants are in Grotius' opinion not compatible with the purity to be maintained by clerics. Exceptions are to be made from these exceptions in cases of extreme need. Thus, as a last resort even clerics might be requested to join in military activities if, for example, the country cannot otherwise be saved from foreign attacks.

2. Just Reason

The second prerequisite for a just war traditionally acknowledged by the just war doctrine is a just reason or a just cause. Naturally, this prerequisite is of greatest interest to Grotius, as only a breach of Right can constitute a just reason. Grotius classifies potential reasons for warfare into three different groups according to their respective legitimacy. He distinguishes between clearly just reasons for wars, unjust reasons, and reasons which are dubious.

2.1. Clearly Just Reasons

Grotius points out that one has to make a distinction between causes which clearly justify a war because they are a consequence of a manifest breach of

64 Cf. IBP, II.XXV.vii.
65 Cf. ibid., II.XXV.viii.
66 Cf. ibid., I.V.iv.

Right on the one hand and causes which are mainly rooted in the desire for gain on the other, but which are not necessarily to be delineated from Right. One might also call the latter incidents – as distinguished from a cause in the sense of just cause – that give rise to war. Then Grotius states that the only just cause for war is an injustice.[67] This rather subtle distinction separates a genuine reason, which can find its source only in the preservation of Right, from reasons which may have a serious background, but in truth only serve as pretext for taking advantage of someone else's fault.

There are basically three types of injustice which Grotius conceives as possible causes for just wars, which correspond to the reasons for initiating legal actions in court: first the defence of what is ours, second the enforcement of a claim to what is due to us, and third the punishment of an offence.[68]

2.1.1. Defence

As regards the just defence of what is ours, Grotius first claims that we may defend our life even by taking the life of those that attack us.[69] However, self-defence exempts no one from the rule of Right, so the strict limitations which govern the conduct of any human being in the course of war also apply to a person defending himself. Here Grotius follows the line set out by Suarez in relation to self-defence.[70]

According to Grotius, nature recommends us rather to kill someone else than to let us be killed; hence, the idea of retribution appears to be absent from Grotius' understanding of self-defence, though retribution will come into play later when we approach punishment as a reason for waging war. Under Natural Right it is even possible to kill someone justly who threatens our life without his fault, for example, because he acts in good faith as a soldier, because he mistakenly confuses us with the true aim of his attack, or because he is not responsible for his act. Furthermore, not only life can be defended by means of war, but also our limbs as far as their loss would come equal to the loss of life.[71] Grotius holds the same for the defence of female honour.[72]

More difficult is the question whether it is permissible to kill an innocent person who intervenes and impedes one's flight or the defence necessary for escaping death.[73] Grotius thinks that such killing is generally permissible under Natural Right, but not under the Law of the Gospel, which commands

67 Cf. ibid., I.II.i.
68 Cf. ibid., I.II.ii.
69 Cf. ibid., I.II.iii.
70 Cf. F. Suarez, *Opus de triplici virtute theologica, fide, spe et charitate,* D. 13.
71 Cf. IBP, I.II.vi.
72 Cf. ibid., I.II.vii.
73 Cf. ibid., I.II.iv.

us to love our neighbour as much as ourselves. The same is held by many representatives of the canonist just war theory, but also by various Islamic legal scholars in relation to non-combatants in the Jihad. Nevertheless, referring to Thomas Aquinas, Grotius claims that in the case of a true defence properly understood there is no intentional killing, because the death of the person attacking us is not the primary aim of the defence. Even so, Grotius regards it as preferable to seek other remedies for defence than killing the attacker, such as measures of deterrence or of weakening him. This treatment of the subject leaves one with the impression that Grotius himself feels somewhat awkward about this issue: while the position under Natural Right is quite clear, as it is for Grotius certainly compliant with the rational nature of human beings to preserve oneself even at the expense of other human beings' lives, the commandment to love one's neighbour as core principle of the Law of the Gospel is rather difficult to apply in such a case: the argument presented by Thomas Aquinas is less than satisfactory, as one cannot earnestly deny that by preserving oneself at the expense of someone else's life one at least has a circumstantial intention to kill this person by knowingly taking this into account in the sense of a *dolus eventualis*. Thus for Grotius the only solution left is to advocate the greatest possible care not to kill any innocent person, without ultimately denying that there may be cases in which such killing is ultimately to be deemed legitimate even under the Law of the Gospel; Grotius might as well have referred to his aforementioned interpretation of the commandment to love one's neighbour as oneself, but not more than oneself. Again Grotius follows a path pursued by Suarez, who had also admitted that non-combatants could be killed incidentally.[74]

On the other hand, there may be an exception to the permissibility of defence in relation to the lives of people that attack us but nevertheless are of great benefit to others. Such exceptions are not only to be made under God's law in the Old and the New Testament, but also under the law of Nature.[75] Their importance is then to be esteemed higher than the legal position that would be held against them.

Another problem arising in this respect is the question of whether measures of defence have to remain in proportion to the aim of the defence. Here Natural Right and Arbitrary Divine Right come to different conclusions. For example, minor injuries, such as insults or the like, can serve as justification for the killing in defence under expletive justice and therefore under Natural Right if this is necessary to restore justice, but not under the

---

74 Cf. F. Suarez, *Opus des triplici virtute theologica, fide, spe et charitate*, D. 13; cf. also O. M. T. O'Donovan, J. Lockwood O'Donovan, *From Irenaeus to Grotius: A Sourcebook in Christian Political Thought*, pp. 726 et seq.

75 Cf. IBP, I.II.ix.

Law of the Gospel.[76] Similar principles apply to the violation of proprietary rights. Under the Natural Right principle of expletive justice it is permissible to kill a thief if this is necessary to preserve one's property. The difference between property and life is here equated for the benefit of the innocent and to the disadvantage of the offender.[77] Grotius then notes that Jewish law had differentiated between defence during the night on the one hand and defence during daytime on the other: the killing of a thief was therefore permissible if the thief was detected in the night, as the absence of witnesses at night time makes it more difficult to identify the thief later and to subsequently recover one's stolen property. However, it was impermissible to kill a thief if he was detected during daylight or if there were witnesses.[78]

Grotius regards the situation under the Law of the Gospel as more complex: while he claims that nearly all lawyers and theologians held that a human being may be killed in defence of one's own property, thus exceeding even what was allowed under Jewish law, Grotius thinks that under the Law of the Gospel the prerequisites for defence against the violation of proprietary rights are to be interpreted much more strictly.[79] Thus, we may defend our property only with measures that stay below the threshold of killing a thief. Killing a thief can only be accepted under the Law of the Gospel if the property to be stolen is necessary to sustain our own life or the life of our dependants, or if there is no hope that the good can be recovered with the assistance of the judge. Otherwise the property has to be abandoned. This is because man has been made in the image of God, wherefore the life of any human being is incalculably higher than any property whatsoever.

There remains the question whether it suffices that a particular human law, made by someone who has authority over life and death, allows a private person to kill a thief. Grotius replies in the negative[80]: First, civil laws could never have the power over life and death in relation to any type of offence, but only in relation to offences that deserve the death of the offender. Second, no civil law may allow for persons who are to be punished with the death penalty to be executed privately, unless in the case of the gravest offences. Thus, a human law may exempt the killer of the thief from punishment, but it cannot confer the right to execute someone to a private person.

As regards the type and degree of danger necessary to allow a defence by means of war Grotius requires that the respective danger is present or at least imminent. In this respect he tends to accord a rather broad sense to the word

76 Cf. ibid., I.II.x.
77 Cf. ibid., I.II.xi.
78 Cf. ibid., I.II.xii.
79 Cf. ibid., I.II.xiii.
80 Cf. ibid., I.II.xvi.

"present".[81] However, a suspected danger is not sufficient. This is not to say that a war could not be waged if one state believes itself to be attacked though it is actually not, but only that no danger is present if there is no actual threat but merely a suspicion of hostile activities. Nor is there a present danger if there is only information about preparatory measures taken, such as a plot being made. Thus defence could not serve as justification for any pre-emptive war waged against a state that simply engages in arming itself. Again Grotius is far from understanding war simply as pursuit of political aims by special means as, for example, Clausewitz[82]: in no case may a war be waged in order to prevent the increase of a power which later could prove to be harmful. Though this aspect may be considered a matter of utility when making the decision upon waging a war which is justified by a true reason, it may not be treated as a question of Right.[83]

2.1.2. Enforcement of a Claim

A claim that is held by any particular human being may be enforced by that person if there is no particular authority appointed which has a monopoly on the use of force.[84] In a state it will normally be for the court to assist individuals in enforcing their claims. Since between holders of sovereign authority there is no particular authority that could decide upon claims, the holders of sovereign authority will have to take charge of the enforcement of claims themselves.

It has already been noted above that Grotius is quite reluctant to allow for subjective rights to exist under Natural Right or under Arbitrary Divine Right. Thus, claims to be enforced normally have their source in Human Right; as far as claims amongst states are concerned, most of such claims will be regulated by the Human Right of Nations. However, these claims and their enforcement are again supported by the principle of expletive justice under Natural Right according to which one has to render to others what is due to them, and according to which one has to keep one's promises.

2.1.3. Punishment

Punishment is the third potential just cause for a war. It is of a different nature than self-defence and the enforcement of claims, as it is not rooted in subjective legal positions, but rather in the objective retribution for individual guilt of an offender according to the principle of attributive justice under Natural Right. Consequently, there is no particular right of anyone to punish

81 Cf. ibid., I.II.v.

82 Cf. C. von Clausewitz, *Vom Kriege*, I.I.24.

83 Cf. IBP, I.II.xvii.

84 Cf. ibid., I.IV.ii. et seq.

someone else; under Natural Right it is possible for anyone to punish an offender, as long as one has not committed the same offence.[85] Nevertheless, as soon as the legal order of a state has been established, the holder of the sovereign authority has a monopoly to punish offenders who are subject to his authority. This authority to punish is then normally delegated to the judges.

While punishment exerted by God does not require any purpose to be achieved and thus no justification, punishment which is exerted by human beings requires a reason, as they may not simply punish merely out of sadistic impulses or because of a desire for revenge.[86] Human punishment thus needs to be measured according to the use which the offender has drawn from his offence, the interest of those for the benefit of whom the offence is prohibited, and the interest of anyone else.[87]

Details of Grotius' theory of punishment need not interest us in this respect. It is however interesting to ask whether punishment, as an objective enforcement of Right provided for by Natural Right, belongs to expletive justice or to attributive justice. From Grotius' observations on penal justice in *De Satisfactione* we may draw the inference that punishment is a mode of confirmative justice.[88] This means that punishment is entailed by expletive justice: it is inflicted upon the offender because punishment is due to him as satisfaction for his offence. However, this does not suffice for explaining the purposes of punishment envisioned by Grotius: the measure of punishment has to be in proportion to the offence, and thus punishment also pertains to attributive justice as justice of judgement. A killer thus is to be punished more severely than a thief. From what Grotius remarks on the purposes of punishment it becomes clear that not every killer is to be punished in the same way; likewise not every thief is to be treated equally in terms of punishment. It has to be asked what serves the offender right: the thief who has been driven to steal by need is to be treated more mildly than the thief motivated by greed. Moreover, when punishing one has to take account of the damage that has been done to the victim of the offence, or more generally speaking, the interest of those who are protected by the rule the offender has breached. Thus, the punishment for defamation by illegitimately publicising true facts might deserve a lighter treatment than pure insults. Finally, the interests of third parties, namely of the public, have to be borne in mind. Thus it has to be asked whether others have to be warned against committing similar offences. Hence, punishment may be dependent on the necessity to exemplify the noxious effects of an offence. Consequently, drug traffic or

85 Cf. ibid., II.XX.iii.
86 Cf. ibid., II.XX.iv.
87 Cf. ibid., II.XX.vi. et seq.
88 H. Grotius, *De Satisfactione*, I. § 2.

smuggling might be punished according to the need to exemplify the prohibition of such offences for the sake of the public.

In contrast to Grotius' views on penal wars, a strong tendency to outlaw penal wars under modern public international law is to be noted. Thus, only defensive wars are held admissible, whereas penal wars are regarded as aggressive in character. This tendency is also visible in John Rawls' liberal concept of the Law of Peoples. In Rawls' opinion, liberal and "decent" societies will not have any motivation to wage aggressive wars, but will only, if necessary, defend their legal position if attacked by "non-decent" or "outlaw" societies.[89] From there the question arises how breaches of public international law which fall short of an attack on other states can be remedied effectively. Rawls' theory of the Law of Peoples cannot give a satisfactory answer to this, considering the limited effectiveness of the peaceful sanctions which modern public international law offers. One possible solution would be to extend the definition of defensive wars to the effect that they also cover wars which are undertaken in defence of abstract legal principles of public international law. However, Rawls seems to be quite reluctant to pursue this path. In any case, Grotius' concept of penal wars appears to offer a more effective solution to this problem, even if one has to concede that penal wars could well be used as a pretext to pursue illegitimate aims with forceful means.

2.2. Unjust Reasons

In chapter 22 of the second book of *De Iure Belli ac Pacis* Grotius lists causes that do not justify the waging of war against another party. To these belong mere horror[90], a false claim for the discovery of a new land[91], the longing of a subjected people for liberation[92], the wish to subject another people under the pretence that it is for their own good[93], or the alleged claims of the Church to all people and property in unknown parts of the world.[94]

In this respect it suffices to say that any reason that does not consist of a breach of Right cannot serve as just reason for a just war, and thus Grotius implicitly rejects the Republican tradition of war. The desire of an ethnic minority for political freedom may for example be quite understandable in

89 Cf. J. Rawls, *The Law of Peoples*, pp. et seq.
90 Cf. IBP, II.XXII.v.
91 Cf. ibid., II.XXII.ix.
92 Cf. ibid., II.XXII.x.
93 Cf. ibid., II.XXII.xii.
94 Cf. ibid., II.XXII.xiv.

itself; nevertheless, this desire is insufficient to qualify as just reason for a war of separation, unless that desire is grounded in Right.

Quite remarkable is Grotius' clear statement that the Church itself has no claims to all people in unknown parts of the world, by which he implicitly subscribes to the parallel opinions of Vitoria and Suarez.[95] Christ has not established any legally relevant title of the Church to the authority over any people or over any territory. Thus, missionary endeavours may only be undertaken by peaceful means. There is no strict, enforceable obligation of pagans to become Christians; nor has the Pope or any other representative any temporal authority from the respective ecclesiastical office. Consequently, the refusal to become Christian or the denial of the Church's temporal authority cannot qualify as just reason for waging a war. With this statement Grotius distances himself from the Christian holy war tradition which had accompanied certain missionary efforts in Latin America in particular in the 16th century.

2.3. Dubious Reasons

Finally, there are also reasons for wars which, though they are not clearly unjust, still cannot be regarded as clearly just. Grotius remarks that even the performance of an act which is in itself just must be deemed wrong if the person who performs it regards it as unjust.[96] Grotius in this respect refers to the principle that an erring conscience still obligates a person to follow its dictates.

The idea behind Grotius' comments on dubious reasons can be illustrated by the example of a person who kills someone else intentionally out of sheer criminal motives, without knowing that in so doing he saves the life of a third person who at that very moment was threatened by the victim of the killer. Thus anyone would have been justified to kill this person, except the one who did it out of an illegitimate intention.

To decide whether a dubious reason is indeed a just or an unjust reason Grotius recommends to gather all the advice and information accessible, in particular the reasons of others[97] as well as counsel.[98] If there still remain doubts, one still should choose the safest option[99], i.e. in the case of the decision upon waging a war one should opt against it[100], and should

95 Cf. F. Köck, *Der Beitrag der Schule von Salamanca zur Entwicklung der Lehre von den Grundrechten*, pp. 173 et seq.

96 Cf. IBP, II.XXIII.ii.

97 Cf. ibid., II.XXIII.iii.

98 Cf. ibid., II.XXIII.iii.

99 Cf. ibid., II.XXIII.v.

100 Cf. ibid., II.XXIII.vi.

endeavour to resolve remaining disputes by peaceful means, in particular by way of negotiation[101], arbitration[102], or by drawing lots.[103]

Thus, Grotius is by no means an advocate for the strict and merciless enforcement of Right, but rather scrupulous as regards the use of force. For him Right will not necessarily require its enforcement under any circumstance. Hence only clear breaches of Right which are susceptible of being remedied by the use of force by human beings qualify as just reasons for war. Peace or at least the abstention from the use of violence thus gains the benefit of the doubt in Grotius' system. Again Grotius emphasises the personal responsibility of the individual moral agent on the international level.

3. War as Appropriate Means

Even if sufficient cause can be found for war and thus a just reason legitimates war in general, Grotius still argues for the necessity to check the appropriateness of war as measure to serve the cause. Though the introductory remark of Grotius to chapter 24 of the second book of *De Iure Belli ac Pacis*, entitled "Admonishment not to wage a war hastily even though there are just causes", would seem to indicate that Grotius here is not dealing with justice but with "other virtues", it is in fact a legal discourse about the appropriateness of war and the use of force.

Grotius claims that there is an obligation to abandon the care for one's own life in order to care as much as one can for the life and the eternal salvation of others.[104] This is particularly true for Christians, to whom Christ has been the most perfect example. However, this still seems to be also an obligation under Natural Right for anyone, even if to a lesser degree.

According to Grotius, we should not pursue our rights and our claims in the course of a war if this necessarily implies great disadvantages to others. This is a most obvious case of applying attributive justice. In particular, a waiver of the right to exert punishment on those who have done wrong against us is to be considered[105]; mercy should be exercised where possible.[106] The obligation to check the propriety of a measure, in particular of the use of force, is most clearly spelt out by Arbitrary Divine Right, in particular by the Law of the Gospel. However, this obligatory moderation of human conduct is also provided for by Natural Right, as here attributive justice may indeed

101 Cf. ibid., II.XXIII.vii.
102 Cf. ibid., II.XXIII.viii.
103 Cf. ibid., II.XXIII.ix.
104 Cf. ibid., II.XXIV.i.
105 Cf. ibid., II.XXIV.ii.
106 Cf. ibid., II.XXIV.iii.

imply clemency and prudence. It can also be in our own best interest to abstain from waging war[107], in which case one has to compare advantages and disadvantages of warfare carefully.[108] Thus, attributive justice not only has an altruistic dimension: prudence as a virtue entailed by attributive justice is also to be applied to one's own affairs.

This means that justice in the strict sense may have to give way to injustice; yet this is only the case if the blind pursuit of one's right is to be expected to cause more damage than gain from the war. The propriety of measures of war is a requirement which brings equity into play as a legal category. It is thus in the end attributive justice which provides a major check against inappropriate warfare. Grotius even claims that the cases in which a war could or should not be avoided are rare.[109] Thus a war may only be waged in case of great need, or because of a very important reason, and even then only if the situation looks favourable.[110] War as a means to enforce Right obviously misses the point if the success of a military action is already improbable from the outset. Moreover, the rule of Right does not need to be asserted in any case and under all circumstances – Grotius is indeed far from the concept of *fiat iustitia et pereat mundi.*

It is interesting how Grotius here brings into play the requirement of the propriety of war in the light of the question of how to reconcile the strict necessity to uphold justice with the human inclination and Christian counsel to exercise mercy and to forgive, which is inherently problematic for any Christian theory of punishment. In Grotius' elaboration on punishment in *De Satisfactione,* in which he defends the penal-substitution doctrine of atonement in Christ's death against the heretic Socianian understanding of Christ's sacrifice, he contends that a ruler is free to forgive an offence, like a creditor may waive his claim. This case is however different from that of a judge: the judge is not entitled to make dispositions on his authority.[111] Yet, while any ruler is entitled to administer his authority as he sees fit, no ruler may freely decide whether or not to administer justice. It is a ruler's office to uphold justice; however, the ruler has relatively large leeway and does not necessarily have to resort to punishment.

Again the question arises who is responsible for upholding justice amongst sovereigns. There is no particular institution entrusted with the task to punish sovereign rulers, and hence potentially any ruler is entitled to punish other sovereign rulers by waging war upon them, as it is for all rulers to uphold justice in international relations. Nevertheless, there may again be

107 Cf. ibid., II.XXIV.iv.
108 Cf. ibid., II.XXIV.v.
109 Cf. ibid., II.XXIV.viii.
110 Cf. ibid., II.XXIV.ix.
111 Cf. H. Grotius, *De Satisfactione,* II.

more than one alternative for upholding justice if a ruler has committed an offence, and thus there is no strict necessity to wage war, as long as there are other proper means, too, in order to safeguard the general rule of justice amongst rulers. A simple admonishment might suffice; political or economic sanctions might be taken or other, milder, means might be employed in order to restore justice. In any case, it is for the sovereign ruler to choose whatever means he deems fit to restore the order of justice. In taking his choice, however, he has to assess the respective propriety of the measure, and should let himself be guided by clemency before going to extremes, such as waging war.

This again distinguishes Grotius' theory of just war clearly from the idealist traditions, which prefer to subordinate the means to the aims, and thus let the aim alone justify the means which are to be used. For example, in the republican tradition war has often been seen as a necessary evil to implement a certain idea into practice, and thus representatives of the republic tradition have frequently advocated a relatively free use of force as a means to achieve the end, regardless of the individual effects that such measures might entail. Yet here Grotius even parts with various representatives of the just war tradition such as Gratian, who held that the restoration of justice as a general end could justify relatively harsh measures regardless of the merits of the individual case: for him the question is whether justice is to be upheld at any price. Grotius believes that through an improper use of force in the defence of justice new injustice could arise. This view is another confirmation of the thesis that Grotius advocates a theology of international law based on a strong personal responsibility of the individual agent.

4. Just Intention

Compared to other authors on the just war doctrine Grotius has surprisingly little to say about the just intention of the war-faring party with regard to its engagement in war. Traditionally, most lawyers concerned with the prerequisites of a just war held that a war is unjust even though all other conditions are fulfilled if the party having the just cause to wage war does so because of an unjust motivation.[112] There are two remarks by Grotius that shed some light upon his views in this respect.

First, as we have already seen, Grotius adheres to the traditional idea that an erring consciousness obliges. Consequently, an act which is in itself just becomes wrong if it is performed by someone who holds this act in consideration of all aspects to be unjust.[113] From this it may also be concluded

112 Cf. F. H. Russell, *The Just War in the Middle Ages*, pp. 65 et seq.
113 Cf. IBP, II.XXIII.ii.

that a war for which the party in question has sufficient authority and good cause, and which also seems appropriate in light of the circumstances, is nevertheless unjust if the party waging the war is driven by an unjust intention.

For example, there might be a sovereign state that has unjustly been deprived of a certain territory by another sovereign state. However, in truth the state as true owner of this territory had not been interested in the territory; perhaps it is even quite glad to have been relieved of the territory because of the economic burdens connected with it, or because the population was disloyal. Nevertheless, the state seizes the opportunity to wage war against the other state, not with the primary aim to recover the territory, but with the hope to gain economic benefit, e.g. by reparation payments after its victory. Though in this case the other requirements for a just war are fulfilled, the war would nevertheless be unjust as it has not been waged with the intention to rectify the territorial injustice suffered, but merely with the intention to draw gains from it. Like the Spanish moral theologians of the School of Salamanca, in particular Francisco Vitoria, Grotius is convinced that the purpose of war, especially the defence against illegitimate attacks and the punishment of wrongdoings, determines the scope of the means to be employed.[114]

A second remark of Grotius in his elaboration on dubious reasons for war is interesting in this respect. Taking up the traditional question of whether there is the possibility that a war is just in relation to all parties involved, Grotius distinguishes between various meanings of the term "just".[115] If one applies "just" in the sense related to the matter itself, then a war cannot be just in relation to both parties, in the way that a legal dispute cannot be just in relation to both parties involved. It is possible, though, that none of the parties involved acts unjustly: even if one has no right to wage war, one may not be faulted for this if one could not have known that no corresponding right existed. In this case the legal status of a justified party is to be applied in relation to both parties.

For our purpose it is legitimate to turn this statement into its opposite: if one has a right, but does not know or does not believe that one has it, one may not exercise it. Therefore, even if a party is justified in waging a war, but does not know it and wages the war out of an unjust motivation, then this party is to be regarded unjustified. Thus, there is indeed a subjective requirement for a just war in the sense that the party engaging in a war has to do so with the right intention.

114 Cf. F. Vitoria, *De Iure Belli*, q. 4.

115 Cf. IBP, II.XXIII.xiii.

V. Right in War

The Right of War consists of those rules which govern the process of the restoration of the Right of Peace by means of using force if a deviation from the "normal" legal status, i.e. a breach of Right, has occurred. The Right of War can be classified into those rules of war which determine the admissibility of using force in general as Right to War on the one hand and those rules which concern the mode of using force in the course of a war as Right in War on the other. In short, the Right to War answers the question if war may be waged in the sense of substantive Right, whereas the Right in War focuses on the question of how war may be waged as procedural Right.

A presentation of the relevant areas of this procedural Right is only one aim pursued by Grotius. A second dominating feature of Grotius' comments on the Right in War is a – sometimes quite harsh – critique of the predominant contemporary practice as regards war in the light of the overarching categories of Natural Right and Arbitrary Divine Right. Thus Grotius here attempts to present the Right in War as it is, but also, and probably more importantly, as it should be. We shall firstly learn some of the general rules of the Right in War before we approach some examples of the critique of the Right in War. In so doing we will furthermore demonstrate that Grotius implicitly rejects the martial tradition as well as the idealist tradition of war, which both were disinclined to subject warfare to legal limitations.

1. General Rules of the Right in War

According to Grotius, there are three basic principles regarding the means that may be employed in a war. First, virtually anything which serves the pursuit of the aims set for the war is deemed permissible.[116] This presupposes the principle that the moral judgement on any means is dependent upon the purpose for which it is used. If a just war is waged by the right authority, because of just causes, in the right intention, and if the war presents an appropriate means to reach a legitimate aim, in particular the restoration of justice, then in principle any measure may be used which is conducive to successfully end the war. If the war is inherently just, then the measures employed in the course of the war are justified, too. This statement might seem to present a contradiction to Grotius' above-mentioned demand to moderate warfare. Yet this is not the case: while Grotius certainly is in favour of employing only legitimate measures in warfare which are in proportion to the aim pursued, he nevertheless contends that a justified war has to be undertaken effectively. Hence, there is no general requirement to fight a war

116 Cf. ibid., III.I.ii.

in an open or so-called honest way; the justified party may deceive the other party, or it may use hidden tactics to overcome the opponent as long as the war is covered by the justified aim. Consequently, a justified war may be undertaken with the help of ambushes or other tricks.[117] Grotius here follows the traditional approach to the use of cunning and trickery.[118] However, this is not to say that Natural Right is suspended as regards measures taken in a war. The war-faring parties still have to adhere to Natural Right in all their actions. Thus, if a promise has been given to the enemy, this promise has to be honoured[119], as this is required by expletive justice. The principles of Natural Right apply to situations of war as much as they apply to situations of peace. The aforementioned general principles of the Right in War apply to Christians and non-Christians alike: there are no specific Christian principles of a Right in War. Likewise, there are no different aims for warfare for Christians than there are for non-Christians. Thus, there are also the same means to be employed by Christians and non-Christians alike. Consequently, Christians may take recourse to ambushes as well as may non-Christians. However, as we shall see the measures that may legitimately be taken by all under Natural Right are still subject to an additional check under Arbitrary Divine Right, and therefore Christians may face further restrictions in the acts they may engage in during a war.

According to the second principle, the right one has against one's enemy is not to be judged from the reason for the war only, but also under other aspects that may arise in the course of the war as well.[120] This is to say that changes in the legal situation after the war has been started have to be taken into account to measure the respective legitimacy of warfare. Thus, if former allies form a new alliance with the enemy, these former allies may be treated as enemies as well.

The third principle regarding the Right in War concerns collateral effects of wars: certain consequences which might not legitimately be intended in themselves, may in proportion be treated as an acceptable price to pay for pursuing hostilities. For example, women or little children may not normally be attacked in war; a direct attack on women or children will hardly ever be covered by the aim of the war, and thus is prohibited in general. However, if women and little children are on a ship which is a legitimate target of military action, then their killing may be acceptable.[121] In such a case, the primary aim, the destruction of a military ship of the enemy, is truly

117 Cf. ibid., III.I.vi et seq.

118 Cf. F. H. Russell, *The Just War in the Middle Ages*, pp. 23 et seq.; cf. C. A. Stumpf, "Vom Heiligen Krieg zum gerechten Krieg", pp. 29 et seq.

119 Cf. ibid., III.XIX.

120 Cf. ibid., III.I.iii.

121 Cf. ibid., III.I.iv.

legitimate. The legitimacy of this measure is not affected by circumstantial events which entail side-effects or "collateral damages" according to the modern terminology that are not intended and could not even be justifiably intended. In such cases it is rather the duty of the opponent to exclude the occurrence of such effects, but there is no duty of the justified party to avoid them. Still, Grotius qualifies his position by pointing out that negative side-effects may not be acceptable under any circumstance. One may not always fully exercise one's own rights, regardless of the circumstances and regardless of the effects that such actions entail. In particular, the commandment to love our neighbours requires a qualification. Thus, the Law of the Gospel may require Christians rather not to insist on one's legal position if this cannot be done without bringing harm upon innocent people.

2. Critique of Practice

When discussing particular issues of the Right in War in *De Iure Belli ac Pacis*, Grotius on the one hand presents the respective legal situation as he sees it ordained in the Right of Nations.[122] On the other hand, however, Grotius focuses keenly on the assessment of which limitations in the sense of a moderation of the Right of Nations are necessary under the overarching principles of Natural Right and Arbitrary Divine Right.[123] This distinction between a rather detached and allegedly objective descriptive approach to the Human Right of Nations and its rules on war, and the normative approach to moderation under the higher categories of Divine Right has often been simply ignored and sometimes even conflated by accusing Grotius of incoherent views on the Right in War.

At the core of Grotius' discussion of the Right in War is the term "licence". In chapter 4 of the third book of *De Iure Belli ac Pacis* Grotius firstly quotes Virgil, who had stated in a poem that in the case of war the enemy has the licence (*licebit*) to fight full of hatred and rapine.[124] Grotius then asks what the term of "having a licence" might mean. It can be interpreted in the sense that something is to be regarded as right and moral in any respect, even though there still may be an alternative way of acting which is more praiseworthy.[125] Thus one has a licence to marry; marriage is perfectly acceptable under moral and legal aspects. However, Christian authors have claimed that it is still more praiseworthy not to marry at all. On the other hand a second marriage may also be morally and legally acceptable, at least under Natural Right; nevertheless, it is still better to marry only once.

122 Cf. P. Haggenmacher, *Grotius et la doctrine de la guerre juste*, pp. 597 et seq.
123 Cf. IBP, III.X.
124 Cf. ibid., III.IV.i.
125 Cf. ibid., III.IV.ii.1.

However, the second meaning of the expression "to have licence" implies the absence of any punishment for a certain conduct, even though it is morally and legally unacceptable.[126] For example, prostitution is regarded as immoral and illegal amongst many nations; nevertheless, it still is not punished. The counterpart to such licence is an obligation: thus one may do something because no punishment is inflicted if one does it; nevertheless, there is still the obligation not to do this, whether or not punishment is prescribed.

It is this second meaning of the term "licence" that Grotius uses in his elaboration on the Right in War. He thus first presents which licenses the Right of Nations grants for the conduct of war-faring parties. By this he presents the contemporary legal practice in relation to war, which he himself finds rather abhorrent. However, Grotius then moves on to discuss the Right in War as provided for by Natural Right and Arbitrary Divine Right. Here the true character of the rules of the Right of Nations in relation to war becomes apparent: much of what is granted as licence is simply morally and therefore also legally unacceptable.

Thus after having asserted relatively far-reaching rights of the war-faring party under the Right of Nations to kill enemies or to enslave them[127], Grotius limits these rights severely under Natural Right and Arbitrary Divine Right.[128] Likewise, while far-reaching rights regarding the destruction and removal of things are granted under the Right of Nations[129], most of these rights appear to be taken away again under the Divine Right.[130] The same applies respectively to the acquisition of property[131], to the right over prisoners of war[132], to the principles of the state power of the defeated party[133], and to the return of goods.[134]

It may suffice to exemplify Grotius' critique of the Human Right of Nations in analysing his exposition of the right to kill the enemy and his treatment of proprietary rights in war.

2.1. Killing the Enemy

As already stated above, it is the sense of a licence as absence of punishment despite contravening an obligation that Grotius applies to his exposition on

126 Cf. ibid., III.IV.ii.2.
127 Cf. ibid., III.IV.
128 Cf. ibid., III.XI.
129 Cf. ibid., III.V.
130 Cf. ibid., III.XII.
131 Cf. ibid., III.VI.; III.XIII.
132 Cf. ibid., III.VII.; III.XIV.
133 Cf. ibid., III.VIII.; III.XV.
134 Cf. ibid., III.IX.; III.XVI.

what war-faring parties may do with regard to the killing of their enemies. There is then a licence to damage the enemy in his person and his property in the course of a formal public war[135]; this licence applies to both parties of the war, regardless of whether or not they act because of a just reason or whether or not they adhere to the limitations set to their conduct by Natural Right. Thus, even if an unjustified party to a formal public war kills an enemy against the rules of justice set out by Natural Right, it cannot be punished for doing so under the Human Right of Nations. Grotius believes that the nations have devised this in the Human Right of Nations, because any decision as to the legality of a war between two states may be dangerous to other states, as then they could become involved in the war as well.[136] It would hardly be possible to ever make peace again if such acts were regarded as breach of Right and consequently might be regarded as reasons for further wars. Grotius then adds that there is even a licence to treat anyone as enemy who stays in the territory of the enemy[137]; children and women of the enemy do not have to be spared.[138] Nevertheless, Grotius thinks that there are still some acts that are not covered by this licence, such as the use of poison against the enemy, in particular, the poisoning of fountains.[139] Overall Grotius' treatment of the subject keeps the form of a rather distanced neutral observation of what is in practice regarding the Right in War, while he appears to be reluctant to become involved in a serious discussion of the issues related to this licence.

Grotius' next comment on this subject is devoted to the question of what is unjustly done in a war. Right at the beginning Grotius states that he has to return to what has been said in the foregoing and to withdraw from the war-faring states nearly everything he has so far apparently granted to them in his comments on the Right in War.[140] Until now he has only been concerned with the licence in the sense of what is permitted because there is no punishment prescribed for it. However, in what follows he examines what is truly just. For this examination the Human Right of Nations is mostly irrelevant, for it allows for a broader variety of acts regardless of whether or not all of these acts are also to be regarded as just under Natural Right and Arbitrary Divine Right. Consequently, all acts undertaken in the course of an unjust war are unjust in relation to internal justice, whereby internal justice is to be understood in the sense of an inner feeling of justice as expressed by conscience.[141] Thus, those who have intentionally acted in or rendered

135 Cf. ibid., III.IV.iii.
136 Cf. ibid., III.IV.iv.
137 Cf. ibid., III.IV.vi.
138 Cf. ibid., III.IV.ix.
139 Cf. ibid., III.IV.xv.–xvi.
140 Cf. ibid., III.X.i.
141 Cf. ibid., III.X.iii.

assistance to an unjust war cannot reach the heavenly kingdom without repentance. Repentance includes the compensation of damages that have been caused in the course of an unjust war.[142]

Grotius starts his exposition of the limitations regarding the killing of enemies by asserting that the statement "Everything is allowed to you if someone denies to you a right" is not accurate[143]: instead one has to follow the principles of Right even in the case of a just war. Regarding the admissibility to kill one's enemy in the course of a war Grotius refers to the general principles of a just war: the intentional killing of human beings is only justified in order to execute a just punishment or if we cannot otherwise protect our life or our property.[144] Even so, the killing of other human beings in order to defend things of minor value is contrary to the commandment to love one's neighbour; it may however be justified under strict justice. Moreover, the death penalty is a just punishment if the offender has committed an offence for which a just judge would sentence this offender to death. Any other killing is then not normally admissible under Natural Right and Arbitrary Divine Right. For example, it is impermissible to kill those who have been forced to join the party of the enemy.[145] The same applies to a person who belongs to the party of the enemy because of a mistake which is to be located somewhere between accident and bad faith.[146] Furthermore, Grotius asserts that prudence might warrant to spare even those from being killed who have truly deserved the death penalty.[147] Far from showing any personal distance here at all, Grotius appears to advocate the greatest possible temperance regarding the potential killing of enemies. While he had claimed that the licences provided under the Right of Nations for the killing of people do not fully comply with the principles of justice under Natural Right, he himself tends to lean on the other side of the spectrum, by not keeping to the strict letter of the principles of Natural Right, and instead appealing to the exercise of mercy even for the benefit of those who have erred and might very well be sentenced to death according to the true principles of justice.

2.2. The Treatment of the Enemy's Proprietary Rights

In Grotius' analysis of the treatment of the enemy's proprietary rights under the Right in War he pursues a similar path: Grotius firstly deals with the

142 Cf. ibid., III.X.iv.–vi.
143 Cf. ibid., III.XI.i.
144 Cf. ibid., III.XI.ii
145 Cf. ibid., III.XI.iii.
146 Cf. ibid., III.XI.iv.
147 Cf. ibid., III.XI.vii.

question of how far the destruction and taking away of property[148] and the acquisition of property[149] is admissible in a war under the Right of Nations. He concludes that the successful party of a war has far-reaching powers to appropriate goods and lands of the defeated party under the Right of Nations. The victorious party may do nearly everything it deems fit: under the Right of Nations everything that belongs to the enemy may be destroyed; there is not even an exception to be made with respect to the sacred goods of the enemy[150], although sometimes temperance is exercised with respect to goods that are used for worship and graves.[151] Basically the same principles apply to an appropriation of the enemy's property. In general, the successful party may appropriate anything that belongs to the enemy under the Right of Nations[152], for which Grotius gives numerous practical examples.[153] In order to conquer and appropriate foreign territory, the belligerent army has to effectively occupy the country of the enemy.[154] However, in order to appropriate proprietary rights in the course of war, the Right of Nations requires that the respective property is truly owned by the enemy[155]; otherwise no appropriation is possible. Grotius then turns to the fate of the authority of the defeated party under the Right of Nations: the victorious party obtains exactly the same authority the defeated party had held.[156] The defeated party may even lose its status as an independent state[157], and the defeated people may be enslaved or forced to amalgamate with the victorious people.[158] Consequently, the authority of the defeated may be terminated as the result of a just war.

Only a few chapters later Grotius then moves on to advocate temperance regarding the exercise of such rights accorded to the victorious party of a war from the perspective of Natural Right and of Arbitrary Divine Right. This firstly becomes clear from his treatment of the qualifications pertaining to the destruction the other party's property.[159] Grotius here criticises the unlimited licence provided by the Right of Nations to destroy the property of the adverse party; it is contrary to the commandment of prudence as part of the rational nature of human beings and therefore contrary to Natural Right to

148 Cf. ibid., III.V.
149 Cf. ibid., III.VI.
150 Cf. ibid., III.V.
151 Cf. ibid., III.V.iii.
152 Cf. ibid., III.VI.i.
153 Cf. ibid., III.VI.ii.
154 Cf. ibid., III.IV.
155 Cf. ibid., III.IV.v.
156 Cf. ibid., III.VIII.i.
157 Cf. ibid., III.VIII.ii.
158 Cf. ibid., III.VIII.iii.
159 Cf. ibid., III.XIII.

destroy such property if we can use it for ourselves or if the enemy can supply himself from elsewhere. Grotius here does not argue in an altruistic fashion, but simply contends that goods may not be destroyed for destruction's sake. Moreover, some things Grotius regards as completely sacrosanct, such as sacred goods[160]; these may never be destroyed. Here we may see a further application of Natural Religion entailed by Natural Right as perceived by Grotius. Even more temperance is required by Christians from Arbitrary Divine Right.[161] In principle, the same applies to booty, which may only be appropriated by the victorious party as far as this is necessary to satisfy the debts the defeated party owes the victorious party.[162] This may again be perceived as specification of the Natural Right principle of expletive justice: even in a war we may only take what is due to us, but may not make any additional gain. The war is conducted for the sake of upholding or restoring justice, whereas it is not permissible to pursue one's own benefit – the preservation of justice serves everyone.

Then Grotius proceeds to examine certain restrictions imposed by Natural Right and Arbitrary Divine Right regarding the acquisition of the authority of the defeated party. Here Grotius regards it as praiseworthy to exercise clemency and mercy against the defeated enemy.[163] Although confirming the principle of Natural Right, according to which the acquisition of the authority of the defeated party by the successful party is permissible[164], Grotius is keen to point out how praiseworthy it is from a general as well as from a Christian point of view to refrain from making use of this possibility.[165] Furthermore, Grotius elaborates upon various other methods of a moderate treatment of defeated people, such as the amalgamation of the defeated people with the victorious people, and similar means.[166] Grotius advocates such moderate treatment not only by pleading humanity, but also by recommending such conduct as prudent in the light of attributive justice as part of Natural Right.[167] As far as the weakening of the defeated party seems necessary, this party still should be left some power of rule, or some liberties, in particular religious freedom.[168] In any case, the defeated party should always be treated generously.[169] Again attributive justice and the exercise of virtues take pride of place, and we may assume that Grotius even

160 Cf. ibid., III.XII.vi.
161 Cf. ibid., III.XII.vi.3.
162 Cf. ibid., III.XIII.i.
163 Cf. ibid., III.XV.i.
164 Cf. ibid., III.XV.i.
165 Cf. ibid., III.XV.ii.
166 Cf. ibid., III.XV.iii–iv.
167 Cf. ibid., III.XV.vii–viii.
168 Cf. ibid., III.XV.ix–xi.
169 Cf. ibid., III.XV.xii.

would hold that a greater degree of virtue, and in particular of generosity, is to be expected from Christians as victorious party in a just war than from others.

In relation to the Right in War as provided for under Natural Right and Arbitrary Divine Right, Grotius is thus a less detached observer and theorist, but assumes rather the role of a legal critic, displaying at times a quite harsh opposition to the effective practice under the contemporary Right of Nations. Hence, Grotius only takes a descriptive approach to the Right in War in the sense of licences granted under the Human Right of Nations in a first step before employing a critically normative approach to the Right in War as devised by Natural Right and Arbitrary Divine Right in a second step.

VI. Conclusion

There are two main conclusions to be drawn from Grotius' treatment of the Right to War and the Right in War for the broader picture of his theology of international law:

Firstly, while the Right of peace inhales the spirit of expletive justice as acknowledgement of the legal positions of individuals, for example by commanding to render to others what is due to them, to keep promises, etc., attributive justice governs the mode of implementing these legal positions. While expletive justice determines the legal status of everything, attributive justice determines the implementation of this legal status by devising the modalities of how to achieve this. It allows virtues to govern human interaction as the decisive criterion for the legitimacy of any action. This is already the case in the state of peace, where attributive justice, for example, is to be applied in order to assess the legitimacy of any action in relation to the persons involved. Thus, honour is rendered to the state to a greater degree than to the individual. The morally deserving are to be treated differently in the distribution of goods than the morally undeserving.

In the state of war the role of attributive justice is equally important. Attributive justice determines the legitimacy of any act of war undertaken. Attributive justice is the moderating influence upon the strict necessities of expletive justice. Not everything one is entitled to do under expletive justice should or even may be done under attributive justice. Even if one is perfectly entitled to use force under expletive justice, attributive justice may advise differently, requiring moderation and pointing out the use of virtues, in particular of prudence. Not everything which one is justified to do is prudent to do. Thus attributive justice here is the justice of moderation.

The second feature of Grotius' exposition of the Right of War to be noted is the difference which attributive justice may effect upon the conduct of non-

Christians and Christians respectively. Attributive justice entails the application of virtues. Arbitrary Divine Right requires a higher degree of virtue from Christians than Natural Right does from all human beings. Thus, the combination of the Evangelical counsels and attributive justice should result in a more virtuous conduct in war by Christians than what is to be expected from non-Christians. Certainly, Christians are not prohibited to engage in fighting a just war. Nor are the claims of attributive justice only applicable to Christians. However, according to Grotius the conduct of Christians in a war should be penetrated by a higher degree of prudence, clemency, and charity than that of non-Christians. Christians are supposed to engage less in cruelties, they should not destroy just for destruction's sake, and should even display greater reluctance about initiating wars. Grotius acknowledges that this is rarely the case in practice. Yet this obviously was the very reason for Grotius to write *De Iure Belli ac Pacis*.

Finally, a brief comparison between Grotius' views on the Right of War on the one hand and the other traditions of war seems in place. We have already seen that Grotius is indeed a follower of the Christian just war tradition. Implicitly he distances himself from the martial tradition of war by viewing war simply as a means to preserve or to restore justice through the means of force. Hence, different from the martial tradition of war, for Grotius the use of force can never be an end in itself. In relation to the idealist traditions of war Grotius certainly argues in favour of a certain idea – the rule of justice – as aim to be pursued by war. This is yet a quite different aim from that of the republican tradition of war or the holy war doctrines that justify war with ends beyond the rule of justice. The difference is even greater between Grotius and the understanding of war as a means to pursue random political aims with force of which Carl von Clausewitz was the most well-known representative. Furthermore, for Grotius the aim of justice also determines the means to be employed, whereas for the Idealist traditions the aim itself may justify any measure.

As to the Islamic understanding of the Jihad as just war, it has an important parallel in Grotius' own perception of the Right of War: according to both theoretical approaches the use of force is subordinated to the aim of implementing divine justice, and thus any measure of warfare will be limited from this perspective. Yet, beside various other differences in detail, the interpretation of the Jihad as just war still ties the legitimacy of warfare to the approval by the Caliphate or Imamate as the highest temporal and spiritual authority, whereas for Grotius any holder of sovereign authority is called to ensure the rule of justice in international relations.

In comparison to the modern public international law on warfare, Grotius is in agreement regarding the general prerequisites for warfare. In particular, a war can only be justified if it is undertaken to remedy a breach of Right. Yet the modern liberal understanding of warfare displayed in particular in John Rawls' *Law of Peoples* is still more restrictive in limiting warfare to self-defence, whereas Grotius in principle contends that penal wars and wars for the enforcement of claims may also be legitimate. The more important difference between Grotius and Rawls lies however in their respective concepts of justice and the consequences to be drawn for the acceptance of principles of Right, which are to be preserved by warfare: while Rawls here relies on his concept of justice as fairness, which is rooted in a consensus between liberal and "decent" peoples, Grotius adheres to the idea of a divine justice which requires compliance regardless of any human consensus upon its principles. Furthermore, while Rawls already endeavours to pierce the veil of statehood with the idea of an international law between peoples – and not only between states – Grotius argues in favour of an immediate personal obligation of all human beings by the respective sets of Natural Right and of Arbitrary Divine Right. This personal obligation in Grotius' concept again corresponds to a personal responsibility of the individuals as moral agents in international relations as rulers and subjects, which is at the heart of the Grotian theology of international law.

Conclusion

As already mentioned in the Introduction, there are two characteristic features of modern public international law which face mounting criticism in the current legal and political discussions: First, the focus of public international law is on states as the only original legal subjects and thus as exclusive legal agents in the international arena, which makes it hard to incorporate subjective human rights or personal responsibility on the international level. Second, modern public international law relies on consensus as the only source of legitimacy for its rules, wherefore its legal standards are the least common denominator to which the states as legal agents consent. Both of these features are a consequence of the secularisation within the European legal tradition in the course of the 17th century, and of the emergence of the concept of a territorial state in Europe.

In Europe there prevailed previously an understanding of law as a metaphysical system, which was supplemented by a Christological concept of legislation. This concept included rights and obligations in the strict sense as well as certain moral standards that pertain to the inward disposition of the respective moral agent.

The traditional Christian concept of international law entails various parallels to similar religious systems of international law, in particular to the Islamic law of nations (*siyar*), which relies on a set of divine laws, pertaining to the individual believer as subject or to the unbeliever as object.

Yet even in the contemporary debate on public international law there are tendencies to develop its principles further: one of the most interesting of the recent proposals is the concept of a "Law of Peoples" brought forward by John Rawls. Rawls endeavours to pierce the veil of statehood by transferring the idea of a social contract on the identification of the common good from the domestic to the international level.

The general object of this examination was to demonstrate that Hugo Grotius' system of international relations is indeed a theology of international law, which offers a potential to supplement modern public international law and to provide bridges to the religious traditions of jurisprudence. In particular, this examination aimed at (i) highlighting the traditional Christian roots of Grotius' concept of International Right, (ii) demonstrating its general compatibility with the framework of modern liberal concepts of public international law, by pointing out in which sense the modern positivist understanding of freedom as absence of prohibitions and commandments may be enhanced by Grotius' idea of a positive moral responsibility of the individual, and (iii) indicating similarities and differences between the Grotian system of international relations and its counterparts in other religions. Thus it was the aim of this analysis to reconcile traditional theological content and modern legal shape in Grotius' concept of international relations.

We have seen that Grotius certainly is to a great extent indebted to the Christian theological and legal traditions: his theory of Natural Right follows lines parallel to those of the Salamancan school; his just war doctrine mostly pursues the path already paved by medieval canon law, and in his understanding of the function of Christ's sacrifice for the redemption of mankind Grotius adheres to orthodox Patristic theology.

While there are manifold differences in principle as well as in detail between Grotius' Christian theology of international law and its Islamic counterparts, there are also two prominent common properties which distinguish both traditions from the modern outlook on international law. This is firstly the acknowledgement of God as supreme legislator also in the domain of International Right: while the so-called "Western" tradition simply refers to consensus as the ultimate source of legal principles, the religious traditions accept a divine source of Right beyond the mere agreement between human beings. The second common property is the acknowledgement of individual human beings as legal subjects, as the ones that are personally responsible and at the same time personally protected by International Right.

Still, Grotius' theology of international law would seem compatible with modern liberal concepts of international law, such as the Law of Peoples proposed by John Rawls. Certainly Grotius takes an interest in matters in which no modern jurist would dare intrude, such as the inward moral dispositions of the individual agent; he is willing to accord the government a meaningful role in the propagation of religious truth, whereas no modern liberal jurist would consider such a function of the government legitimate in a pluralist state. Nonetheless, even modern lawyers could well subscribe to Grotius' general idea of Natural Right as a legal framework for the international society of nations. The same is true for Grotius' concepts of expletive justice and attributive justice, which have the benefit of being sustainable legal principles without necessitating any recourse to divine revelation in order to corroborate their validity.

Grotius regarded any human jurisprudence which did not account for the respective framework of Divine Right as crippled and mutilated, and hence, as Martin Wight had pointed out, combined the traditional idea of the *respublica Christiana* with the more contemporary concept of a universal fellowship amongst human beings. Hence, in between the Christian legal tradition, the Islamic law of nations, and the modern concepts of legal philosophy, Hugo Grotius' views on the moral foundations of international relations amount to a specific Grotian theology of international law.

Bibliography

I. Grotiana

Defensio Fidei Catholicae de Satisfactione Christi adversus Faustum Socinum Senensem. Opera theologica, ed. Edwin Rabbie. Assen: Van Gorcum, 1990.

De Imperio Summarum Potestatum circa Sacra Commentarius. Paris 1648.

De Iure Belli ac Pacis, in quibus ius naturae et gentium item iuris publici praecipua explicantur. Ed. B. J. A. de Kanter-van Hettinga Tromp and Robert Fenstra. Leiden 1939, repr. Aalen: Scientia, 1993. [Quoted in the text as IBP.]

De iure praedae commentarius. Repr. Oxford: Clarendon Press, 1950.

The Jurisprudence of Holland / Inleiding tot de Hollandsche rechts-geleertheyd. vols. I—II. Ed. Robert Warden Lee. Oxford: Clarendon Press, 1953, repr. Aalen: Scientia, 1977.

Mare liberum sive de iure quod Batavis competit ad Indicana Commercia dissertatio. Leiden: Elzevier, 1618, repr. Osnabrück: Biblio, 1978.

Meletius, sive, De iis quae inter Christianos conveniunt epistola. Ed. Edwin Rabbie. Leiden, New York, Cologne: Brill, 1994.

Ordinum Hollandiae ac Westfrisiae Pietas. Ed. Edwin Rabbie. Leiden, New York, Cologne: Brill, 1995. [Quoted in the text as OP.]

De Veritate Religionis Christianae. Oxford, 1700.

II. Other Works

Abou El Fadl, Khaled. "The Unbounded Law of God and Territorial Boundaries". In: Allen Buchanan, Margaret Moore (eds.), *States, Nations, and Borders: The Ethics of Making Boundaries.* Cambridge: Cambridge University Press, 2003, pp. 214–227.

Althusius, Johannes. *Politica methodice digesta atque exemplis sacris et profanis illustrata.* Repr. Cambridge, MA.: Harvard University Press, 1932.

d'Andreae, Giovanni. *Novella in sextum.* Venice, Pincius, 1499, repr. Graz: Akademische Druck- und Verlagsanstalt, 1963.

Aristoteles, *Ηθικα νικομαχεια. Die Nikomachische Ethik.* Griechisch—Deutsch. Ed. Olof Gigon, re-ed. Rainer Nickel. Düsseldorf, Zurich: Artemis & Winkler, 2001.

Augustinus, Aurelius. *De civitate Dei libri XII.* Leipzig: Teubner, 1877.

———. *Confessiones.* Leipzig: Bredt, 1869.

Austin, John and Robert Campbell. *Lectures on Jurisprudence, or the Philosophy of Positive Law.* London : Murray, 1880.

Barschak, Lotte. *Die Staatsauffassung des Hugo Grotius.* In: *Bijdragen voor Vaderlandsche Geschiedenis en Ouheidkunde.* Vol. III. The Hague: Nijhoff, 1926.

Benedek, Wolfgang. *Die Rechtsordnung des GATT aus völkerrechtlicher Sicht.* Berlin/Heidelberg: Springer, 1990.

de Beza, Theodore. *Du droit des magistrats.* Geneva: Droz, 1970.

Bockmuehl, Markus. *Jewish Law in Gentile Churches: Halakhah and the Beginning of Christian Public Ethics*: Edinburgh: T&T Clark, 2000.

Bodin, Jean: *Les six livres de la République*. Lyon 1593.

Bonner, Stanley F. *Education in Ancient Rome: From the Elder Cato to the Younger Pliny*. Berkeley: University of California Press, 1977.

Bothe, Michael. "Friedenssicherung und Kriegsrecht". In: Wolfgang Graf Vitzthum (ed.), *Völkerrecht*. 2nd ed., Walter de Gruyter: Berlin, New York 2001, pp. 603–679.

Brandweiner, Heinrich. *Die christlichen Kirchen als souveräne Rechtsgemeinschaften*. Graz, Vienna: Moser 1948.

Brownlie, Ian. *Principles of Public International Law*. 6th ed., Oxford: Oxford University Press, 2003.

Brundage, James A. *Medieval Canon Law*. London, New York: Longman, 1995.

Bull, Hedley. "The Importance of Grotius in the Study of International Relations". In: Hedley Bull, Benedict Kingsbury, Adam Roberts (eds.), *Hugo Grotius and International Relations*. Cambridge: Cambridge University Press, 1990, pp. 65–93.

Buridan, Jean. *In metaphysicam Aristotelis questiones*. Paris: Badius Ascensius, 1518, repr. Frankfurt am Main: Minerva, 1964.

Calvin, Jean. *Institutio Religionis Christianae*. Geneva: Preux 1590.

———. *In quinque libros Mosis, commentarii: Genesis seorsim: reliqui quatuor in formam harmoniae digesti*. Geneva: In officina Sanctandreana, 1595.

Caspani, Andrea. "Il De Imperio summarum potestatum circa sacra di Grozio". In: *Revista di Filosofia Neo-scolatica*, 79 (1987), [part 1] pp. 218–249, [part 2] pp. 382–419.

Cato, Marcus Porcius. *Originum libri septem*. Brandenburg: Mueller 1858.

Churchill, Robin R. and Alan V. Lowe. *The Law of the Sea*. 3rd ed., Manchester: Manchester University Press, 1999.

Cicero, Marcus Tullius. *De Officiis*. Ed. Walter Miller. London: Heinemann, 1956.

Clark, George Norman. "Grotius's East India Mission to England". In: *Transactions of the Grotius Society*, 20 (1935), pp. 45–84.

——— and W. J. M. van Eysinga. "The Colonial Conferences between England and the Netherlands in 1613 and 1615". In: *Bibliotheca Visseriana*, 34 (1951), pp. 79–98.

von Clausewitz, Carl. *Vom Kriege*. 3rd ed., Berlin: Ullstein, 2002.

Corpus Iuris Canonici. Ed. Emil Friedberg, 2 vols. Leipzig: Tauchnitz, 1879, repr. Graz: Akademische Druck- und Verlagsanstalt, 1959.

Corpus Iuris Iustiani. Ed. Okko Behrends. Heidelberg: Müller, 1993.

Cullet, Philippe. "Differential Treatment in International Law: Towards a New Paradigm of Inter-state Relations". In: *The European Journal of International Law*, 10 (1999), pp. 549–582.

van Dam, Harm-Jan. "De Imperio Summarum Potestatum circa Sacra". In: Henk J. M. Nellen, Edwin Rabbie: *Hugo Grotius, theologian: Essays in Honour of G. H. M. Posthumus Meyjes*. Brill: Leiden, New York, Cologne: Brill, 1994, pp. 19–39.

Dante Alighieri. *Monarchia*. Stuttgart: Reclam, 1989.

Dolzer, Rudolf. "Wirtschaft und Kultur im Völkerrecht". In: Wolfgang Graf Vitzthum (ed.): *Völkerrecht*. 2nd ed., Berlin, New York: Walter de Gruyter, 2001, pp. 469–544.

Dreier, Horst. "Kanonistik und Konfessionalisierung: Marksteine auf dem Weg zum Staat". In: *Juristenzeitung*, 57 (2002), pp. 1–13.

Dürig, Günter. "Artikel 1: Menschenwürde". In: Theodor Maunz, Günter Dürig: *Grundgesetz, Kommentar*. Munich: C.H. Beck, 1958.

Fergusson, David. *Community, Liberalism and Christian Ethics*. Cambridge: Cambridge University Press, 1998.

Figgis, John Neville. *Studies of Political Thought from Gerson to Grotius: 1414–1625*. Cambridge: Cambridge University Press, 1923.

Gerson, Jean. *Tractatus de ecclesiastica potestate & origine iuris ac legume*. Paris: Pouchin & Chaudiere, 1510.

von Gierke, Otto. *Das deutsche Genossenschaftsrecht*. Vol. I: *Rechtsgeschichte der deutschen Genossenschaft*. Berlin: Weidmann, 1868.

———. *Das deutsche Genossenschaftsrecht*. Vol. II: *Geschichte des deutschen Körperschaftsbegriffs*. Berlin: Weidmann, 1873.

———. *Das deutsche Genossenschaftsrecht*. Vol. IV: *Die Staats- und Korporationslehre der Neuzeit: durchgeführt bis zur Mitte des 17., für das Naturrecht bis zum Beginn des 19. Jahrhunderts*. Berlin: Weidmann, 1913.

Giles (Aegidius) of Rome. *De ecclesiastica potestate*. Ed. Richard Scholz. Repr. Aalen: Scientia, 1961.

Green, Leslie. "International Crimes and the Legal Process". In: *The International and Comparative Law Quarterly*, 29 (1980), pp. 567–598.

Hafner, Gerhard. "Räumliche Regime und Nutzungen über die und jenseits der Staatsgrenzen". In: Hanspeter Neuhold, Waldemar Hummer, Christoph Schreuer (eds.): *Österreichisches Handbuch des Völkerrechts*. 2nd ed., Vienna: Manz, 1991, pp. 328–374.

Haggenmacher, Peter. *Grotius et la doctrine de la guerre juste*. Paris: Presses Universitaires de France, 1983.

Hailbronner, Kay. "Der Staat und der Einzelne als Völkerrechtssubjekte". In: Wolfgang Graf Vitzthum (ed.): *Völkerrecht*. 2nd ed., Berlin, New York: Walter de Gruyter, 2001, pp. 161–265.

Heckel, Martin. *Staat und Kirche nach den Lehren der evangelischen Juristen Deutschlands in der ersten Hälfte des 17. Jahrhunderts*. Munich: Claudius, 1968.

Heering, Jan Paul. "Hugo Grotius' De Veritate Religionis Christianae". In: Henk J. M. Nellen, Edwin Rabbie: *Hugo Grotius, theologian: Essays in Honour of G. H. M. Posthumus Meyjes*. Leiden, New York, Cologne: Brill, 1994, pp. 41–52.

Herms, Eilert. "Lage und Perspektive der Kirchen im Zusammenhang der europäischen Einigung am Ende des 20. Jahrhunderts: Eine evangelische Selbsteinschätzung". In: Christoph A. Stumpf, Holger Zaborowski (eds.): *Church as Politeia: The Political Self-Understanding of Christianity*. Proceedings of a Becket Institute Conference at the University of Oxford, 28 September–1 October 2000. Berlin, New York: Walter de Gruyter, 2004, pp. 285–322.

Heuss, Alfred. *Die völkerrechtlichen Grundlagen der römischen Außenpolitik in republikanischer Zeit*. Klio-Beiheft. Leipzig 1933.

von der Heydte, Friedrich August. *Die Geburtsstunde des souveraenen Staates: Ein Beitrag zur Geschichte des Völkerrechts, der allgemeinen Staatslehre und des politischen Denkens*. Regensburg: Habbel, 1952.

Hobbes, Thomas. *De cive*. Ed. Howard Warrender. Oxford: Clarendon Press, 1983.

———. *Leviathan*. London 1651, repr. Oxford: Clarendon Press, 1909.

Höpfl, Harro. *The Christian Polity of John Calvin*. Cambridge: Cambridge University Press, 1985.

Hooker, Richard. *On the Law of Ecclesiastical Polity*. vols.I–ÌII. Ed. John Keeble, revised by Richard William Church and Francis Paget, 7th ed. Oxford: Clarendon Press, 1888.

Horace Flaccus, Quintus. *Satires, Epistles and Ars Poetica*. Ed. Henry Fairclough. Repr. Cambridge, MA: Harvard University Press, 1999.

Hostiensis (Henricus de Segusio). *Summa super titulos decretalium*. Strasbourg 1478–1479.

Hurrell, Andrew. "International Law and the Making and Unmaking of Boundaries". In: Allen Buchanan, Margaret Moore (eds.), *States, Nations, and Borders: The Ethics of Making Boundaries*. Cambridge: Cambridge University Press, 2003, pp. 275–297.

———. "Order and Justice in International Relations: What is at Stake?", in Rosemary Foot, John Gaddis, Andrew Hurrell (eds.), *Order and Justice in International Relations*. Oxford: Oxford University Press, 2003, pp. 24–48.

Ibn Abi Usaybi'ah. *Uyun al-Anba' fi Tabaqat al-Atibba*. Ed. August Müller. Königsberg 1884, Repr. Farnborough: Gregg International Publishers, 1972.

Israel, Jonathan Irvine. *The Dutch Republic and the Hispanic World, 1606–1661*. Oxford: Clarendon Press, 1982.

James (Jacobus) of Viterbo. *De regimene Christiano*. Ed. R. W. Dyson. Woodbridge: Boydell, 1995.

Jellinek, Georg. *Allgemeine Staatslehre*. 3rd ed., Berlin: Haering, 1914.

Kaser, Max: *Römisches Privatrecht*.16th ed., Munich: C. H. Beck, 1992.

Kennedy, David. "Primitive Legal Scholarship". In: *Harvard International Law Review*, 27 (1986), pp. 1–57.

Khadduri, Majid. *The Islamic Conception of Justice*. Baltimore, London: John Hopkins University Press, 1984.

———. *The Islamic Law of Nations: Shaybani's Siyar*. Baltimore, London: John Hopkins University Press, 1966.

Kimminich, Otto. "Die internationalen Beziehungen der Kirchen und das Recht auf freien Verkehr". In: Ernst Friesenhahn, Ulrich Scheuner, Joseph Listl, Dietrich Pirson (eds.): *Handbuch des Staatskirchenrechts*. Vol. II. 2nd ed., Berlin: Duncker & Humblot, 1995, pp. 217–250.

Klein, Eckardt. "Die internationalen und Supranationalen Organisationen". In: Wolfgang Graf Vitzthum (ed.): *Völkerrecht*. 2nd ed., Berlin, New York: Walter de Gruyter, 2001, pp. 267–377.

———. *Menschenrechte: Stille Revolution des Völkerrechts und Auswirkungen auf die innerstaatliche Rechtsanwendung*. Baden-Baden: Nomos, 1997.

Knox, John. *The First Blast of the Trumpet: Against the Monstrous Regiment of Women*. Geneva, 1558, repr. Amsterdam: Theatrum orbis terrarium, 1972.

Köck, Heribert Franz. *Der Beitrag der Schule von Salamanca zur Entwicklung der Lehre von den Grundrechten*. Berlin: Duncker & Humblot, 1987.

———. *Rechtliche und politische Aspekte von Konkordaten*. Berlin: Duncker & Humblot, 1983.

Kokott, Juliane. "Naturrecht und Positivismus im Völkerrecht – sind wir auf dem Wege zu einer Weltverfassung?". In: Christian J. Meier-Schatz, Rainer J. Schweizer (eds.): *Recht und Internationalisierung, Festgabe zum Juristentag 2000 in St. Gallen*. Zurich: Schulthess, 2000, pp. 3–21.

Krawietz, Birgit. *Hierarchie der Rechtsquellen im tradierten sunnitischen Islam*. Berlin: Duncker & Humblot, 2002.

Lagrée, Jacqueline. "Grotius, Stoïcisme et religion naturelle". In: *Grotiana*, 10 (1989), pp. 80–96.

Laplanche, Francois. "Grotius et les religions du paganisme dans les Annotationes in Vetum Testamentum". In: Henk J. M. Nellen, Edwin Rabbie: *Hugo Grotius, theologian: Essays in honour of G. H. M. Posthumus Meyjes*. Leiden, New York, Cologne: Brill, 1994, pp. 53–63.

Lauterpacht, Hersch. "The Grotian Tradition in International Law". In: *British Yearbook of International Law*, 23 (1946), pp. 1–53.

Link, Christoph. *Herrschaftsordnung und bürgerliche Freiheit: Die Grenzen der Staatsgewalt in der älteren deutschen Staatslehre*. Vienna: Böhlau, 1979.

———. *Hugo Grotius als Staatsdenker*. Tübingen: Mohr Siebeck, 1983.

———. "Die Staatstheorie des Christian Wolff". In: Werner Schneiders (ed.): *Christian Wolff 1679-1754: Interpretation zu seiner Philosophie und deren Wirkung*. Hamburg: Meiner, 1983, pp. 160–183.

Lockwood O'Donovan, Joan. "The Christian Pedagogy and Ethics of Erasmus: A Poesis for the Present?" In: Christoph A. Stumpf, Holger Zaborowski (eds.): *Church as Politeia: The Political Self-Understanding of Christianity*. Proceedings of a Becket Institute Conference at the University of Oxford, 28 September–1 October 2000. Berlin, New York: Walter de Gruyter, 2004, pp. 103–119.

———. *Theology of Law and Authority in the English Reformation*. Atlanta: Scholars Press, 1992.

Lubbert, Sibrandus. *Responsio ad pietatem Hugonis Grotii*. Franeker 1614.

Luther, Martin. *Von weltlicher Obrigkeit*. 4th ed., Gütersloh: Gütersloher Verlagshaus, 1983.

Macdonald, D. and A. Abel. "dār al-Sulh". In: *Encyclopedia of Islam and the Muslim World*. Vol. II. 2nd ed., Leiden: Brill, 1960, p. 131.

Machiavelli, Niccolò. *Discorsi sopra la prima deca di Tito Livio*. Turin: Einaudi, 2000.

MacIntyre, Alasdair. *Whose Justice? Which Rationality*. Notre Dame, Ind.: University of Notre Dame Press, 1988.

Marsilius of Padua. *Defensor pacis*. Vols. I–II. Hanover: Hahn, 1933.

Meinecke, Friedrich. *Die Idee der Staatsräson in der neueren Geschichte*. Munich: Oldenbourg, 1924.

Melanchthon, Philipp. *Loci Communes*. Basel 1521, re-ed. Vereinigte Evangelisch-Lutherische Kirche in Deutschland, 2nd ed., Gütersloh: Gütersloher Verlagshaus, 1997.

de Mornay, Philippe. *De la verité de la religion chrestiene: Contre les Athées, Epicuriens, Payens, Juifs, Mahumedistes, et autres Infideles*. Geneva 1590.

Mosler, Hermann. "Die Erweiterung des Kreises der Völkerrechtssubjekte". In: *Zeitschrift für ausländisches öffentliches Recht und Völkerrecht*, 22 (1962), pp.1–45.

Münkler, Herfried. *Gewalt und Ordnung: Das Bild des Krieges im politischen Denken*. Frankfurt am Main: Fischer, 1992.

Murphy, Cornelius F. "The Grotian Vision". *American Journal of International Law*, 76 (1982), pp. 477–498.

Nabulsi, Karma. *Tradition of War: Occupation, Resistance, and the Law*. Oxford: Oxford University Press, 1999.

Nettesheim, Martin. "Das kommunitäre Völkerrecht". In: *Juristenzeitung*, 57 (2002), pp. 569–578.

Neuhold, Hanspeter and Christoph Schrummer. "Westliches Völkerrecht: Geschichte, Methoden, Positionen". In: Hanspeter Neuhold, Waldemar Hummer, Christoph Schreuer (eds.), *Österreichisches Handbuch des Völkerrechts*. 2nd ed., Vienna: Manz, 1991, pp. 13–20.

Neuhold, Hanspeter, Waldemar Hummer, and Christoph Schreuer. "Grundlagen und Rahmenbedingungen des heutigen Völkerrechts". In: Hanspeter Neuhold, Waldemar Hummer, Christoph Schreuer (eds.), *Österreichisches Handbuch des Völkerrechts*. 2nd ed., Vienna: Manz, 1991, pp. 1–12.

Niemann, Franz-Josef. "Die erste ökumenische Fundamentaltheologie: Zum 400. Geburtstag von Hugo Grotius". In: *Catholica, Vierteljahreszeitschrift für ökumenische Theologie*, 37 (1983), pp. 203–215.

O'Donovan, Oliver M. T. "Christianity and Territorial Right". In: Allen Buchanan, Margaret Moore (eds.), *States, Nations, and Borders: The Ethics of Making Boundaries.* Cambridge: Cambridge University Press, 2003, pp. 127–139.

———. *The Desire of the Nations: Rediscovering the Roots of Political Theology*. Cambridge: Cambridge University Press, 1996.

———. *The Just War Revisited*. Cambridge: Cambridge University Press, 2004.

———. "The Justice of Assignment and Subjective Rights in Grotius". In: Oliver M. T. O'Donovan, Joan Lockwood O'Donovan (eds.), *Bonds of Imperfection: Christian Politics, Past and Present*. Grand Rapids: Eerdmans, 2004, pp. 167–203.

——— and Joan Lockwood O'Donovan. *From Irenaeus to Grotius: A Sourcebook in Christian Political Thought*. Grand Rapids: Eerdmans, 1999.

Onuma,Yasuaki. "War". In Onuma Yasuaki (ed.), *A Normative Approach to War*. Oxford: Clarendon Press, 1993, pp. 57–121.

Pinto, M. C. W. "The New Law of the Sea and the Grotian Heritage, International Law and its Sources". In: Wybo P. Heero (ed.), *Liber Amicorum Maarten Bos*. Deventer, Boston, The Hague, Norwell: Kluwer, 1989, pp. 54–73.

Posthumus Meyjes, Guillaume H. M. "Hugo de Groot's 'Meletius' (1611), his earliest theological work, rediscovered". In: *Lias*, 11 (1984), pp. 147—150.

———. "Hugo Grotius as an Irenicist". In: The Grotius Committee of the Royal Netherlands Academy of Arts and Sciences (eds.), *The World of Hugo Grotius (1683–1645)*. Amsterdam: Holland University Press, 1984, pp. 48–61.

———. *Jean Gerson. Zijn Kerkpolitiek en ecclesiologie*. The Hague: Nijhoff, 1963.

Rabbie, Edwin. "Grotius and Judaism". In: Henk J. M. Nellen, Edwin Rabbie (eds.), *Hugo Grotius, theologian: Essays in Honour of G. H. M. Posthumus Meyjes*. Leiden, New York, Cologne: Brill, 1994, pp. 99–120.

———. "Some Remarks Concerning the Textual History of Hugo Grotius' De Satisfactione". In: *Grotiana*, 7 (1986), pp. 99–111.

Ramadan, Said. *Das Islamische Recht*. 2nd ed., Marburg: Muslimische Studentenvereinigung in Deutschland, 1996.

Rawls, John. *The Law of Peoples*. Cambridge, MA: Harvard University Press, 2000.

———. *A Theory of Justice*. Cambridge, MA: Belknap Press, 1999.

Reibstein, Ernst. *Johannes Althusius als Fortsetzer der Schule von Salamanca: Untersuchungen zur Ideengeschichte des Rechtsstaates und zur altprotestantischen Naturrechtslehre*. Karlsruhe: Mueller, 1955.

———. Volkssouveränität und Freiheitsrechte: Texte und Studien zur politischen Theorie des 14.–18. Jahrhundert. Vols. I–II. Freiburg im Breisgau: Alber, 1972.

Remec, Peter Pavel. *The Position of the Individual in International Law According to Grotius and Vattel*. The Hague: Nijhoff, 1960.

Rohe, Mathias. "Rechtliche Perspektiven eines deutschen und europäischen Islam". In: *Rabels Zeitschrift für ausländisches Privatrecht*, 64 (2000/2), pp. 258-298.

Roloefsen, Christopher G. "Grotius and the International Politics of the Seventeenth Century". In: Hedley Bull, Benedict Kingsbury, Adam Roberts (eds.), *Hugo Grotius and International Relations*. Cambridge: Cambridge University Press, 1990, pp. 95–131.

———. "The Sources of Mare Liberum: The Contested Origins of the Doctrine of the Freedom of the Seas, International Law and its Sources". In: Wybo P. Heero (ed.), *Liber Amicorum Maarten Bos*. Deventer, Boston, The Hague, Norwell: Kluwer, 1989, pp. 143–159.

van Rooden, Peter T. *Theology, Biblical Scholarship and Rabbinical Studies in the Seventeenth Century*. Leiden, New York, Cologne: Brill, 1994.

Rotter, Manfred. "Die allgemeinen Rechtsgrundsätze". In: Hanspeter Neuhold, Waldemar Hummer, Christoph Schreuer (eds.), *Österreichisches Handbuch des Völkerrechts*. 2nd ed., Vienna: Manz, 1991, pp. 88–92.

Rufinus. *Summa Decretorum*. Ed. Heinrich Singer. Paderborn, 1902, repr. Aalen: Scientia, 1963.

Russell, Frederick H. *The Just War in the Middle Ages*. Cambridge: Cambridge University Press, 1975.

Schmidt, Carl Adolf. *Der prinzipielle Unterschied zwischen dem römischen und dem germanischen Rechte*. Rostock, 1853, repr. Aalen: Scientia, 1964.

Schockenhoff, Eberhard. "Dient die Politik dem Glück des Menschen? Zum Verhältnis von geistlicher und weltlicher Gewalt bei Thomas von Aquin". In: Christoph A. Stumpf, Holger Zaborowski (eds.), *Church as Politeia: The Political Self-Understanding of Christianity*. Proceedings of a Becket Institute Conference at the University of Oxford, 28 September–1 October 2000. Berlin, New York: Walter de Gruyter, 2004, pp. 69–102.

Schröder, Meinhard. "Verantwortlichkeit, Völkerstrafrecht, Streitbeilegung und Sanktionen". In: Wolfgang Graf Vitzthum (ed.), *Völkerrecht*. 2nd ed., Berlin, New York: Walter de Gruyter, 2001, pp. 545–602.

Seckel, Emil. *Über Krieg und Recht in Rom: Rede zur Feier des Geburtstages Seiner Majestät des Kaisers und Königs, gehalten am 27. Januar 1915*. Berlin, 1915.

Seidl-Hohenveldern, Ignaz. "Die Staaten". In: Hanspeter Neuhold, Waldemar Hummer, Christoph Schreuer (eds.), *Österreichisches Handbuch des Völkerrechts*. 2nd ed., Vienna: Manz 1991, pp. 129-156.

Selden, John. *Mare Clausum seu De dominio maris libri duo*. London: Stanesbeius, 1636.

Simma, Bruno. "Das Völkergewohnheitsrecht". In: Hanspeter Neuhold, Waldemar Hummer, Christoph Schreuer (eds.), *Österreichisches Handbuch des Völkerrechts*. 2nd ed., Vienna: Manz, 1991, pp. 43–54.

Song, Robert. *Christianity and Liberal Society*. Oxford: Oxford University Press, 1997.

Sprackling, David M. "Divine and Human Law in Hugo Grotius". Unpublished MLitt thesis, University of Oxford, 1996.

Stumpf, Christoph A. "The Christian Society and Its Government: A Comparison between the Theo-Political Concepts of Richard Hooker and of Hugo Grotius". In: Christoph A. Stumpf, Holger Zaborowski (eds.), *Church as Politeia: The Political Self-Understanding of Christianity*. Proceedings of a Becket Institute Conference at the University of Oxford, 28 September–1 October 2000. Berlin, New York: Walter de Gruyter, 2004, pp. 151–175.

———. "Die Freiheit des Religionswechsels als Herausforderung für das religiöse Recht des Islam und des Christentums". In: *Zeitschrift für evangelisches Kirchenrecht*, 48 (2003/2), pp. 129–148.

———. "Vom Heiligen Krieg zum gerechten Krieg". In: *Zeitschrift der Savigny-Stiftung für Rechtsgeschichte. Kanonistische Abteilung*, 87 (2001), pp. 1–30.

———. *Kirchenrecht als Bekenntnisrecht: Die Verbindung von Erlanger Theologie und geschichtlicher Rechtswissenschaft im Leben und Werk von Adolf von Scheurl*. Ebelsbach: Aktiv Druck & Verlag, 1999.

———. "Völkerrecht unter Kreuz und Halbmond: Muhammad al-Shaybani und Hugo Grotius als Exponenten religiöser Völkerrechtstradition". In: *Archiv des Völkerrechts*, 41 (2003/1), pp. 83–100.

———. "Der Westfälische Frieden und die Wiedervereinigung der Konfessionen in verfassungshistorischer Perspektive". In: Harm Klueting (ed.), *Irenik und Antikonfessionalismus im 17. und 18. Jahrhundert*. Hildesheim, Zurich: Olms, 2003, pp. 39–54.

——— and Paul R. Melot de Beauregard. "Die Entwicklung der staatlichen Souveränität im Spiegel der kanonistischen Völkerrechtslehre". In: *Der Staat*, 42 (2003), pp. 459–472.

Suarez, Francisco. *Opus de triplici virtute theologica, fide, spe, et charitate*. Venice: Sebastinum Coleti, 1742.

———. *Tractatus De legibus, ac Deo legislatore*. Venice: Sebastinum Coleti, 1740.

Suganami Hidemi. "International Equality". In: Hedley Bull, Benedict Kingsbury, Adam Roberts (eds.), *Hugo Grotius and International Relations*. Cambridge : Cambridge University Press, 1990, pp. 221–240.

Tadashi Tanaka, "State and Governing Power". In: Yasuaki Onuma (ed.), *A Normative Approach to War*. Oxford: Oxford University Press, 1993, pp. 122–146.

Baron de Taube, Mikhail Aleksandrovich. "La position international actuelle du Pape et l'idée d'un ‚droit entre pouvoirs' (ius inter potestates)". In: *Archiv für Rechts- und Wirtschaftsphilosophie*, 1 (1907/08), pp. 302–345.

Thomas Aquinas. *In decem libros Ethicorum Aristotelis ad Nicomachum expositio / Sancti Thomae Aquinatis*. Ed. Raimondo Spiazzi. 2nd ed., Turin: Marietti, 1949.

———. *Summa Theologica*. Ed. Thomas Gilby et al. London: Blackfriars in conjunction with Eyre & Spottiswoode, 1964–1981.

Trapman, Johannes. "Grotius and Erasmus". In: Henk J. M. Nellen and Edwin Rabbie, *Hugo Grotius, theologian: Essays in Honour of G. H. M. Posthumus Meyjes*. Leiden, New York, Cologne: Brill, 1994, pp. 77–98.

Tuck, Richard. "Grotius, Carneades, and Hobbes". In: *Grotiana*, 4 (1983), pp. 43–62.

———. *Natural Rights Theories: Their Origins and Development*. Cambridge: Cambridge University Press, 1979.

———. *Philosophy and Government, 1572–1651*. Cambridge: Cambridge University Press, 1993.

———. *The Rights of War and Peace: Political Thought and the International Order from Grotius to Kant*. Oxford: Oxford University Press, 1999.

Vincent, Raymond John. "Human Right and Interventions". In: Hedley Bull, Benedict Kingsbury, Adam Roberts (eds.), *Hugo Grotius and International Relations*. Cambridge: Cambridge University Press, 1990, pp. 241–256.

de Vitoria, Francisco, de. *De civili potestate*. Madrid: Consejo Superior de Investigaciones Científicas, Instituto Francisco de Vitoria, 1975.

———. *De indis recenter inventis et de iure belli Hispanorum in barbaros*. Relectiones (ed. Walter Schätzel). Tübingen: Mohr Siebeck, 1952.

Graf Vitzthum, Wolfgang. "Begriff, Geschichte und Quellen des Völkerrechts". In: Wolfgang Graf Vitzthum (ed.), *Völkerrecht*. 2nd ed., Berlin, New York: Walter de Gruyter, 2001, pp. 1—85.

———. "Raum und Umwelt im Völkerrecht". In: Wolfgang Graf Vitzthum (ed.), *Völkerrecht*. 2nd ed., Berlin, New York, Walter de Gruyter, 2001, pp. 379–467.

de Wall, Heinrich. "Protestantische Theorien über die Beziehung zwischen Kirche und Staat im Heiligen Römischen Reich Deutscher Nation". In: Christoph A. Stumpf, Holger Zaborowski (eds.), *Church as Politeia: The Political Self-Understanding of Christianity*. Proceedings of a Becket Institute Conference at the University of

Oxford, 28 September–1 October 2000. Berlin, New York: Walter de Gruyter, 2004, pp. 177–189.

Walther, Helmut G. *Imperiales Königtum, Konziliarismus und Volkssouveränität: Studien zu den Grenzen des mittelalterlichen Souveränitätsgedankens*. Munich: Fink, 1976.

Weigand, Rudolf. *Die Naturrechtslehre der Legisten und Dekretisten von Irnerius bis Accursius und von Gratian bis Johannes Teutonicus*. Munich: Hueber, 1967.

Welzel, Hans. *Naturrecht und materiale Gerechtigkeit*. 4th ed., Göttingen: Vandenhoeck & Ruprecht, 1962.

Whewell, William. *Grotius on the Right of War and Peace*. Cambridge: Cambridge University Press, 1853.

Whiteman, Marjorie M. "Jus Cogens in International Law". In: *Georgia Journal of International and Comparative Law*, 7 (1977), pp. 609–626.

Wieacker, Franz. *Privatrechtsgeschichte der Neuzeit, unter besonderen Berücksichtigung der deutschen Entwicklung*. 2nd ed., Göttingen: Vandenhoeck & Ruprecht, 1967.

Wight, Martin. *Systems of States*. Leicester: Leicester University Press, 1977.

William of Ockham. *Breviloquium de potestate papae*. Paris: Vrin, 1937.

———. *Dialogus inter militem et clericum*. London 1925, repr. Millwood: Kraus Repr., 1987.

Willoweit, Dietmar. *Rechtsgrundlagen der Territorialgewalt: Landesobrigkeit, Herrschaftsrechte und Territorium in der Rechtwissenschaft der Neuzeit*. Cologne, Vienna: Böhlau, 1975.

Wolf, Dieter. *Die Irenik des Hugo Grotius*. 2nd ed., Hildesheim: Gerstenberg, 1972.

Wolfke, Karol. *Custom in Present International Law*. 2nd ed, Dordrecht: Kluwer, 1993.

Yoder, John Howard. *Nevertheless, the Varieties and Shortcomings of Religious Pacifism*. Waterloo: Herald Press, 1992.

Zemanek, Karl. "The Legal Foundation of the International System". In: *Recueil des Cours de l'Académie de droit international*, 266 (1997/IV), pp. 9–41.

———. "Das Völkervertragsrecht". In: Hanspeter Neuhold, Waldemar Hummer, Christoph Schreuer (eds.), *Österreichisches Handbuch des Völkerrechts*. 2nd ed., Manz: Vienna: Manz, 1991, pp. 55—87.

Index of Names

Index of Subjects

Bei Fragen zur Produktsicherheit wenden Sie sich bitte an:
If you have any questions regarding product safety,
please contact:

Walter de Gruyter GmbH
Genthiner Straße 13
10785 Berlin
productsafety@degruyterbrill.com